THE STENCILED STRAWBERRY

COOKBOOK

Patterns for Fine Dining

The Junior League of Albany, N.Y., Inc.

The purpose of The Junior League is exclusively educational and charitable and is: to promote volunteerism; to develop the potential of its members for voluntary participation in community affairs; and to demonstrate the effectiveness of trained volunteers.

The proceeds from the sale of *The Stenciled Strawberry Cookbook* will be returned to the community through projects sponsored by The Junior League of Albany.

For additional copies, use the order blanks in the back of the book or write directly to:

The Stenciled Strawberry Cookbook
The Junior League of Albany
419 Madison Avenue
Albany, New York 12210

Suggested retail price: **$14.95** plus $1.75 for shipping charges.
(New York State residents add local sales tax)

The Stenciled Strawberry Cookbook may be obtained by organizations for fund-raising projects or by retail outlets at special rates. Write to the above address for further information.

Copyright © 1985
Junior League of Albany Publications

ISBN 0-9614012-0-6

Printed in the United States of America
Wimmer Brothers Books
P.O. Box 18408
Memphis, TN 38181-0408
Cookbooks of Distinction™

CONTENTS

Historical perspectives are listed in italics

Recipe Contributors

The Junior League of Albany would like to thank its members and their friends who donated recipes for this book.

League Members

Elisabeth Bamberger
Mary Martel Barvoets
Nancy Bell
Laura Ladd Bierman
Catherine Culver Birkhauser
Mary Bisantz
Sherry Bostwick Bishko
Pamela Brown Bixby
Susan Lambeth Blabey
Martha Voorhees Blackman
Catha Sheer Britton
Susan Brodine
Martha Bailey Brown
Philly Brown
Sheila Paoli Burgess
Deborah Murray Cairns
Nikko Murray Carman
Roxanne McDonald Carr
Susan Devlin Cesario
Edythe English Clarke
Marcia Shaw Codling
Mary Ellen Guiendon Cole
D. Elizabeth Conners
Margery Wilkens Cooper
Ellen McLaughlin Courtney
Sue Forster Coyne
Alice Maltbie Crannell
Janet Alston Crannell
Grace Stephens Crary
Carol Frone Criscione
Betty Jane Bonpane Crummey
Karen O'Neil Curren
Ann Scarborough Dahne
Lorraine D'Aleo
Pamela Deeley
Nancy Tufano Dentinger
Regis Dyer Donovan
Judy Blair Douglas
Nancy Bryer Douglass
Mary Doyle
Nancy LaMarche Dreimiller
Ellin Dribben
Veronica Gabrielli Dumas
Mary Kirk Durgee
Tricia Manion Dwyer
Marita Estelle-Hancock
Adele Reed Everett
Julia Parker Ewen
Catherine Fahey
Rosaleen Scully Farley
Rita Wast Fassett
Susan Roth Filipp
Elizabeth Chrisp Finegan
Sue Anne S. Finley
E. Kristen Frederick
Charlotte Frye
Jane Rhinesmith Glassman
Janet Smith Gobeille
Rona Goldstein
Teresa Green
Alexandra Biernat Hallock
Joan Scheffler Hanley
Janis Happ
Lorraine Prince Harper

Barbara Mokhiber Harrington
Helen Merriam Hawn
Barbara Christenson Healy
Beverly Hearn
Penelope Davis Heath
Cynthia Clark Hessberg
Lois Barrett Hessberg
Joye Hewlett
Barbara Kegler Hoehn
Ellen Soley Hogarty
Genevieve Mosciwski Homiller
Eileen Huber
Bunny Hurlbut
Margaret Irving
Stana Hemstreet Iseman
Lizanne Hardegan Jones
Lynne Trudeau Jonquieres
Jennifer Lattin Julier
Barbara Bursch Kelly
Joanne Kimmey
Leslie Kimmey
Maureen Miller Klein
Connie Kristan
Sharon Leslie
Pamela LaFalce Linnan
Nancy Maloy Loftus
Lillian Wallender Longley
Ann Loucks
Helen Lucas
Betsy Keefauver Lyons
Rita Bentley Maciariello
Nancy E. Mack
Joanne Fitzpatrick Maloy
Karen Marcoux Mankes
Barbara Helsdon Marsch
Charlotte Brohard McGinnis
Judy Meagher
Patricia Slanina Messing
Dorothy Leeb Meyer
Cassandra Miller
Peggy J. Neal Montgomery
Mary Kathryn Smith Nahl
Antoinette Palmer Nathan
Patricia Nevergold
Marilyn Geneviva Newkirk
Marcia Kahl O'Connell
Diane Bell O'Keeffe
Elizabeth Maloney Paolino
Maria Parker
Laura Thalmann Patton
Lynn Johnston Pauquette
Lynnea Safstrom Payne
Barbara Nickerson Pearce
Ellen Picotte
Sherry Scott Putney
Gail Thomas Reynolds
Marianne Haite Rings
Patricia Carlson Rohstedt
Peg Lenahan Roos
Barbara Bechtold Ryan
Cheryl Sadler
Linda Chrystal Savino
Jane Barnes Scullen

Mary Margaret Sheehan
Sara Maxson Sheldon
Margaret Papa Sherwin
Janice Chandler Skilbeck
Cheryl Slattery
Elizabeth Aufsesser Sonneborn
Marilyn Tincher Spalt
Elisabeth Spencer-Ralph
Jaye Beard Sprinkle
Jane Anderson Staab
Janet Ruether Stasio
Christine Szaniawski
Patricia Hunt Thorpe
Patricia Griffin Traub
Kathleen Davis Trimble
Judith Twombly
Rebecca Sloan Tyrrell
Virgine Van Derhyden
Anne Dwyer Vinci
Janet Watts
Ann Cioffe Wang
Ana Webb
Sandra Adamovitch Weber
Patricia Fulginiti Whelan
Robin Bowdish Williams
Mary Gay Norris Wood
Kathryn Blase Yezzi
Joan Spath Young

League Friends

Mary Fowler Anderson
Rita Bell
E. Louise Bengisser
Betty Brown Bostwick
Margaret C. Brohard
Sally Bruner
Charlotte Buchanan
Patricia Campos
Pauline Cole
Daniel Cooper
John Crary
Mario M. Cuomo
George Deukmejian
Angela Estell
Alexander Filipp
Ann Harold
Cynthia Hoffman
Deborah Lambeth Jones
Carolyn Jonientz
Dana Kennedy
Virginia Smith Lambeth
Louise McDermott
Joan Morgan McKenzie
Diane Martin
Helen Nahl
Cornelius O'Donnell
Ellie Posner
Dorothy Reed
Leela Savkar
Norma Scarbrough
Beatrice Smith
Martha Parker Spence
Maureen Stapleton
Eli Taub
Rob Trimble
Thomas M. Whalen III
Marylou Whitney

Cookbook Committee

Cookbook Chairmen	1982-1984 Mary K. Nahl
	1984 Gail Reynolds
Recipe Chairman	Martha Blackman
Design & Format	Sherry Bishko
	Patricia Rohstedt
	Betty Sonneborn
	Kathie Trimble
Marketing Chairmen	Lorraine D'Aleo
	Beth Paolino

The cookbook committee wishes to express its sincere appreciation to the Junior League Actives and Sustainers for submitting recipes, testing, editing, proofing, and promoting the cookbook. A grateful thank you to the Sustainers who helped finance the cookbook with their generous contributions.

We also wish to thank Dr. David Ellis, Joan McKenzie, and Kirkman 3hree Advertising for their literary and artistic contributions, and Albany International for their technical assistance.

Corporate Sponsors

The Junior League of Albany wishes to thank the following corporations who contributed so generously to the publication of this cookbook. For years to come, these corporations will be a part of each Junior League community donation through their initial support of this project.

Americana Inn

Matthew Bender Company

Stewarts Ice Cream Co., Inc.

First Albany Corporation

Key Bank, N.A.

Bankers Trust Company

Eating in Albany, Historically Speaking

What other city can match Albany's distinctions: a cosmopolitan port nourished by almost four centuries of commerce; a city charter in 1686 as early as that of New York City; a political arena in which mayors from Peter Schuyler to Thomas Whalen and also governors such as Martin Van Buren, Grover Cleveland, and Alfred E. Smith jousted with their foes; the capital of state government since 1797; and a modern seat of government of startling design and staggering cost.

Change–constant, relentless, stimulating–has forced every generation of Albanians to make adjustments in transport, trade, and manufacturing as well as in their cuisine. Peter Kalm, a Swedish botanist, visited the city in 1749-1750 and described Dutch cooking as follows:

> Their food and its preparation is very different from that of the English. Their breakfast is tea, commonly without milk. About thirty or forty years ago, tea was unknown to them, and they breakfasted either upon bread and butter or bread and milk. They never put sugar into the cup, but take a small bit of it into their mouths while they drink. Along with the tea they eat bread and butter with slices of dried beef. The host himself generally says grace aloud. Coffee is not usual here. They breakfast generally about seven. Their dinner is buttermilk and bread or fresh milk and bread, with boiled or roasted meat. With each dinner they have a large salad, prepared with an abundance of vinegar, and very little of oil. Their supper consists generally of bread and butter, and milk with small pieces of bread in it.

This diet consisting chiefly of dairy products and vegetables compared unfavorably with beef and beer of the English colonists. Of course Albany's elite then and now indulged themselves with fancier pastry, confectionary, and wines. Mrs. Ann Grant of Scotland visited Albany in 1768 and observed the parties at the Schuyler and Van Rensselaer homes. She wrote:

> Here was a perfect regale, being served up with various sorts of cakes unknown to us, cold pastry, and great quantities of sweetmeats and preserved fruits of various kinds, and plates of hickory and other nuts ready cracked. In all manner of confectionery and pastry these people excelled; and having fruit in great plenty, which cost them nothing, and getting sugar home at an easy rate, in return for their exports of the West Indies, the quantity of these articles used in families otherwise plain and frugal, was astonishing.

Over a half century later Mrs. Basil Hall of England attended a reception at the home of Governor and Mrs. De Witt Clinton. She noted the various "editions" of tea and cakes, the trays of peaches and grapes, and the "magnificent pyramid of ice supported on each side by preserved pineapple and other sweetmeats". In fact Mrs. Clinton believed that the easiest way to entertain her guests "was to keep them eating". Not a bad idea for a day whose citizens had never heard of dietary fads. Mrs. Hall also commented that American servants were scarce and badly trained. Whether criticism of cuisine and manners came from British travelers or mayors of rival cities, most Albanians shrugged their shoulders with disdain.

The Dutch bequeathed to the Hudson Valley cole slaw, cookies, and crullers, three of the most toothsome delicacies in our culinary cupboard. Since the colonial period each wave of newcomers–Yankees, Irish, German, Italian, Poles, Greeks, and Blacks, to mention a few–have added delicious dishes to our national smorgasbord. The Italians have added the delight of spaghetti to our tables. The Germans contributed sauerkraut, sauerbraten, and frankfurts. Shish kabob came from the Eastern Mediterranean where lamb is highly prized. And for many years the Governor crowned the Maple Syrup Queen in order to celebrate New York's production of this delicacy.

David Maldwyn Ellis

David Maldwyn Ellis
P.V. Rogers Professor of History Emeritus
Hamilton College

7

Stenciling

Stenciling, which has been enjoying a revival on floors, walls, and cloth, as well as wood and tin, has been with us in many forms for a very long time.

In the Figi Islands, the natives cut patterns out of banana leaves and used the juices of berries and roots to color the bark cloth used in their clothing.

When paper became available in Europe–China's gift to the world–the stencil was used in many different ways; playing cards, the coloring of wood cuts and domino sheets to name a few. The domino sheets were decorative prints used to add color to the drab and somber shelters of the peasants and bourgeois. These 'dominos' were the forerunners for wall hangings made to look like the more expensive rich textiles, which in turn led to the products of Jean Papillon, known in France as the father of wallpaper.

In the early 19th century through the port of New York came rosewood and mahogany from Barbados and the West Indies. Because of the oriental influence of the times, the cabinet makers of fine furniture–pianos, wardrobes, secretaries–learned gilding, japanning and stenciling. Apprentices were hired to be indentured for four years to learn their trade and then usually to open their own shops.

When rosewood and fine mahogany became too expensive, cabinet makers began to make cheaper furniture and to decorate it in simpler ways. As styles began to change the art of decorating furniture all but died out.

Its revival is owed to Janet Waring and others who did endless research. Mrs. Waring's story was that she bought six decorated chairs and could not figure out how to duplicate the decoration. Later, in Lee, Mass. she found some stencils in an old ledger in an antique shop. Some time after that, she was in Portland, Maine and saw chairs that had been newly decorated in the same patterns that she had found in Lee. She was directed to George Lord who had done the chairs and was still working at the age of eighty-seven. Still later, in Cambridge, Mass. Mrs. Waring discovered six volumes of William Eaton's stencils. Mr. Eaton was George Lord's stepfather and, when she took these stencils back to Mr. Lord, he agreed to teach her his methods of gilding, painting, and striping. Mrs. Waring's book *Early American Stencils on Walls and Furniture* was first published in 1937 and is a definitive work on the subject.

If, as you use this cookbook, you were to say to yourself, "Why, that's exactly like my grandmother's (or my mother's or aunt's) recipe," remember, someone copied it down and handed it on; it didn't become lost and forgotten in the mists of time as some of the decorative arts almost did.

APPETIZERS

Saratoga and Potato Chips

Saratoga Springs, New York, is a small town 25 miles north of Albany. Referred to as the Queen of Spas, Saratoga has race tracks, musical events, auctions, art shows, bicycle races, and, of course, the renowned mineral baths. The lush countryside attracts sportsmen and campers, while the annual yearling sales draw Whitneys, Vanderbilts, Guggenheims, and other prominent socialites.

Entertaining and lavish food preparations consume almost as much time and energy in Saratoga as racing or cultural events. The invention of the potato chip is a direct result of this intense interest in food.

Back in 1853, a new snack food made its debut thanks to the inventiveness of Chef George Crum. Crum and his Aunt Kate ran the popular Moon's Lake House on Saratoga Lake. According to documented reports, a gentleman kept sending his potatoes back to the kitchen saying that they were too thick. Chef Crum finally sliced the potatoes wafer thin and deep fried them. The result delighted the gentleman, and he quickly told his friends about the tasty treats. So began the demand for Crum's Saratoga Chips. Eventually, they were sold in bags for ten cents. It became a familiar sight to see elegant ladies strolling with parcels of these chips in their white-gloved hands.

To this day, Saratoga remains a summer resort interested in good food and good fun. Whatever the event, a casual picnic or an elegant garden party, people are sure to be discussing food, from caviar to Saratoga chips.

The recipes in this section will provide you with a wide range of appetizers. Some are simple and easy, others are more elegant. All are delicious.

Hot and Cheesy Artichoke Spread

1 (6 ounce) jar marinated
   artichoke hearts or artichoke
   hearts in water, drained and
   finely chopped

1 cup mayonnaise
1 cup Parmesan cheese
3-4 dashes of garlic salt

Combine all ingredients. Place in ovenproof dish. Bake at 400°F. for 30 minutes. Serve on crackers or toasted bread rounds.

VARIATION: Add a 4-ounce can of chopped green chilies and substitute Cheddar cheese for the Parmesan cheese.

Preparation: 15 minutes   **Serves:** 4-6
Cooking: 30 minutes

Boursin Cheese Spread
Try this recipe for an inexpensive "bread and butter" gift idea

2 (8 ounce) packages cream
   cheese
8 ounces whipped unsalted butter

½ teaspoon garlic powder
¼ teaspoon each: oregano, thyme,
   marjoram, dill, basil, pepper

All ingredients should be at room temperature. Beat all ingredients until smooth. Allow to set for several hours or overnight. Serve with crackers.

VARIATION: Garlic lovers may prefer to add 2 cloves of garlic to the ingredients.

Preparation: 15 minutes   **Serves:** 8
                                      Must do ahead.

Fresh Vegetable/Chip Dip

1 cup sour cream
1 cup mayonnaise
1 tablespoon parsley

1 tablespoon shredded onion
1 teaspoon beau monde spice
1 teaspoon dill weed

Combine ingredients until smooth. Chill for 24 hours. Serve with fresh vegetables or chips.

Preparation: 10 minutes   **Serves:** 10-15
                                      Must do ahead

Guacamole Mountain
An excellent dip for small, hungry groups

GUACAMOLE:

5 ripe mashed avocados

1 pint sour cream

Green taco sauce, to taste

Splash of lemon juice

ADDITIONAL INGREDIENTS:

1 pound Cheddar cheese, shredded

½ pound Monterey Jack cheese, shredded

2 bell peppers, chopped

1 red onion, chopped

3 tomatoes, diced

1 (4 ounce) can black olives, chopped

Combine all guacamole ingredients. Layer ingredients into a mountain as follows: guacamole, Cheddar cheese, Monterey Jack cheese, bell peppers, red onions, tomatoes, olives. Repeat layering. Serve on a large, round platter with tortilla chips.

Preparation: 20 minutes

Serves: 6-8

Serve immediately

Blue Cheese Fondue
This easy, fast, and foolproof recipe is great for cocktail parties

2 (8 ounce) packages cream cheese

1 cup milk

1 teaspoon Worcestershire sauce

¼ teaspoon garlic powder

½ pound crumbled Blue cheese

Cubed bread

Raw vegetables (green peppers, cauliflower, carrots, or mushrooms)

In a saucepan, melt cream cheese with milk, Worcestershire sauce, and garlic powder. Stir over medium heat until smooth. Add Blue cheese and mix. Place mixture in a fondue pot and adjust heat to keep mixture just warm. Dip bread and vegetables into fondue.

Preparation: 10 minutes

Cooking: 5 minutes

Serves: 8

Serve immediately

Curried Chutney Cheese Ball
This has a deliciously mild sweet curry taste

2 (8 ounce) packages cream
   cheese, at room temperature
½ cup chutney

2 teaspoons curry powder
½ teaspoon dry mustard
½ cup finely chopped almonds

Add all ingredients to softened cream cheese. Mix well with hands. Shape into ball. Wrap and refrigerate. Remove 30 minutes prior to serving with crackers.

HINT: Add 1-3 tablespoons milk to cream cheese to make mixing easier.

Preparation: 10 minutes

Yield: 1 ball
Can be frozen

Company Cheese Ball

8 ounces each: cream cheese,
   smoked Cheddar cheese, sharp
   Cheddar cheese

Dash of Worcestershire sauce
½ cup chopped walnuts

Warm all ingredients, except walnuts, to room temperature and blend together with a fork. Roll into ball and then into desired shape. Roll cheese ball in bed of chopped walnuts.

NOTE: Grating cheese prior to blending provides a better consistency.

Preparation: 10 minutes

Yield: 1 ball
Can be frozen

Sweet Brie

1 (8-inch) round of Brie,
   top rind removed
1 cup chopped pecans

2 cups firmly packed brown sugar
Crackers

Preheat broiler. Place Brie in 10-inch quiche dish or pie plate and sprinkle with nuts. Cover top and sides with sugar, patting gently with fingertips (do not be concerned if sides are not fully covered). Broil on lowest rack until sugar bubbles and melts; about 3 minutes (cheese should retain its shape). Serve immediately with crackers.

Preparation: 10 minutes
Cooking: 3 minutes

Serves: 16-20
Serve immediately

Oyster Roll
Even non-oyster lovers enjoyed it

1 clove garlic, crushed
1 tablespoon minced onion
2 (8 ounce) packages cream
    cheese, softened
2 tablespoons mayonnaise
2 teaspoons Worcestershire sauce

¼ teaspoon salt
¼ teaspoon pepper
⅛ teaspoon Tabasco sauce
1 (8 ounce) can oysters, drained
1 cup chopped walnuts

In food processor with metal blade, or in mixing bowl, blend all ingredients except oysters and walnuts. Spread mixture on aluminum foil shaped into an 8 x 5-inch rectangle. Purée or mash oysters and spread over cream cheese mixture. Cover loosely with plastic wrap. Refrigerate overnight or at least 4 hours. With a spatula, release cream cheese from foil. Roll up and shape into a log. Roll in chopped nuts. Refrigerate up to 3 days before serving. Serve with party rye.

Preparation: 15 minutes

Yield: 1 roll
Must do ahead

Middle Eastern Hummus

1 (20 ounce) can chick-peas
3 garlic cloves, chopped
½ cup lemon juice
½ cup tahini (sesame seed paste)

¼ cup olive oil
Salt, to taste
Parsley sprigs or pimiento,
    to garnish

Drain chick-peas in a colander, reserving ¼ cup of juice, and rinse. In a food processor fitted with a metal blade, blend chopped garlic cloves, lemon juice, and chick-pea juice for 30 seconds. Add chick-peas alternately in batches with the tahini. With food processor running, add the olive oil in a stream. Purée mixture until smooth. Add salt to taste. Chill in a bowl for at least 2 hours. Remove from refrigerator at least 30 minutes prior to serving. Serve with wedges of pita bread. Garnish with parsley sprigs or pimiento.

Preparation: 10 minutes

Yield: 2 cups
Must do ahead

Soft and Spicy Cheese Dip
A peppery, spicy dip that complements any Mexican meal

¼ cup butter, softened
½ pound mild Cheddar cheese, grated
2 tablespoons finely chopped parsley

1 ½ tablespoons minced jalapeño peppers
½ teaspoon hot pepper sauce
1 tablespoon Worcestershire sauce

Place all ingredients in a food processor. Process, with a metal blade, until dip is smooth. Serve at room temperature with crackers or corn chips.

VARIATION: Try Salsa or Tabasco sauce as hot pepper sauce.

Preparation: 10 minutes

Yield: 2 cups
Can do ahead

Chutney Curry Dip

1 cup sour cream
1 cup mayonnaise
4 ounces softened cream cheese
2 teaspoons finely chopped onion

½ (9 ounce) jar chopped chutney
2 tablespoons curry powder
2 teaspoons horseradish

Combine all ingredients until smooth. Chill overnight. Serve with assorted raw vegetables.

NOTE: A very attractive dish when served in a hollow pineapple half. This dip can be made up to 10 days in advance.

Preparation: 20 minutes

Yield: 2½ cups
Must do ahead

Hot Crab Dip "Appeteaser"

1 (8 ounce) package cream cheese, softened
¼ cup mayonnaise
⅓ cup white wine
¾ teaspoon prepared mustard

¾ teaspoon confectioners' sugar
1 small onion, finely grated
⅛ teaspoon garlic powder
Seasoned salt, to taste
1 (6 ounce) can crabmeat

Mix all ingredients together by hand. Heat mixture in a double boiler for 15 minutes. Stir occasionally. Serve hot in a chafing dish. Garnish with parsley or paprika. Serve with assorted crackers.

Preparation: 15 minutes
Cooking: 15 minutes

Yield: 2 cups
Can do ahead

Hot Crabmeat Spread
Horseradish adds a nice touch to this spread

1 (8 ounce) package cream
   cheese, softened
1 (6 ounce) package frozen
   crabmeat
2 tablespoons chopped onion

1 tablespoon milk
1 teaspoon horseradish
¼ teaspoon salt
Dash of pepper
⅓ cup sliced almonds (optional)

Blend all ingredients, except almonds. Place in ovenproof dish. Sprinkle almonds (optional) on top. Bake at 375°F. for 15 minutes. Serve with assorted crackers.

NOTE: A combination of shrimp and crabmeat may be used.

Preparation: 10 minutes
Cooking: 15 minutes

Serves: 8
Serve immediately

Russian Peasant Dip
Suitable for large cocktail parties

1⅓ cups mayonnaise
1⅓ cups sour cream
2 tablespoons each: dill weed,
   parsley flakes, onion flakes,
   beau monde spice

1 (4 ounce) can ripe black olives,
   chopped and pitted
2 loaves rye, black rye, or
   pumpernickel bread

Mix all ingredients, except bread, the day before serving and refrigerate. Scoop out center of one loaf rye bread to create a boat-shaped container. Use scooped out bread and additional loaf to cut into bite-sized pieces for dipping. At serving time, fill center of bread with dip and surround with cut-up pieces.

VARIATION: It can also be served with fresh vegetables and chips. Also, you may add 1 (3½ ounce) jar dried beef or ½ cup pepperoni, finely chopped, or 6 ounces corned beef to the dip.

Preparation: 20 minutes

Serves: 30
Must do ahead

Liver Pâté

½ pound chicken livers, cleaned
 and quartered
1 small onion, halved
½ cup chicken stock, fresh or
 canned
1 (¼ ounce) envelope unflavored
 gelatin
½ teaspoon paprika
¼ teaspoon curry

½ teaspoon salt
1 teaspoon Worcestershire sauce
⅛ teaspoon freshly ground
 pepper
1 (8 ounce) package cream
 cheese, softened
Parsley sprigs and pimiento,
 to garnish

Simmer livers and onions in chicken stock for 10 minutes, or until livers are thoroughly cooked. Remove from heat and cool slightly. Remove ¼ cup liquid from pan. Place in a small bowl and dissolve the gelatin in it. Combine contents of the saucepan, the dissolved gelatin, and all the remaining ingredients in bowl of a food processor. Blend until smooth. Pour into small mold or crock and chill overnight. Garnish with fresh parsley sprigs and pimiento.

Preparation: 40 minutes
Cooking: 10 minutes

Yield: 1¾ cups
Must do ahead

Hot Clam Dip

2 (8 ounce) cans minced clams
1 cup bread crumbs
½ cup butter, melted
1 teaspoon oregano
1 teaspoon chopped parsley

2 cloves garlic, mashed
2 cups shredded Mozzarella
 cheese
¼ cup grated Parmesan cheese

Drain clams and save juice. Mix clams, bread crumbs, butter, oregano, parsley, garlic, and Mozzarella cheese. Sprinkle with Parmesan cheese. Bake at 350°F. for 15 minutes or until bubbly. Serve with crackers.

NOTE: If mixture seems too dry, add 1-2 cans of remaining clam juice.

Preparation: 15 minutes
Cooking: 15 minutes

Serves: 8-10
Serve immediately

Country-Style Pâté
An appetizer recipe worth the effort and planning

1 pound chicken livers, trimmed
½ cup orange juice
1¼ cups finely chopped dried
   mushrooms
½ cup dry sherry
10 garlic cloves, minced
3 large eggs
½ cup brandy
¼ cup heavy cream
1 tablespoon salt

2 teaspoons white pepper
1 teaspoon allspice
1 pound veal, ground
1 pound pork shoulder, ground
¾ pound pork fat, ground
½ cup all-purpose flour
¾ cup pistachio nuts
   (red or green)
1½ pounds sliced bacon

In medium bowl, add chicken livers and orange juice. In small bowl, add dried mushrooms and sherry. Let mixtures marinate at least 30 minutes, preferably overnight. Combine garlic, eggs, brandy, heavy cream, salt, pepper, and allspice in another bowl and blend lightly. Drain livers and add to garlic mixture. Place in food processor and blend until smooth. Pour garlic mixture in large bowl. Add ground meats, flour, nuts, and drained mushrooms. Blend well.

TO ASSEMBLE: Place 12 slices bacon, overlapping each other, in two 4 x 4 x 2-inch pans. Allow bacon to overhang pan sides 1-2 inches. Pour in liver mixture to within 1 inch of pan top. Fold overhanging bacon ends on liver mixture. Cover with foil and place in 2 shallow baking pans. Fill baking pans ½ full with boiling water. Bake at 400°F. for 3 hours. Remove foil last 30 minutes for browning. Remove from oven and weight both pâtés with heavy object (same size pan with foil wrapped bricks is ideal). Refrigerate with weights for 7 days. Serve unmolded with lettuce, cherry tomatoes, and simple crackers.

HINT: Best served 21 days after baking (14 days after removing weights).

Preparation: 1 hour
Cooking: 3 hours

Serves: 24
Must do ahead

Olive's Hot Cheese Spread
This appetizer is very popular with men

1 (8 ounce) package cream
   cheese, softened
2 tablespoons milk
1 (2½ ounce) jar dried beef,
   chopped
2 tablespoons finely chopped
   green pepper

¼ teaspoon black pepper
⅛-¼ teaspoon red pepper flakes
   or hot pepper sauce
½ cup sour cream
¼ cup chopped walnuts

Blend together all ingredients, except walnuts. Place in an 8 or 9-inch ovenproof serving dish. Garnish with chopped nuts. Bake at 350°F. for 15-20 minutes, or until bubbly. Serve with crackers.

NOTE: This can be mixed early in the day, but do not bake until just before serving.

Preparation: 10 minutes
Cooking: 15-20 minutes

Serves: 8
Serve immediately

Baba Ghannuj
This Middle Eastern dip recipe has been adapted
for use in a food processor

1-1½ pounds eggplant
3 garlic cloves

¾ cup tahini (sesame seed paste)
1½ tablespoons lemon juice

Place unpeeled eggplant on a cookie sheet or jelly roll pan. Make 2-3 lengthwise slits in eggplant skin. Broil until inside is soft when pierced with a fork. Cool for 15 minutes. Peel garlic cloves. Mince by dropping one at a time into the container of a running food processor (use metal blade). Add inside pulp of eggplant. Do not use eggplant skin. Purée the eggplant–garlic mixture. Add tahini and lemon juice and purée. Remove to serving dish. Cool to room temperature or refrigerate until ready to serve.

NOTE: Serve with wedges of pita bread or vegetables for dipping.

Preparation: 45 minutes
Cooking: 20 minutes

Yield: 2 cups
Can do ahead

Scallop Dip
Especially good in the summer

FISH:
1 pound sea scallops, cooked and
  chilled

DIP:
2 cups mayonnaise
1 teaspoon yellow prepared
  mustard
1 tablespoon capers, chopped

1 teaspoon minced parsley
2 tablespoons minced chives
Parsley, to garnish

FISH: Barely cover scallop with boiling water. Cook 5 minutes and drain.
Cut in half if large.

DIP: Mix together all dip ingredients. Chill at least 1 hour. Arrange scallops on platter and serve with dip. Garnish with parsley.

NOTE: Buy ready-cooked seafood to facilitate preparation. Other seafood such as shrimp or crabmeat may be added or substituted.

Preparation: 15 minutes
Cooking: 5 minutes

Yield: about 30
Can do ahead

Molded Shrimp Mousse

1 (15 ounce) can tiny shrimp,
  drained
¾ cup finely chopped celery
¾ cup finely chopped onion
1 cup mayonnaise
3 (3 ounce) packages cream
  cheese, softened

1 (10¾ ounce) can condensed
  tomato soup
1 tablespoon plus 2 teaspoons
  gelatin, mixed with water to
  form paste
Lettuce

Mix shrimp, celery, onion, mayonnaise, and cream cheese in large bowl
until blended. Heat condensed soup in small saucepan to low boil. Remove from heat and stir in gelatin paste until melted and blended. Add
soup mixture to other ingredients. Mix until blended smoothly. Pour
into 1-quart mold. Chill for at least 6 hours, or until firm. Unmold onto
bed of lettuce. Serve with crackers.

Preparation: 15 minutes
Cooking: 1 minute

Serves: 30
Can do ahead

Crab Snow Pea Pods

2 (6 ounce) packages Chinese
  snow pea pods
1 (6 ounce) package frozen
  crabmeat

1 (8 ounce) package cream cheese
½ teaspoon Worcestershire sauce
1 tablespoon grated onion

Pour boiling water over pea pods to hasten thawing. Drain and split pods. Mix crabmeat, cream cheese, Worcestershire sauce, and onion together. Place small amount of mixture into each split pea pod with a teaspoon. Chill.

Preparation: 30 minutes

Yield: 5 dozen
Can do ahead

Party Spinach Dip

1 (10 ounce) package frozen
  spinach, thawed and drained
½ cup chopped parsley
½ cup scallions

2 cups mayonnaise
Juice from 1 lemon
½ teaspoon garlic powder

Combine all ingredients and blend in food processor. Chill overnight. Serve with raw vegetables.

VARIATION: Omit parsley and lemon juice and add a dash of Tabasco sauce and 2 ounces crumbled Roquefort cheese.

Preparation: 15 minutes

Serves: 10
Must do ahead

Hearts of Caviar

1 (16 ounce) can artichoke hearts
½ cup sour cream
½ cup black caviar

½ teaspoon lemon juice
1 tablespoon minced onion
Pepper, to taste

Remove centers from artichoke hearts. Mix sour cream, caviar, lemon juice, and minced onion together. Fill artichoke shells with mixture. Sprinkle pepper over top and refrigerate. Serve cold.

Preparation: 10 minutes

Serves: 4-5
Can do ahead

Marinated Brussels Sprouts
This is a nice salad substitute too

2 (10 ounce) packages frozen
  brussels sprouts
½ cup tarragon vinegar
½ cup cooking oil
1 clove garlic, minced
1 tablespoon sugar

1 teaspoon salt
Dash of Tabasco sauce
2 tablespoons chopped onion
Lettuce
Tomato wedges, to garnish

Cook brussels sprouts according to package directions. Set aside. Combine vinegar, oil, garlic, sugar, salt, Tabasco sauce, and onion in large bowl. Add brussels sprouts. Pour into a container which allows brussels sprouts to be as well covered by marinade as possible. Cover and chill 8 hours. Stir occasionally. Serve on a bed of lettuce and garnish with tomato wedges.

VARIATION: Frozen artichoke hearts can be substituted for the brussels sprouts.

Preparation: 15 minutes

Serves: 6-8
Must do ahead

Aunt Doris's Eggplant Caponata

2 large eggplants, unpeeled,
  cut into 1-inch cubes
Salt
Pepper
Vegetable oil
2 medium onions, chopped
2 cloves garlic, crushed
3 celery stalks, chopped

1 cup Italian plum tomatoes
10 large green olives, quartered
  and pitted
3 tablespoons pine nuts
¼ cup capers
¼ cup wine vinegar
2 tablespoons sugar

Season eggplant cubes with salt and pepper. Fry in oil until tender. Remove eggplant and set aside. In same pan, sauté onion. Add garlic, celery, tomatoes, and olives. Cook slowly for 10 minutes. Add eggplant, pine nuts, and capers. In separate pan, heat vinegar. Stir in sugar. Add to vegetable mixture. Add salt and pepper to taste. Continue cooking for 5 minutes. Refrigerate mixture. Serve chilled with crackers.

Preparation: 45 minutes
Cooking: 15 minutes

Yield: 1 quart
Can do ahead

Grand Salmon Appetizers

1 (4 ounce) can salmon, drained,
  boned, and skinned
1 (3 ounce) package cream
  cheese, softened
1½ teaspoons mayonnaise
¼ teaspoon dry mustard
10 capers, minced
½ teaspoon onion salt

3 drops Tabasco sauce
1 tablespoon minced pimiento
24 cherry tomatoes
24 slices cucumber, ½-inch thick
Black olives, sliced
Stuffed olives, sliced
Parsley sprigs

Chop salmon coarsely. In a small bowl, blend cream cheese, mayonnaise, and mustard. Stir in capers, onion salt, Tabasco, salmon, and pimiento. Chill overnight.

TO ASSEMBLE: Cut thin slices from tops of the cherry tomatoes and scoop out some of the seeds and pulp. Fill each tomato with salmon mixture. Also, to vary, top each cucumber slice with a scant teaspoon of salmon mixture. Garnish each with olive slices and parsley sprigs.

Preparation: 1 hour

Yield: 4 dozen
Must do ahead

Fruited Tea Sandwiches

2 (8 ounce) packages cream
  cheese, softened
8 ounces crushed pineapple,
  drained
2¾ ounces orange marmalade
1½ ounces ginger preserves
1 cup chopped pecans
¼ cup finely chopped green
  pepper

1 tablespoon minced onion
½ teaspoon celery salt
½ teaspoon onion salt
8 maraschino cherries, chopped
Sliced raisin bread, crusts
  removed

Combine all ingredients, except raisin bread, using ½ cup pecans, and mix well. Spread on slices of raisin bread which have been halved diagonally. Sprinkle remaining pecan pieces on top before serving.

NOTE: This mixture may also be used as a spread for crackers.

Preparation: 20 minutes

Serves: 12
Can do ahead

Marinated Mushrooms
Those who like vinaigrette will find this delicious

¾ cup salad oil
⅓ cup red wine vinegar
1½ teaspoons salt
¾ teaspoon sugar
½ teaspoon basil
2 green peppers, thinly sliced

2 onions, thinly sliced
6 peppercorns
1 bay leaf
1 clove garlic, quartered
1½ pounds medium-sized fresh
  mushrooms, cleaned

In medium saucepan, over medium heat, boil all ingredients except mushrooms. Cover and simmer over low heat for 10 minutes. Stir in mushrooms until coated. Simmer an additional 10 minutes. Do not overcook. Cool and refrigerate for 2-3 days. Drain off some of marinade before serving, retaining green peppers and onions.

Preparation: 10 minutes
Cooking: 20 minutes

Serves: 6-8
Must do ahead

Tortellini in Garlic-Herb Dressing
This makes a superb beginning to an Italian dinner

1 (8 ounce) package frozen
  tortellini
¼ cup red wine vinegar
¾ cup olive oil
1-2 cloves garlic, minced
1 tablespoon Dijon mustard

8 leaves fresh basil, finely
  chopped
2 tablespoons chopped parsley
4 scallions, finely chopped
½ cup grated Parmesan cheese

Cook tortellini in boiling water until tender, but still firm. Drain and rinse with cold water. Set aside. Mix vinegar and oil well. Stir in garlic and mustard. Pour over tortellini. Add basil, parsley, and scallions. Toss gently. Refrigerate until well chilled. Top with Parmesan cheese just before serving.

Preparation: 15 minutes

Serves: 8-10
Can do ahead

Seviche
This dish is delicious and low calorie

2 cups raw bay scallops
2 tablespoons minced fresh onion
2 tablespoons minced green chili
   (optional)
⅓ cup fresh lime juice

1 clove garlic, minced
1 tablespoon chopped parsley
Salt
Coarsely ground pepper
Lettuce

Mix first six ingredients in glass bowl. Add salt and pepper to taste. Refrigerate 8-12 hours, stirring at least once. Serve on a bed of chilled lettuce.

Preparation: 10 minutes

Serves: 4-6
Must do ahead

Shrimp Stuffed Tomatoes

2 (6 ounce) cans shrimp
1 tablespoon lemon juice
18-20 cherry tomatoes
2 tablespoons each: minced
   onion, minced celery,
   mayonnaise

Salt (optional)
Parsley (optional)

Drain and finely chop shrimp. Place in medium bowl and pour ½ tablespoon lemon juice over shrimp. Let stand. Remove tops and insides from tomatoes. Add onion, celery, and mayonnaise to shrimp and mix thoroughly. Add remaining lemon juice and salt, if desired. Stuff cherry tomatoes with shrimp filling. Refrigerate several hours before serving. Add parsley as garnish, if desired.

Preparation: 30 minutes

Yield: 1½ dozen
Must do ahead

Shrimp Stuffed Snow Peas

2 (8 ounce) packages cream
  cheese
1 pound shrimp, cooked and
  well drained
¼ cup mayonnaise

2 tablespoons lemon juice
½ teaspoon garlic powder
¼ teaspoon each: pepper, salt,
  dill weed
100 snow peas

String and split open the snow peas. Blanche in boiling water for 30-60
seconds. Immediately cool in a bowl of ice water. Drain on paper towels.
Blend remaining ingredients in a food processor using a steel blade. Do
not totally purée. Refrigerate mixture 2-3 hours. To assemble, fit a piping
bag with a #1 star tip. Fill bag with chilled mixture and pipe into split
open snow peas.

NOTE: The snow peas can be blanched up to 1 day ahead. Prepare filling
and assemble the day they are to be served.

Preparation: 1 hour

Yield: 100
Can do ahead

Bacon and Cheese Rounds

10 ounces Gouda cheese, grated
12 strips bacon
6 tablespoons mayonnaise

12-14 drops of Worcestershire
  sauce
1 loaf party rye rounds

Fry bacon until crisp and crumble into cheese. Add mayonnaise and
Worcestershire sauce. Mix thoroughly. Spread on party rye rounds. Place
under broiler until cheese is melted.

NOTE: This mixture is also excellent on hamburgers.

Preparation: 15 minutes
Cooking: 3-4 minutes

Yield: 30-40
Can do ahead

Broiled Cantaloupe and Prosciutto

2 cantaloupes

½ pound prosciutto, thinly sliced

Seed cantaloupe and remove rind. Slice to form crescents. Wrap each
crescent with one piece of prosciutto. Secure with a toothpick. Place in
baking dish and broil until meat is crackling hot, or about 5 minutes.

Preparation: 10-15 minutes
Cooking: 5 minutes

Serves: 4-6
Serve immediately

Cayenne Cheese Balls

Keep these in the freezer for unexpected guests

2 cups grated sharp Cheddar
  cheese
4 tablespoons butter
1 cup all-purpose flour

⅛ teaspoon cayenne
40-50 pimiento stuffed green
  olives, well drained

Cream together cheese and butter. Blend in flour and cayenne. Wrap a teaspoon of dough around each olive, covering completely. Bake at 400°F. for 15 minutes.

Preparation: 30 minutes
Cooking: 15 minutes

Yield:40-50
Can do ahead

Pepperoni Appetizer Bread

Try adding combinations of sausage, mushrooms, peppers, and onions for delicious variations on this recipe.

1 pizza dough
1 stick pepperoni, cut in small
  pieces

½ pound Provolone, sliced
4 ounces Mozzarella, grated

Let dough stand at room temperature for 3 hours. Divide in two. Roll each piece out into 4 x 8-inch rectangle, using flour. Heap one half of pepperoni pieces onto each rectangle. Add one half of Provolone slices and one half of grated Mozzarella onto each rectangle of dough. Turn dough over filling with floured fingers, lengthening while closing. Seal along length and at ends by pinching the dough closed. Bake on un-greased cookie sheet for 50 minutes at 350°F. Slice when cooled. Serve warm.

Preparation: 20 minutes
Cooking: 50 minutes

Yield: 30 slices
May be frozen

Buffalo Wings

WINGS:
1 (5 pound) bag frozen chicken
   wings, tips removed

SAUCE:
½ pound butter
1 tablespoon white vinegar

3-5 tablespoons Louisiana-style
   hot sauce

DIP:
4 ounces crumbled Blue cheese
1 cup mayonnaise

1 cup sour cream

WINGS: Oven fry frozen wings at 425°F. for 45 minutes. Pour sauce over wings in last 15 minutes of cooking time. Serve hot with dip.

SAUCE: Combine butter, vinegar, and hot sauce in small saucepan over low heat.

DIP: Combine all ingredients. Let stand in refrigerator at least an hour.

NOTE: For hotter wings, add additional hot sauce.

Preparation: 10 minutes
Cooking: 45 minutes

Serves: 12-16
Serve immediately

Bacon and Crab Rumaki

½ cup butter, melted
4 tablespoons all-purpose flour
1½ teaspoons salt
1 cup milk
1 tablespoon chopped onion
2 tablespoons chopped parsley

3 cups crabmeat
1 (8 ounce) can water chestnuts,
   chopped
2 tablespoons bread crumbs
2 pounds bacon, cut strips in half

In a saucepan over medium-low heat, blend 4 tablespoons butter, flour, and ¼ teaspoon salt. Add milk, stirring briskly. Cook until thick and smooth. Set aside. Sauté onion in remaining 4 tablespoons butter. Add parsley, crabmeat, and water chestnuts. Sauté 1 minute. Add bread crumbs and cream sauce. Season to taste with remaining 1¼ teaspoons salt. Cool. Form into balls the size of walnuts. Wrap each ball with a slice of bacon. Fasten with toothpick. Bake at 350°F. for 20-25 minutes or more until bacon is brown. Drain and serve.

NOTE: These can be frozen for at least 2-3 weeks.

Preparation: 1 hour
Cooking: 15 minutes

Yield: 64-72
Can do ahead

Shrimp Toast with Duck Sauce

SHRIMP TOAST:

½ pound shrimp, fresh or frozen
4 water chestnuts, minced
1 egg, slightly beaten
1 scallion, minced
1 teaspoon minced fresh ginger or
   2 teaspoons ground ginger

½ teaspoon salt
½ teaspoon sugar
1 tablespoon cornstarch
2 cups peanut oil
7 slices 2-day old bread

DUCK SAUCE:

½ cup each: Chinese plum sauce,
   apricot preserves, peach
   preserves, applesauce

1 teaspoon dry mustard
1 tablespoon catsup

SHRIMP TOAST:

Shell and devein shrimp. Wash, drain, and mince. Mix with water chestnuts, egg, scallion, ginger, salt, sugar, and cornstarch. Trim crust off bread and cut into triangles. Spread 1 teaspoon shrimp mixture on each slice. Heat oil and gently lower bread in, shrimp side down. After 1 minute, turn and fry a few seconds more. Drain and serve with Duck Sauce.

DUCK SAUCE:

Mix all ingredients thoroughly. Makes 2 cups sauce that will keep indefinitely.

Preparation: 30 minutes
Cooking: 5 minutes

Yield: 28 pieces
Can do ahead

Peanut Butter-Curry Chicken Wings

¼ cup margarine
⅓ cup creamy peanut butter
⅔ cup milk
6 tablespoons cornmeal
6 tablespoons all-purpose flour

1 teaspoon salt
1 teaspoon curry powder
18 chicken wings (tips removed,
   skinned if desired)

Put margarine in a foil-lined, 9 x 13-inch baking pan. Watching carefully, melt margarine in 400°F. oven. In a blender or with a mixer, blend peanut butter and milk. Put in shallow dish. Combine cornmeal, flour, salt, and curry powder in another shallow dish. Dip chicken wings in peanut butter mixture and then in flour mixture. Lay dipped wings in melted margarine in pan. Bake at 400°F. for 40 minutes.

Preparation: 45 minutes
Cooking: 40 minutes

Serves: 4
Serve immediately

Curried Crabmeat Canapés

2 (6 ounce) cans crabmeat,
   cleaned and drained
1 cup mayonnaise
1 cup Monterey Jack cheese,
   finely shredded
⅓ cup finely grated almonds
¼ cup parsley leaves, minced

1 tablespoon lemon juice
2 large shallots, minced
1½ teaspoons curry powder
2 drops of Tabasco sauce
72 party rye squares
72 almond slices

Combine crabmeat, mayonnaise, cheese, grated almonds, parsley, lemon juice, shallots, curry powder, and Tabasco sauce in large bowl. Blend well, alternately using a rubber spatula and a large whisk. Spread ½ teaspoon of mixture on each bread square. Top each square with an almond slice. Bake at 500°F. for 8 minutes. Serve hot.

NOTE: Canapés may be frozen once assembled, by placing on a baking dish and covering with aluminum foil. Thaw completely before baking.

Preparation: 45 minutes
Cooking: 8 minutes

Yield: 6 dozen
Serve immediately

Fried Eggplant Nuggets

1 cup water
2 cups cubed eggplant, peeled
1 cup bread crumbs
1 cup grated Cheddar cheese
2 tablespoons minced onion
1 clove garlic, minced
½ teaspoon dry mustard

½ teaspoon curry powder
⅛ teaspoon salt
⅛ teaspoon pepper
¼ teaspoon Tabasco sauce
1 egg
Flour for dredging
¼ cup margarine

Boil water in medium saucepan. Add eggplant cubes, cover, and cook 10 minutes. Drain. Place eggplant in bowl, and mash. Add bread crumbs, Cheddar cheese, onion, garlic, dry mustard, curry powder, salt, pepper, and Tabasco sauce. Beat egg. Add to eggplant mixture. Combine well and shape into small balls. Roll balls in flour. Melt butter in skillet. Add eggplant balls gradually and brown for about 10 minutes, turning occasionally to avoid burning. Drain on paper towels and serve hot.

Preparation: 30 minutes
Cooking: 45 minutes

Yield: 4 dozen
Serve immediately

Spinach Balls

2 (10 ounce) packages chopped
    spinach, squeezed dry
2 cups crumb-style stuffing mix
1 cup shredded Jarlsberg cheese
    or other sharp cheese

6 eggs, well beaten
¾ cup unsalted butter
Salt and pepper, to taste

Combine all ingredients. Let stand approximately 10 minutes, or until all moisture is absorbed. Roll into balls and freeze. Place frozen balls on cookie sheet. Bake at 400°F. for 15-20 minutes, turning once.

NOTE: This mixture may be used as a stuffing for mushrooms. Pre-bake mushrooms, moistened with butter and soy sauce for 8 minutes. Stuff with spinach mixture and sprinkle with some cheese. Bake at 400°F. for 15-20 minutes.

Preparation: 20 minutes
Cooking: 15-20 minutes

Yield: 40 medium balls
Can be frozen

Spanakopeta (Spinach and Cheese Pastry)

2 (10 ounce) packages chopped
    spinach, thawed and drained
3 eggs, beaten
3 cups Feta cheese, crumbled
½ cup finely chopped onion

¼ cup sour cream
5 teaspoons lemon juice
1 pound phyllo pastry
½-¾ pound butter, melted

Combine spinach, eggs, cheese, onion, sour cream, and lemon juice. Mix well. Working with single sheets of phyllo pastry, brush with butter, and cut lengthwise into 4 strips. Place 1 teaspoon filling on bottom of each strip and fold into triangle. (See diagram.) Brush tops with butter and bake at 375°F. for 20 minutes, or until brown.
Diagram for folding:

NOTE: When folding phyllo strips, keep the triangles small, just encompassing the filling.

Preparation: 2 hours
Cooking: 20 minutes

Yield: 7 dozen
Can be frozen

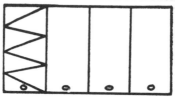

Water Chestnuts in Bacon

1 pound bacon, uncooked
1 (8 ounce) can whole water
  chestnuts

½ cup brown sugar
¼ cup mayonnaise
¼ cup chili sauce

Remove bacon from package and slice entire pound in half. Drain and rinse water chestnuts. Wrap each chestnut in a piece of sliced bacon and secure with toothpick. Place bacon-wrapped chestnuts on a broiler pan. Bake in 350°F. oven for 30-40 minutes, or until bacon is done. Meanwhile, combine the remaining ingredients in a small bowl and set aside. When bacon is cooked, remove broiler pan from oven. Transfer the chestnuts to a smaller, 9 x 7-inch pan. Pour sauce mixture over them, making sure it spreads fairly evenly. Return pan to oven at 350°F. for 5-10 minutes, or until sauce is warm.

Preparation: 55 minutes
Cooking: 50 minutes

Yield: 2½ dozen
Serve immediately

Shrimp Canapé
These can be made a day ahead and baked at the last minute

2 cups Swiss cheese, grated
2 (4 ounce) cans shrimp, drained
  and chopped
1 medium onion, chopped
1 teaspoon lemon juice

1 teaspoon dry mustard
Salt
Pepper
Mayonnaise
1 large loaf of sliced bread

Mix cheese, shrimp, onion, and lemon juice. Add salt and pepper to taste. Add enough mayonnaise to hold mixture together. Set aside. Toast bread. Cut out four circles from each slice. Heap shrimp mixture on each circle. Bake 10 minutes at 350°F., until cheese bubbles.

NOTE: A shot glass makes an excellent utensil for cutting bread circles. Mixture may be frozen prior to baking.

Preparation: 30 minutes
Cooking: 10 minutes

Yield: 50
Serve immediately

BEVERAGES

Entertaining in the Past

In the 18th and 19th centuries, American entertaining often meant a company dinner at two o'clock in the afternoon, preceded by punch and followed by tea. Since singing, dancing, and music were then uncommon in most households, the drinking of tea (and eating accompanying goodies) became the basis for evening parties as well. A hostess might offer her guests several varieties of green or black tea and lemonade. Coffee and hot chocolate might also be served, although the latter was considered a luxury. A visitor to Albany observed that

> Tea here was a perfect regale: accompanied by various sorts of cake unknown to us; cold pastry and great quantities of sweetmeats and preserved fruits of various kinds and plates of hickory and other nuts ready-cracked.

Fear of the "milk fever" (tuberculosis) from cow's milk, and threat of contaminated water forced people to consume beer, cider, rum, and wine as their daily beverages. Americans drank alcoholic beverages on all special occasions as well. Weddings, baptisms, funerals, house raisings, were all times to offer a toast–or two. Those liquors not produced in this country were readily imported from abroad. Gin and aniseed cordials came from Holland; madeira, a favorite of many people, came from Spain and Portugal. Other wines most frequently in demand were claret and port, French wines, and brandies.

Several kinds of alcohol were frequently combined with tea to make punch, a very popular drink in the 19th century. The following recipe for Albany Regency Punch, prepared by a local club for festive occasions, indicates just how potent these mixtures could be.

Albany Regency Punch

3 quarts champagne	1 quart lemon juice
2 quarts Rhine wine	2 quarts green tea
2 quarts Curaçao	2 quarts seltzer water
2 quarts Madeira	1 pint Jamaica rum
1 quart brandy	4 pounds raisins

Crush raisins and allow to stand overnight in tea and lemon juice. Add other ingredients and serve ice cold. Do not add extra ice.

The beverage recipes which follow offer a wide variety of ingredients for many occasions–from a large gathering to a post-prandial sip with a friend.

Satin Peach Daiquiris

1 (10 ounce) package frozen
  peaches, unsweetened,
  partially thawed
6 ounces light rum

½ (6 ounce) can frozen lemonade
  concentrate
2 cups crushed ice

Combine all ingredients. Whirl in a blender until peaches are puréed and the mixture is uniform. Serve immediately or store in covered container in the freezer until ready to serve.

NOTE: If preparing ahead do not freeze to solid consistency. Optional garnishes are a cherry and sprig of mint.

Preparation: 10 minutes
Can do ahead

Serves: 8-10

Jack's Eggnog

6 eggs, separated
¾ cup sugar
2 cups each: heavy cream, milk,
  whiskey

1 ounce rum
Dash of nutmeg

Beat yolks with ½ cup sugar until thick and frothy. Beat egg whites and add ¼ cup sugar. Continue beating until very stiff. Combine beaten yolks and whites. Stir in cream, milk, whiskey, and rum. Refrigerate until cold. Serve with a dash of nutmeg on top.

Preparation: 15 minutes

Yield: 10-12 cups
Must do ahead

Irish Creame
Like a milkshake, this drink is addictive!

3 eggs
1 cup heavy cream
1 (14 ounce) can condensed milk
1 ½ tablespoons chocolate syrup

¼ teaspoon vanilla
¾ cup whiskey
1 drop coconut extract

Mix all ingredients in a blender and refrigerate. Serve cold.

NOTE: Can be made ahead 2 days.

Preparation: 10 minutes

Serves: 10
Can do ahead

Café Liqueur
The longer this drink is stored, the better it is!

2 cups boiling water
3 cups granulated sugar
1 (2 ounce) jar instant coffee

1 fifth vodka or bourbon
1 large vanilla bean

In a saucepan, combine 1 cup boiling water and sugar. Cook, uncovered, over medium heat <u>without stirring</u> for 10 minutes to make a thin syrup. Dissolve the instant coffee powder in remaining 1 cup boiling water. Add the coffee to the syrup. Remove from heat and cool to lukewarm. Stir in liquor and vanilla bean. Pour into a clean, odorless, ½-gallon, glass bottle. Cap tightly. Store at least 3 weeks, or up to 6 months, before using.

Preparation: 5 minutes
Cooking: 10 minutes

Yield: ½ gallon
Must do ahead

Frozen Daiquiris

3 (12 ounce) cans frozen
   lemonade concentrate
1 (12 ounce) can frozen limeade
   concentrate

Few drops green food coloring
1 quart club soda
1 quart white rum

Mix all ingredients together and freeze. Mixture will be slushy. Serve immediately after removal from freezer.

NOTE: Looks great in a punchbowl. Add red cherries for a decorative garnish.

Preparation: 5 minutes

Yield: 4 quarts
Must do ahead

Oscar's
It's very potent, but it looks and tastes great!

1 shot vodka
1 shot gin
1½ tablespoons cherry brandy
Dash of grenadine

Ice
Orange juice
Pineapple juice

Put vodka, gin, cherry brandy, and grenadine in a glass. Add some ice and fill rest of the glass with equal amounts of orange juice and pineapple juice. Stir and enjoy!

NOTE: A sprig of mint serves as a nice garnish.

Preparation: A few minutes

Yield: 1 drink
Serve immediately

Bourbon Slush

SLUSH:

2 cups bourbon
1 (12 ounce) can frozen lemonade
   concentrate
1 (6 ounce) can frozen orange
   juice concentrate

2 cups (16 ounces) strong tea,
   warm
1 cup sugar
7 cups water

SERVING:

Lemon-lime soda

Maraschino cherries

SLUSH: Mix slush ingredients altogether in a very large pot. Pour mixture into containers with wide openings. Freeze 24-72 hours.

SERVING: When serving, scrape out like ice ball into cocktail glass. Add splash of soda, just enough to wet. Add maraschino cherry.

NOTE: Use two half gallon containers for freezing.

Preparation: 5 minutes

Yield: 15 cocktails
Must do ahead

Café Brûlot
A dramatic dessert drink that even non-coffee drinkers will love

1 whole cinnamon stick
10-12 whole cloves
2 orange peels, slivered
2 lemon peels, slivered
6 teaspoons sugar

1 cup brandy
¼ cup orange liqueur
1 quart freshly brewed strong
   coffee (expresso is excellent)

In saucepan, combine cinnamon, cloves, fruit rinds, sugar, brandy, and liqueur. Bring to a boil over medium high heat. <u>Carefully,</u> ignite mixture and let it burn until flame is extinguished. Gradually, add black coffee and stir. Pour into coffee pot for pouring and serve in demitasse cups. Can be mixed and set aside prior to igniting the mixture.

NOTE: Brewing time is different for each coffee maker but you can make it 2 hours ahead.

Preparation: 15 minutes
Cooking: 10-20 minutes

Serves: 10-12
Can do ahead

Mint Juleps en Masse
Serve this for "Derby Day" parties

2 cups sugar
2 cups water
6 cups fresh mint sprigs

1 quart bourbon
Fresh mint, to garnish

PREPARATION: Make a syrup by boiling sugar and water for five minutes. Do not stir. Allow to cool. Carefully rinse and drain the mint. Put into a large container and add the syrup. Cap and refrigerate for at least 24 hours.

SERVING: Strain syrup and discard the mint. Fill a julep cup or old-fashioned glass with crushed ice. Pour in a tablespoon of mint syrup and 2 ounces of bourbon. Add a sprig of fresh mint and serve.

NOTE: You can frost the glasses by grasping the rim of the filled cups with your fingertips and quickly twist back and forth. The outside will cover with frost.

Preparation: 15 minutes
Cooking: 5 minutes

Yield: 12 drinks
Must do ahead

Krupnik (Fire Vodka)
An after-dinner drink to share with good friends

1½ cups honey
⅔ cup water
1 teaspoon vanilla extract (not
  imitation)
¼ teaspoon freshly grated nutmeg

8 cinnamon sticks
2 whole cloves
Peel of 1 lemon, in strips (yellow
  only)
1 (⅘ quart) bottle vodka

Combine honey, water, vanilla, nutmeg, cinnamon, cloves, and lemon peel in large saucepan. Bring to boil, cover and <u>simmer</u> 5 minutes. Add vodka. Remove from heat (do not boil once vodka is added). Serve warm.

NOTE: It can be made weeks ahead and reheated.

Preparation: 15 minutes
Cooking: 10 minutes

Yield: 1 quart
Can do ahead

Peg's Punch

1 (10 ounce) package frozen
   strawberries
1 quart orange juice
1 quart grape juice
Ice

2 quarts ginger ale
1 fifth vodka
1 orange, thinly sliced
1 lemon, thinly sliced

In large punchbowl, place frozen strawberries (do not defrost). Stir in orange juice, grape juice, and lots of ice. Stir in ginger ale and vodka. Garnish with orange and lemon slices.

NOTE: You can substitute gin for vodka.

Preparation: 10 minutes

Yield: 25 cups
Serve immediately

121st Cavalry Punch

"It was served at my wedding in the days just before the second World War when there still was a Cavalry. The Cavalry has long since been motorized but the good old punch is still the same."

4 parts carioca rum
6 parts catawba wine (or 3 parts
   dry sauterne wine and 3 parts
   catawba wine)
1 part brandy

1 part lemon juice
12 parts vichy
⅛ pound sugar per part of stock
   or 1½ pounds per batch

Combine all ingredients and serve.

NOTE: Add sugar to taste. (And it's the tasting to get it right that is the fun part!)

Hot Wassail Bowl

1½ pints cranberry juice cocktail
1 (6 ounce) can frozen orange
   juice concentrate
2 cups water
1 tablespoon sugar

¼ teaspoon allspice
3 cups dry sauterne
1 orange, sliced
Cloves, to stud orange slices

Mix juices and seasonings in 8-quart pot. Bring almost to simmer. Add sauterne and heat. Do not boil. Float clove-studded orange slices.

NOTE: If making ahead, do not add wine. Reheat and then add the wine.

Preparation: 10-15 minutes
Cooking: 10 minutes

Yield: 12-24 punch cups
Can do ahead

Holiday Wassail

1 cup of honey or sugar
4 cinnamon sticks
1 lemon, sliced
½ cup water
2 cups pineapple juice

2 cups orange juice
6 cups dry red wine
½ cup lemon juice
1 cup dry sherry

In a small saucepan, boil honey (or sugar), cinnamon sticks, and lemon slices in water for 5 minutes. Strain and discard cinnamon and lemon. Set aside. Heat remaining ingredients in 5-quart pot. Add the spiced honey syrup. Heat but do not boil. Float lemon slices or add cinnamon sticks.

NOTE: If making ahead, refrigerate and reheat.

Preparation: 10 minutes
Cooking: 10 minutes

Yield: 20 servings
Can do ahead

Whiskey Sour Punch

2 (12 ounce) cans frozen
   lemonade concentrate
2 (12 ounce) cans frozen orange
   juice concentrate
1½ quarts water

2 quarts club soda
1 quart bourbon
1 orange, thinly sliced
Maraschino cherries

Combine all liquid ingredients. Float orange slices and cherries in drinks.

NOTE: Cherries would look nice if frozen in ice cube. Vary the alcohol to suit your taste.

Preparation: 10 minutes

Yield: 5-6 quarts
Can do ahead

White Sangria

½ gallon dry white wine
½ cup peach-flavored brandy
   (can use more)
Peel from 2 large oranges, zest
   only

Ice cubes
1 quart club soda, chilled
4 large ripe peaches, peeled,
   pitted, quartered

Mix wine, brandy, orange peel. Chill well. Just before serving, add soda and serve over ice with peaches.

NOTE: You can use fresh hulled strawberries in place of the peaches.

Preparation: 15 minutes

Serves: 8-12
Can do ahead

Boardroom Punch
A light punch, foamy and rich-looking

2 quarts orange juice
1 quart unsweetened apple juice
46 ounces unsweetened
  pineapple juice

1 litre Rhine wine
2 quarts rainbow sherbert
1 quart ginger ale

Mix all juices at least 3 hours ahead. Add wine. Just before serving scoop in sherbert. Pour ginger ale over sherbert.

NOTE: Other fruit sherberts could be substituted.

Preparation: 20 minutes

Serves: 20-25
Must do ahead

Hot Wine Punch
Tangy and relaxing on a blustery cold night

1 cup + 6 tablespoons sugar
1½ lemons, sliced
1 cup lemon juice, (about 5½
  lemons)

10 cinnamon sticks
15 whole cloves
1 gallon red wine

Combine all ingredients except wine in large pot. Heat until sugar is completely dissolved and ingredients blended. Add wine and serve hot.

NOTE: Float fruit slices for garnish. If you make ahead, reheat when serving. Serve with munchies or donuts.

Preparation: 20 minutes
Cooking: 10 minutes

Yield: 1 gallon
Can do ahead

Orange Sunrise
A summer refresher

1 (6 ounce) can frozen orange
  juice concentrate
1 cup milk
¼ cup confectioners' sugar or ½
  cup white sugar

1 teaspoon vanilla
1 cup water
5-7 ice cubes

Combine all ingredients in blender, cover, and blend for 30 seconds or until smooth.

NOTE: ¼ cup vodka could be added for zip. Put mint on top and you have a summer's delight.

Preparation: 5 minutes

Yield: 4-6 cups
Serve immediately

Hot Mulled Cider
Delicious with donuts, cheese and apple slices

½ cup brown sugar
1 teaspoon cloves
¼ teaspoon salt

Dash of nutmeg
1 cinnamon stick
2 quarts apple cider

Combine all ingredients in saucepan. Slowly bring to boil. Cover and simmer 20 minutes. Remove spices and serve in warm mug.

Preparation: 5 minutes
Cooking: 20 minutes

Serves: 8
Can do ahead

Healthy Milkshake
For all ages

2 cups frozen fruit (blueberries, strawberries, peaches, bananas, etc.), thawed

1 cup milk
2-4 tablespoons honey

Combine ingredients in blender and blend till smooth. Chill until ready to serve.

NOTE: Garnished with a cherry, it's great as a snack.

Preparation: 10 minutes

Yield: 2½-3 cups
Can do ahead

Russian Tea
The boiling spices spread a lovely aroma through the house

5 whole cloves
1 stick cinnamon
16 cups water
6 tea bags

Juice of 4 oranges
Juice of 2 lemons
1½ cups sugar

Boil spices and water for 15 minutes, remove spices. Add tea bags and let steep for 5 minutes. Remove tea bags. Add fruit juices and sugar. Stir until sugar is dissolved (you may need to reheat gently for a few moments to get sugar to dissolve). Serve hot or cold.

NOTE: The recipe can be halved nicely. In summer it's nice with fresh sprigs of mint. In winter serve it with slices of lemon with a whole clove stuck in each slice.

Preparation: 10 minutes
Cooking: 20 minutes

Yield: 3½ quarts
Can do ahead

BREADS

Uncle Sam

Bread has been called the staff of life, and during the War of 1812 it was a Troy, New York native, Uncle Sam Wilson, who supplied our soldiers with this and other sustaining provisions.

Sam Wilson owned and operated a meat packing operation in the Troy area during the early 1800's. He was a popular local personality, known for his great sense of humor, and was congenially dubbed "Uncle Sam" by his workmen and many friends. During the War of 1812, the firm of E & S Wilson, along with Elbert Anderson, a contractor from New York, enjoyed great prosperity as suppliers of all rations for the U.S. Army in New York and New Jersey.

The barrels of supplies were stamped E.A.-U.S. Local dock workers, when asked what this stamp stood for, replied that it most likely stood for Elbert Anderson and Uncle Sam Wilson. The joke was repeated among workmen and, when these same men were drafted into the Army, the joke passed quickly from them to soldiers from other parts of the country. Soon, all government property was being referred to as Uncle Sam's, and the words *Uncle Sam* and *United States* became synonymous.

The following recipes are bound to delight family and guest alike. Remember the story of Uncle Sam Wilson and never underestimate the power of a barrel of flour, or of the seemingly lowly loaf of bread. It could make your name a household word!

Apple Raisin Loaf

2 cups peeled, chopped apples
½ cup shortening
1 cup sugar
1 egg
½ cup milk
2 cups all-purpose flour

½ teaspoon cinnamon
½ teaspoon salt
1 teaspoon baking powder
1 teaspoon baking soda
1 cup raisins
1 cup nuts (optional)

Cream shortening and sugar. Add egg and milk. Sift in dry ingredients. Add chopped apples, raisins and nuts. Mix thoroughly. Pour batter into greased 9 x 5 x 3-inch loaf pan. Bake at 350°F. for 55-60 minutes. Cool before cutting.

NOTE: It is great with pork dishes and could easily be served as a breakfast "goodie" too.

Preparation: 15 minutes
Cooking: 55-60 minutes

Yield: 1 loaf
Can do ahead

Brethren Cheddar Bread
It's a good accompaniment for hearty winter soups

4 cups sifted all-purpose flour
2 tablespoons sugar
3 teaspoons baking powder
1¼ teaspoons salt
½ cup unsalted butter, chilled
   and cut in 1-inch slices

4 cups coarsely shredded
   Cheddar cheese
1 tablespoon minced fresh dill or
   1 teaspoon dill weed
2 eggs, beaten
2 cups milk

Sift together in large bowl first four ingredients. Use pastry blender to cut in butter until crumbly (like uncooked oatmeal). Stir in cheese and dill. Combine eggs and milk in separate bowl. Add this, all at once, stirring just enough to moisten dry ingredients. Divide batter into 4 well-greased 7⅜ x 3⅝ x 2¼-inch pans. Bake at 400°F. for 35-40 minutes or until browned and bread sounds hollow when thumped. Cool upright on wire racks in the pans for 10 minutes, then invert and remove pan.

Preparation: 30 minutes
Cooking: 35-40 minutes

Yield: 4 small loaves
Can be frozen

Caribbean Banana Bread

½ cup butter
1 cup sugar
2 eggs
3 large, ripe bananas, mashed
2 cups all-purpose flour

1 teaspoon baking soda
½ teaspoon salt
1 cup chopped nuts (optional)
1 teaspoon butter, melted
Cinnamon-sugar mixture

Cream butter and sugar. Beat in eggs, one at a time. Mix in mashed bananas. Sift dry ingredients together and stir into banana mixture. Add nuts. Pour into greased 9 x 5 x 3-inch loaf pan. Bake at 350°F. for 60 minutes or until a toothpick inserted into loaf comes out clean. While cake is still warm, pour melted butter over top and sprinkle with cinnamon-sugar mixture.

Preparation: 20 minutes
Cooking: 1-1¼ hours

Yield: 1 loaf
Can be frozen

Almond-Lime Bread
This is almost white, very unusual for a quick nut bread

BREAD:
3 cups sifted all-purpose flour
1 cup sugar
3 teaspoons baking powder
1 teaspoon salt
½ teaspoon baking soda
¾ cup almonds, sliced

1-2 tablespoons grated lime zest
    (rind)
1 egg
1 cup milk
4 tablespoons butter, melted
2 tablespoons lime juice

TOPPING:
2 tablespoons almonds, sliced
1 tablespoon butter, melted
2 tablespoons sugar

1 tablespoon lime juice
1-2 tablespoons grated lime rind

BREAD: Sift together flour, sugar, baking powder, salt, and baking soda into a large bowl. Stir in almonds and 1-2 tablespoons lime rind. In a small bowl, beat egg with milk, stir in melted butter and 2 tablespoons lime juice. Add all at once to flour mixture, stirring just until evenly moist. Pour into greased 9 x 5 x 3-inch loaf pan. Be sure batter is evenly spread.

TOPPING: In a small bowl, mix together the almonds, melted butter, and sugar. Spoon evenly over bread batter in loaf pan. Bake at 350°F. for 70 minutes or until done. Cool 10 minutes and remove from loaf pan. Drizzle 1 tablespoon lime juice over loaf. Sprinkle 1-2 tablespoons lime zest over loaf top. Cool completely.

TO STORE: Wrap loaf in foil or plastic wrap. Store overnight to mellow flavors and make slicing easier. Cut in thin slices.

Preparation: 45 minutes   **Yield:** 1 loaf
Cooking: 1 hour 10 minutes   Must do ahead

Beer Bread
This could be the easiest bread you've ever made

3 cups self-rising flour   1 egg, beaten
2 tablespoons sugar
12 ounces beer, at room
    temperature

Mix flour and sugar. Add egg and beer. Stir 25 strokes, no more. Pour into a greased 9 x 5 x 3-inch loaf pan. Bake at 350°F. for 1-1¼ hours or until top is golden brown. Cool and keep wrapped.

VARIATIONS: Add 1 tablespoon cinnamon and ½ cup raisins to the batter before stirring; or add ¼ cup sautéed onion and minced garlic before stirring; or sprinkle with sesame seeds before baking. Be imaginative!

Preparation: 10 minutes   **Yield:** 1 loaf
Cooking: 1-1¼ hours   Can be frozen

Poppyseed Perfection

½ cup poppyseeds   1¼ cups sugar
¾ cup milk   1 teaspoon vanilla
¾ cup butter, softened   2 teaspoons baking powder
3 eggs   2 cups all-purpose flour, sifted

Combine seeds and milk in large bowl. Let stand 3-4 hours. Let butter and eggs warm for easy mixing. Add butter, eggs, sugar, vanilla, baking powder and flour to seeds and milk. Beat with mixer 1 minute. Pour into greased and floured bread pan. Bake at 350°F. for 1¼ hours or until center springs back. Cool in pan 5 minutes and turn out.

NOTE: If using 2 small loaf pans, begin checking for doneness after baking 50 minutes.

Preparation: 10 minutes plus   **Yield:** 1 large loaf or 2 small
   3 hours   loaves
Cooking: 1¼ hours   Can be frozen

Mexican Cornbread
A spicy addition to any meal

1½ cups yellow cornmeal
3 teaspoons baking powder
1 teaspoon salt
2 eggs
⅔ cup vegetable oil

1 cup buttermilk
3 chopped jalapeno peppers
1 (17 ounce) can creamed-style
  corn
1 cup grated Cheddar cheese

Mix all ingredients in order listed, except cheese. Pour half of batter in greased 11 x 18-inch baking dish. Add half of the cheese. Add remaining batter and cover with cheese. Bake at 350°F. for 45 minutes.

NOTE: You can substitute chopped chili peppers for a milder taste.

Preparation: 15 minutes
Cooking: 45 minutes

Yield: 1 pan
Can be frozen

Lemon Bread

½ cup shortening
1 cup sugar
2 eggs, beaten
½ cup milk

Grated rind of 1 lemon
½ teaspoon salt
1½ cups all-purpose flour
1 teaspoon baking powder

TOPPING:
Juice of 1 lemon

½ cup sugar

Cream shortening and sugar. Add eggs, milk and lemon rind. Combine dry ingredients and add to the batter. Pour into a greased 9 x 5-inch loaf pan (line pan bottom with wax paper). Bake at 350°F. for 1 hour.

TOPPING: Heat juice of lemon and sugar until sugar dissolves. When loaf is removed from the oven, pour liquid over loaf. After most of liquid has been absorbed, turn bread out of loaf pan onto a plate.

Preparation: 15 minutes
Cooking: 1 hour

Yield: 1 loaf
Can do ahead

Harvesttime Pumpkin Bread
A moist bread that will keep for ages

⅔ cup sugar
1 teaspoon cinnamon
1 teaspoon cloves or nutmeg
⅔ cup margarine
4 eggs
2 cups (16 ounces) pumpkin
⅔ cup boiling water

3⅓ cups all-purpose flour
2 teaspoons baking soda
1½ teaspoons salt
½ teaspoon baking powder
⅔ cup walnuts
⅔ cup raisins

Mix sugar and spices. Cream with margarine. Add eggs and pumpkin. Stir in water and flour. Add baking soda, salt, and baking powder. Fold in walnuts and raisins. Bake in 1-pound round coffee cans or 9 x 5 x 3-inch loaf pans. Fill ½-⅔ full. Bake at 350°F. for 1 hour and 10 minutes.

Preparation: 20 minutes
Cooking: 1 hour 10 minutes

Yield: 3 large loaves and 1 small
loaf
Can do ahead

Buttery Scones

2 cups all-purpose flour
2 tablespoons sugar
1 tablespoon baking powder
¼ teaspoon salt
½ cup vegetable shortening

½ cup currants
1 egg, beaten
½ cup light cream or half and half
cream
Extra flour for kneading

Sift together dry ingredients. Using pastry blender cut the shortening into dry ingredients until mixture resembles coarse cornmeal. Stir in currants. Make a well in center of mixture and add, all at once, the mixture of egg and cream. Stir with fork until dough follows fork. Form dough into a ball and put on lightly floured surface. Knead <u>lightly</u> with fingertips 10-15 times. Roll dough into a 2-inch thick round. Cut into 12 wedges. Bake at 425°F. on ungreased baking sheet 15-20 minutes or until golden.

NOTE: Sugared Scones – omit currants, and before baking, brush top with melted butter and sprinkle with sugar.

Preparation: 15 minutes
Cooking: 20 minutes

Yield: 1 dozen
Can be frozen

Irish Soda Bread

3½ cups all-purpose flour
1 teaspoon baking soda
⅔ cup sugar
1 tablespoon baking powder

1 cup raisins
2 eggs, beaten
1½ cups buttermilk
2 tablespoons butter, melted

Stir dry ingredients together. Add raisins and coat them well. In a separate bowl, combine eggs, buttermilk and butter. Add to flour mixture. Pour in a greased 9 x 5-inch loaf pan. Bake at 350°F. for 50 minutes or until light brown on top or when a wooden toothpick inserted comes out dry.

Preparation: 15 minutes
Cooking: 1 hour

Yield: 1 loaf
Can be frozen

Strawberry Bread

1 cup all-purpose flour
½ cup sugar
1½ teaspoons cinnamon
½ teaspoon salt
½ teaspoon baking soda

2 eggs, beaten
¾ cup cooking oil
1 (10 ounce) package frozen
   strawberries, thawed
¾ cup chopped nuts

Mix dry ingredients. Add liquid ingredients. Add nuts. Mix well and pour into greased 9 x 5 x 3-inch loaf pan. Bake at 350°F. for 1 hour.

NOTE: Can sprinkle with powdered sugar. Good for breakfast.

Preparation: 15 minutes
Cooking: 1 hour

Yield: 1 loaf
Can do ahead

Popovers

4 eggs, beaten
2 cups milk

2 cups all-purpose flour
1 teaspoon salt

Hand mix eggs, milk, flour, and salt until smooth. Don't overbeat. Grease 16 muffin tins. Fill ¾ full. Bake at 450°F. for 25 minutes. Then lower oven heat to 350°F. and bake 15 minutes longer or until golden brown. Serve hot.

NOTE: You can use 12 custard cups but fill only ½ full.

Preparation: 20 minutes
Cooking: 40-45 minutes

Yield: 12-16

Zucchini Bread

All those extra zucchini can be used since this bread freezes nicely too

2 cups shredded unpeeled
   zucchini
2 cups sugar
1 cup salad oil
3 eggs
1 teaspoon vanilla
3 cups all-purpose flour

3 teaspoons baking powder
1 teaspoon each: baking soda,
   salt, cinnamon, ginger, ground
   cloves
1 cup nuts
1 cup raisins

Mix zucchini, sugar, oil, eggs and vanilla. Sift together flour, baking powder, baking soda, salt, cinnamon, ginger, and cloves. Blend dry ingredients into the zucchini mixture. Add nuts and raisins. Bake at 350°F. for 1 hour in two 9 x 5 x 3-inch ungreased loaf pans.

NOTE: Garnish with powdered sugar for a nice effect.

Preparation: 30 minutes
Cooking: 60 minutes

Yield: 2 loaves
Can be frozen

Zucchini Fruit Bread

4 eggs, beaten
2 cups sugar
1 cup oil
1 teaspoon vanilla
3½ cups all-purpose flour
1½ teaspoons baking soda
1½ teaspoons salt
¾ teaspoon baking powder

2 teaspoons cinnamon
1 cup raisins
1 cup chopped walnuts
2 cups coarsely grated zucchini
½ cup crushed pineapple
½ cup chopped maraschino
   cherries

Combine eggs, sugar, oil, and vanilla. Mix flour with baking soda, salt, baking powder, and cinnamon. Mix a small amount of flour with the raisins and nuts. Set aside. Alternately add zucchini and flour mixture to the egg mixture. Mix well after each addition. Fold in raisin-nut mixture, pineapple, and cherries. Pour into 2 greased and floured 9 x 5 x 3-inch loaf pans. Bake at 350°F. for 55 minutes.

Preparation: 30 minutes
Cooking: 55 minutes

Yield: 2 loaves
Can be frozen

Bea's Blueberry Muffins

½ cup butter or margarine
1½ cups sugar
1 egg, beaten
2 cups all-purpose flour
4 teaspoons baking powder

⅛ teaspoon salt
¾ cup milk
1 cup blueberries, fresh or
   canned, drained

Cream margarine and sugar. Add egg. Combine dry ingredients in separate bowl. Now alternate, adding first the dry ingredients and then the milk to creamed ingredients, stirring after each addition. Fold in blueberries. Fill greased and floured muffin tins ¾ full. Bake at 375°F. for 18-20 minutes.

NOTE: You could also substitute cranberries, apples, etc.

Preparation: 15 minutes
Cooking: 18-20 minutes

Yield: 24
Can be frozen

Icebox Rolls
These are as light as a feather

1 cake or package of yeast
1 teaspoon sugar
⅓ cup warm water (105-115°F)
⅓ cup sugar
½ cup shortening

1 egg, beaten
2 cups warm water
6 cups all-purpose flour
1 tablespoon salt

Dissolve yeast and 1 teaspoon sugar in water. Set aside. Cream ⅓ cup sugar and shortening. Add the egg. Add yeast mixture. Add 2 cups of warm water, flour and salt. Mix well. Grease a large bowl and store dough in refrigerator, loosely covered. When ready to use, pinch off small pieces and roll into balls. Place three pieces in each greased muffin tin. This makes a cloverleaf. Let rise in a warm place until double the size, about 2 hours. Bake at 400°F. for 15 minutes or until brown.

NOTE: This is a very soft dough. Be sure to butter your fingers before handling dough. A nice touch is to dip rolls into melted butter to help them brown.

Preparation: 20-30 minutes
Cooking: 15-20 minutes

Yield: 24
Can do ahead

Buffalo Babka

DOUGH:

1 package active dry yeast
3 tablespoons sugar
¼ cup warm water (105-115°F.)
¼ cup milk
1 cup butter or margarine,
  softened

½ teaspoon salt
4 egg yolks
½ teaspoon vanilla
4½ cups all-purpose flour,
  approximate

FILLING:

4 egg whites
¼ teaspoon cream of tartar
1 cup sugar
¾ cup golden raisins

Hot water
1¾ teaspoons cinnamon
1 cup chopped pecans

DOUGH: Dissolve yeast and 1 tablespoon sugar in warm water. Stir in milk. Set aside. In a large bowl, cream butter, remaining 2 tablespoons sugar, and salt. Add egg yolks and vanilla. Beat until light and fluffy. Add 2½ cups flour alternately with yeast mixture, beating after each addition. Let stand 20 minutes. Stir in about 1½ cups flour, or enough to make a soft dough. Shape in a ball and place in a greased bowl. Turn dough ball to grease all sides, cover tightly, and refrigerate overnight or 12 hours.

FILLING: In a deep bowl, beat egg whites until foamy with ¼ teaspoon cream of tartar. Gradually add sugar, a tablespoon at a time. Keep beating until sugar is dissolved and whites are stiff and glossy. In a small bowl, plump raisins in hot water for 5 minutes. Drain and pat raisins dry.

TO ASSEMBLE: Bring dough to room temperature or press with hands to warm and soften. On a lightly floured board, roll out half of dough to a 16 x 11-inch rectangle. Spread half of filling over width and 11 inches of length. Sprinkle with half of cinnamon, ½ cup nuts and half the raisins. Start at 11-inch side and roll up, jelly roll fashion. Repeat with remaining dough and filling. Carefully lift and place each roll in a well-greased 10-inch tube pan, seam side down. Pinch ends together to join securely. Cover and let rise in a warm, draft-free place 1½ hours or until almost double. Bake at 325°F. for 1¼ hours.

NOTE: In place of the 10-inch tube pan, just place each roll on a separate greased cookie sheet and bake 30-35 minutes.

Preparation: 1 day
Cooking: 1¼ hours

Yield: 1 or 2 loaves
Can be frozen

Buttermilk Biscuits
These are great to keep in the freezer

4 cups all-purpose flour
½ cup shortening
2 cups buttermilk

1 teaspoon baking soda
8 teaspoons baking powder
2 teaspoons salt

Mix and knead well all of the ingredients. Spoon onto a cookie sheet or roll out ¼-inch thick and cut into 2-inch rounds. Bake at 450°F. for 15 minutes and serve hot.
TO FREEZE: Bake biscuits at 450°F. for 7 minutes. Remove from cookie sheet, cool, then freeze. To serve, remove from freezer (do not defrost) and bake at 400°F. for 7 minutes.

Preparation: 15 minutes
Cooking: 15 minutes

Yield: 4-6 dozen
Can be frozen

Butter Horns
An attractive and delicious roll

1 cup butter, softened
1½ cups (12 ounces) cottage
  cheese, large curd

2 cups all-purpose flour
Dash of salt

Cream butter and cottage cheese. Add flour and salt. Refrigerate for 4 hours or overnight. Divide dough into 3 parts. Roll each part into ¼-inch thick circle. Cut circle into 12 to 16 wedges. Roll wedges, starting from outer edge and rolling in to the point. Place horns, point down, on greased cookie sheet. Bake at 350°F. for 30 minutes.

NOTE: They can be made 1 day ahead. Serve with the main course (roast) or with light lunch (salad).

Preparation: 5 hours
Cooking: 30 minutes

Yield: 36-48 rolls
Can do ahead

Katie's Bran Muffins
A delicious dark bread

2 cups whole wheat flour
1½ cups bran
2 tablespoons sugar
¼ teaspoon salt
1¼ teaspoons baking soda

2 cups buttermilk
1 egg
1 cup dark molasses
2 tablespoons butter, melted

Combine first five ingredients. Mix well. In a separate bowl, mix remaining ingredients. Add to dry ingredients, stirring enough to moisten dry mixture. Fill greased muffin tins ⅔ full. Bake at 350°F. for 20-25 minutes.

NOTE: You can substitute all-purpose flour and white milk for the whole wheat flour and buttermilk.

Preparation: 30 minutes
Cooking: 20-25 minutes

Yield: 24
Can do ahead

Cornmeal Rolls

2 packages active dry yeast
½ cup warm water (105-115°F.)
1 cup milk, scalded
½ cup shortening
⅓ cup sugar

2 tablespoons salt
½ cup cold water
5½-6 cups all-purpose flour
2 eggs, beaten
1 cup cornmeal

Add 1 teaspoon of the sugar to warm water and dissolve yeast in it. Pour milk over shortening, remaining sugar, and salt. Stir until melted. Add cold water and cool to lukewarm. Stir in 2 cups flour, eggs, yeast mixture and cornmeal. Continue stirring in flour to make a <u>soft</u> dough (may not use all flour). Knead on floured board until satiny, about 10 minutes. Roll into ball. Place in greased bowl. Grease top of dough, cover. Let rise in warm place until doubled. Punch down. Grease top and cover with wax paper and damp towel. Refrigerate overnight or up to 3 days. Punch down, shape into rolls as desired. Brush tops with melted shortening. Cover and let rise until doubled. Bake at 400°F. for 15-20 minutes.

NOTE: These can be placed in greased muffin tins. After baking, they can be frozen for up to 3 months.

Preparation: 20 minutes
Cooking: 20 minutes

Yield: 30-36 rolls
Can be frozen

Pinch-Me Coffeecake

A Christmas morning tradition, but it tastes wonderful any time of year

DOUGH:

1 envelope active dry yeast
½ cup warm water (105-115°F.)
1 teaspoon sugar
1 cup milk
¼ cup butter

¼ cup sugar
1 teaspoon salt
4 cups all-purpose flour
2 eggs

TOPPING:

¾ cup butter, melted
1½ cups sugar

5 teaspoons cinnamon
½ cup finely chopped pecans

DOUGH: Dissolve yeast in warm water with sugar. Set aside. Scald milk. In a large bowl, combine butter, sugar, salt, scalded milk, and 1½ cups flour. Beat well. Add eggs and mix well. Add yeast mixture and 2½ cups flour. Mix together well. Place in greased bowl, cover with a clean towel, and allow to rise in a warm place until doubled, about 2 hours. Punch down. Knead for 5-10 minutes. Allow to rise a second time until doubled. Punch down again. Cut dough into small pieces and roll into balls about 1 inch in size.

TOPPING: Mix together sugar, cinnamon, and nuts. Dip each dough ball into melted butter and then dip into nut mixture. Place balls in 10-inch tube pan. Allow to rise until doubled. Bake at 375°F. for 35 minutes. Allow to cool at least 30 minutes before removing from pan.

Preparation: 6 hours
Cooking: 35 minutes

Yield: 1 coffeecake
Can be frozen

Viennese Brioche Loaf
If you want a yeast bread that isn't kneaded, this one is for you!

DOUGH:
1 package active dry yeast
½ cup warm water (105-115°F.)
¼ cup sugar
1 teaspoon salt
1 teaspoon grated lemon peel

1 cup butter or margarine,
  softened
6 eggs
4½ cups sifted all-purpose flour

FILLING:
3 tablespoons butter or margarine,
  softened
⅔ cup light brown sugar,
  firmly packed
2 egg yolks
2 tablespoons milk

¼ teaspoon vanilla
2 cups finely chopped walnuts
  or pecans
¼ cup butter or margarine,
  melted
Confectioners' sugar

DOUGH: Make a day ahead. Sprinkle yeast over warm water in a large bowl. Stir until dissolved. Add sugar, salt, lemon peel, butter, eggs and 3 cups flour. Beat 4 minutes with the electric mixer at medium speed. Add remaining 1½ cups flour. Continue beating, with electric mixer at low speed, 2 minutes more, or until smooth. Cover bowl with wax paper and then a damp towel. Let rise in a warm (85°F.) place, free from drafts, until doubled in bulk; about 1½-2 hours. Cover and refrigerate overnight.

FILLING: Make the second day. In a medium bowl, mix 3 tablespoons butter, brown sugar, and egg yolks. Stir in milk and vanilla. Blend in nuts.

TO ASSEMBLE: Remove dough from refrigerator and stir down. Dough will be soft. Turn out onto a lightly floured board. Divide dough in half. Return a half to bowl and place in refrigerator until ready to use. On a lightly floured surface, roll dough half into a rectangle, 14x9 inches. Brush rolled dough with 1 tablespoon melted butter. Spread half of the filling on the rolled dough up to ½ inch from edges. From each end roll up dough lengthwise, jelly-roll fashion, toward center. Turn loaf over, place in greased 9 x 5 x 3-inch loaf pan, smooth side up. Lightly brush with melted butter. Repeat with other half of dough. Let the 2 loaves rise in warm place, covered with towel, free from drafts, until double in bulk, 1½ hours. Bake at 350°F. for 35 minutes or until golden brown. Remove from pan to rack. Sprinkle with confectioners' sugar.

NOTE: The loaves may be frozen for one month.

Preparation: 2 days
Cooking: 35 minutes

Yield: 2 loaves
Must do ahead

Sue's Refrigerator Rolls
This is a reliable, versatile recipe

2 packages active dry yeast
2 cups warm water (105-115°F.)
½ cup sugar
¼ cup shortening

1 egg
2 teaspoons salt
6½-7 cups all-purpose flour

In a large bowl, dissolve yeast in warm water. Add sugar, shortening, egg, and salt. Mix thoroughly, breaking up shortening well. Add half the flour. Blend with electric mixer. Add remaining flour, one cup at a time, working it into dough with hands. Place dough in greased bowl, turn once to bring greased side of dough to top. Cover loosely with foil or plastic wrap. Let rise in refrigerator 2 hours or more. Punch down once during that period. The dough can be kept refrigerated safely up to 3 days. 2 hours before baking, shape into rolls. Cover, let rise in warm place until doubled. Bake at 400°F. for 15 minutes. If browner top is desired, brush tops with melted butter or milk before baking.

VARIATION: For hamburger rolls, roll out dough and cut with "old-fashioned" size glass. Proceed as above.

For old-fashioned dinner rolls, substitute milk for half the water. This can only be refrigerated for one day.

Preparation: 2½-3 hours
Cooking: 15 minutes

Yield: 36
Can be frozen

Soups

Cherry Hill

From 1787 to 1963, five generations of one family lived at Cherry Hill, an 18th century manor house standing within the city limits of Albany. The house and its contents are preserved today to show the broad spectrum of change in family life in the United States from the 18th to the 20th century.

One's first impression of the rooms at Cherry Hill is of a mixture of styles. Every room, filled with furniture of 200 years, shows a glimpse of what each generation treasured. The kitchen is a wealth of history with its authentic Dutch oven and woodburning stoves. The shelves are lined with samples of preserved foods from earlier times. The children's rooms are testimonies to the ageless love of dolls and games.

The formal dining room shows the gracious lifestyle of the mid-18th century residents. One can only imagine what would have been served from the magnificent Canton China soup tureen. A visitor might have been warmed by a hearty stew on a cold winter evening or delighted with a cool bisque on a lovely summer day.

Just as Cherry Hill is an agreeable melange of designs and fashions, so too are the soups presented here. Whether you are looking for something simple—or simply elegant—you are bound to find just the right soup to start your meal.

Avgolemono Soup
A frothy version of the Greek traditional chicken-lemon soup

6 cups chicken stock
1 cup cooked chicken, cut in
  bite-size pieces
6 tablespoons uncooked rice

Dash of salt
2 eggs, separated
Juice of 2 lemons

Boil chicken stock. Add rice and salt. Cook until rice is tender. Separate eggs. Beat egg whites. Slowly beat yolks and lemon juice. Slowly add approximately 1 cup of the stock to the yolk mixture by pouring in a thin stream. Return yolk mixture to the remaining stock. Gradually blend hot stock into egg whites. Serve immediately. Do not heat or simmer.

NOTE: The soup will be richer and more rewarding if homemade chicken stock is used.

Preparation: 20 minutes
Cooking: 20 minutes

Serves: 6-8
Serve immediately

New England Corn Chowder
The longer this soup simmers the better it gets

½ pound salt pork, ⅛-inch cubes,
  rind discarded
6 medium onions, chopped
12 medium potatoes, ¼-inch
  cubes
2 (20 ounce) packages frozen corn

2 (12 ounce) cans niblet corn
  with juice
½ gallon milk (if needed, add
  1 quart more)
¼ cup butter
Salt and white pepper, to taste

In a Dutch oven, sauté cubed salt pork until transparent and starting to get brown. Add onions and sauté until transparent only. Add cubed potatoes and cover with water. Boil, covered, for 5 minutes. Add corn. Continue to cook slowly another 5-8 minutes but <u>not</u> until potatoes are mushy. Add milk, butter, salt, and pepper. Simmer very slowly, <u>do not boil</u>, for 30 minutes. The flavor improves with longer simmering–but it may be served after just 30 minutes of simmering.

NOTE: The soup can be cooked and frozen up to 6 months.

Preparation: 45 minutes
Cooking: 15-30 minutes

Yield: 16-24 cups
Can do ahead

French Vegetable Beef Soup
The Parmesan cheese is the secret ingredient to this delicious soup

¼ cup salad oil
2 pounds stew beef, cut into
  ½-inch cubes
1 (10½ ounce) can condensed
  onion soup
5 soup cans water
1 (6 ounce) can tomato paste
1 tablespoon basil
½ teaspoon salt

¼ teaspoon pepper
8 large carrots, sliced
2 cups sliced celery
1 (16 ounce) can undrained
  wax beans
1 (16 ounce) can undrained
  kidney beans
½ cup grated Parmesan cheese

In a Dutch oven, heat the oil over medium high heat. Add the meat and brown. Reduce heat to medium. Stir in undiluted onion soup, 5 soup cans of water, tomato paste, basil, salt, and pepper. Cover and simmer for 1½ hours. Add carrots, celery, wax beans, and kidney beans. Reheat to boiling and simmer for 20 minutes. Stir in cheese and simmer for 10 minutes.

NOTE: A 1-pound can of green beans and leftover corn, if available, can be added also.

Preparation: 45 minutes
Cooking: 2½ hours

Serves: 6-8
Can do ahead

Martha's Lentil Soup
A spicy lentil soup!

¾ cup brown lentils
1 medium onion, chopped
4 garlic cloves, sliced
6 peppercorns, crushed
2 bay leaves, crushed
½ teaspoon each: ground cloves,
  cinnamon, ground ginger

1 fresh or canned green chili
  pepper, sliced and seeds
  removed
3 (10½ ounce) cans beef broth
Salt, to taste
3 tablespoons chopped parsley,
  to garnish

In a large pan combine all ingredients <u>except</u> parsley. Bring to a boil. Cover and simmer until lentils are soft. If necessary, add water to keep a thick soup consistency. Serve garnished with parsley.

NOTE: Substitute homemade beef stock for a heartier beef flavor.

Preparation: 10 minutes
Cooking: 1½ hours

Serves: 4
Can do ahead

Curried Celery Soup

4 tablespoons butter
6 large stalks celery, chopped
½ teaspoon curry powder
2 cups chicken broth

2 cups milk
⅛ teaspoon white pepper
4 tablespoons heavy cream
4 tablespoons slivered almonds

Melt butter in saucepan. Add celery and curry powder. Cook over low heat for 15 minutes, stirring occasionally. Do not let celery brown. Add chicken broth and bring to a boil. Cover, reduce heat and simmer 60 minutes. Blend in milk and pepper. Transfer to food processor or blender and mix until almost smooth. Some small chunks of celery should remain. Return mixture to saucepan and heat. Just before serving stir in heavy cream and almonds.

Preparation: 15 minutes
Cooking: 1½ hours

Serves: 8
Serve immediately

Autumn Cider Soup
Unusual and delicious, great for lunch or a light dinner

1 cup butter or margarine
⅓ cup minced leek
¼ cup minced celery
2 tablespoons minced green
  pepper
2 tablespoons snipped parsley
2 tablespoons all-purpose flour
¼ teaspoon dry mustard
¼ teaspoon salt
Dash of white pepper

1 tablespoon Worcestershire
  sauce
1½ cups chicken broth
1¼ cups grated sharp
  Cheddar cheese
1 cup hard cider (any apple cider)
⅓ cup heavy cream
Snipped chives or parsley,
  to garnish

In a large saucepan, melt the butter. Add the leek, celery, and green pepper. Sauté over medium heat until tender. Add parsley, flour, mustard, salt, pepper, and Worcestershire sauce. Cook over medium heat for 1 minute, stirring constantly. Stir in chicken broth. Heat to boiling, stirring constantly. Boil and stir for 1 minute. Add cheese. Cook over low heat until cheese melts. Remove from heat and cool to room temperature. Pour cooled soup into blender and purée until smooth. Return to saucepan. Add cider and cream. Cook over low heat until hot. Serve sprinkled with chives or parsley.

Preparation: 15 minutes
Cooking: 15 minutes

Serves: 6
Can do ahead

Hot and Sour Soup

An Oriental market will supply the special ingredients
needed to make the soup

3 (13¾ ounce) cans chicken broth
¼ pound raw pork, shredded
¼ cup Chinese mushrooms,
  soaked 30 minutes in warm
  water, shredded (reserve liquid)
12 dried lily buds, soaked, hard
  end trimmed, cut in halves
¼ cup bamboo shoots, shredded
1 cake fresh bean curd, drained,
  shredded
½ teaspoon sugar

2½ tablespoons light soy sauce
3 tablespoons red wine vinegar
¼ teaspoon freshly ground
  black pepper
2 tablespoons cornstarch mixed
  with ¼ cup water in which
  mushrooms soaked
2 tablespoons chopped scallions
1 teaspoon sesame seed oil
  with chili
1 egg, beaten

Bring chicken stock to a boil. Add pork and bring to a boil again. Remove
scum. Add mushrooms, lily buds, and bamboo shoots. Bring to a boil.
Turn heat to medium and cook for 3 minutes. Return to a boil. Add bean
curd. Mix together sugar, soy sauce, vinegar, and pepper. Add to soup
and bring to a boil. Stir cornstarch mixture again and add to soup, stirring slowly. Simmer for approximately 1 minute until thick. Add scallions and oil. Stir and remove from heat. Slowly add egg, stirring in figure
8 pattern. Serve hot.

Preparation: 30 minutes
Cooking: 30 minutes

Serves: 6
Serve immediately

Ham and Potato Chowder

½ cup butter
1 onion, diced
2 cups diced baked ham
1 cup chopped celery
12 ounces (or more) diced or
  sliced fresh mushrooms

3 cups diced raw potatoes
½ teaspoon pepper
6 tablespoons all-purpose flour
6 cups milk
Salt, to taste
Dash of chopped chives

In a Dutch oven, melt butter and sauté onion, ham, celery, and mushrooms. Add potatoes and cook 10 minutes over medium heat, stirring
occasionally, until potatoes are done but not mushy. Remove from heat.
Add pepper, flour, and milk. Heat slowly. Do not boil. Add salt to taste.
Garnish with chopped chives.

Preparation: 10 minutes
Cooking: 30 minutes

Serves: 6-8
Serve immediately

Cheesy Cauliflower Soup

2 (10 ounce) packages frozen
   cauliflower (or fresh
   cauliflower)
2 cups water
½ cup chopped onion
¼ cup butter or margarine

½ cup all-purpose flour
6 chicken bouillon cubes
2 cups grated Cheddar cheese
2 cups milk
⅛-¼ teaspoon nutmeg

In a saucepan, cook cauliflower in 1 cup water until tender. Drain and reserve liquid and 1 cup cauliflower separately. In a food processor or blender, blend remaining cauliflower and reserved liquid. Set aside. In a heavy saucepan, cook onion in butter until tender. Stir in flour. Gradually add remaining 1 cup water and dissolved bouillon cubes. Stir until blended and thick. Stir in puréed cauliflower, reserved cauliflower, and cheese. Heat until cheese melts. Add milk and nutmeg.

NOTE: Varying the sharpness of the Cheddar cheese will affect this soup.

Preparation: 15 minutes
Cooking: 20 minutes

Serves: 6-8
Can be frozen

Squash Bisque
Great before a pork roast dinner

2 pounds butternut squash,
   peeled and cubed
2 medium-small onions, peeled
   and quartered
4 small tart green apples, peeled
   and quartered
2 large stalks celery, quartered

6 scallions, white part only
6 cups chicken broth
4 egg yolks
½ cup half and half cream
¼ teaspoon white pepper
Salt, to taste

Chop squash, onions, apples, celery, and scallions together. Pour chicken broth in a large stock pot. Add the vegetables and apples and bring to a boil. Turn heat down and simmer for 30 minutes. With a slotted spoon, remove vegetables and apples from stockpot and place in a food processor or blender with 2 tablespoons of broth. Purée until smooth. Beat the egg yolks, half and half cream, and ¾ cup of the broth together until well blended. Return puréed mixture to stock pot. Add egg mixture. Stir and heat just to boiling. Season with pepper. Serve hot.

Preparation: 20 minutes
Cooking: 45 minutes

Serves: 8
Can do ahead

Potato Soup
Easy – for non-cooks!

2 cups finely diced potatoes
1 cup boiling water
1 teaspoon salt
1 small onion, finely sliced

¼ teaspoon freshly ground
   pepper
2 cups sour cream
Parsley, minced

In a 2-quart Dutch oven, combine potatoes, water, salt, onion, and pepper. Cook for 15 minutes. Add sour cream and simmer until potatoes are tender. Serve hot. Garnish with parsley.

Preparation: 15 minutes
Cooking: 30 minutes

Serves: 4-6
Serve immediately

Potato Vegetable Soup

4 cups chicken broth
½ teaspoon salt
4 medium potatoes, peeled and
   cut into eighths
3 onions, chopped

4 stalks celery, chopped
2 carrots, chopped
2 tablespoons parsley, finely
   chopped
2 tablespoons butter

Bring chicken broth to a simmer. Add salt, potatoes, onions, celery, and carrots. Cover and simmer for 20 minutes. Mash potatoes into broth using a hand masher. Add parsley and simmer for 5 minutes. Add butter. Serve hot.

Preparation: 40 minutes
Cooking: 25 minutes

Serves: 3
Serve immediately

Onion Soup

2 teaspoons butter
2 cups thinly sliced onions
1 teaspoon all-purpose flour
3 cups canned beef broth

4 slices French bread, lightly
   toasted
½ cup grated Swiss cheese
½ cup grated Parmesan cheese

In a medium saucepan sauté onions in melted butter. Stir in flour and continue to cook. Stir in broth and bring to a boil. Reduce heat and simmer for 15 minutes. Preheat broiler. Divide soup between two ovenproof bowls. Top each bowl with 2 slices of toasted bread. Sprinkle with cheeses and brown under broiler, being careful not to burn top.

Preparation: 5 minutes
Cooking: 20 minutes

Serves: 2
Can do ahead

Italian Sausage and Bean Soup

1 pound mild Italian sausage
1 clove garlic, minced
1 large onion, chopped
⅓ cup parsley, chopped
2 carrots, thinly sliced
1 cup mushrooms, thinly sliced

1 (16 ounce) can garbanzo beans
  (chick peas), undrained
3 cups water
2 beef bouillon cubes
½ teaspoon rubbed sage
Salt and pepper, to taste

Remove casings from sausage and slice or crumble into bite-size pieces. Cook in a 3-quart saucepan, turning frequently until browned. Add garlic, onion, ¼ cup parsley, carrots, and mushrooms. Cook until onion is limp. Remove as much grease as possible. Add garbanzo beans with liquid from can, water, bouillon cubes and sage. Bring to a boil and simmer for 10 minutes or until carrots are tender. Season with salt and pepper to taste. Garnish with remaining parsley.

Preparation: 20 minutes
Cooking: 20 minutes

Serves: 4
Can do ahead

Mild Red Pepper Soup

1 cup chopped onions
2 cups chopped sweet red
  peppers
3 tablespoons olive oil
1½ pounds tomatoes, peeled
  and chopped
1 teaspoon salt

1½ cups water <u>or</u> chicken stock
3 tablespoons butter
3 tablespoons all-purpose flour
1 teaspoon lemon peel
Freshly ground pepper
Sour cream
Freshly chopped parsley

Sauté onions and red peppers in olive oil until tender. Add tomatoes and simmer for 10 minutes. Add the salt. Purée in blender or food processor until blended but not completely smooth. Add water <u>or</u> chicken stock. Melt butter in a saucepan. Stir in flour and cook to make a roux. Slowly add the soup whisking to blend. Simmer for 10 minutes. Add lemon peel and season with pepper. Serve hot. Garnish with sour cream and freshly chopped parsley.

Preparation: 15 minutes
Cooking: 30 minutes

Serves: 6 servings
Can do ahead

Seafood Bisque

¼ cup chopped celery
2 tablespoons finely chopped
  onion
2 tablespoons butter
1 (10½ ounce) can cream of
  shrimp soup

1 (10¾ ounce) can cream of
  mushroom soup
2 cups milk
¼ cup dry sherry
1 (5 ounce) can crabmeat
1 tablespoon snipped parsley

In a medium saucepan, sauté celery and onion in butter until tender. Alternately add soup and milk. Heat soup. Add sherry, crabmeat and parsley.

Preparation: 10 minutes
Cooking: 20 minutes

Yields: 4
Serve immediately

Hearty Cabbage Soup
This soup is simple to make, and inexpensive but nutritious

3 tablespoons butter, melted
2½ cups chopped cabbage
3-4 potatoes, peeled and cubed
½ cup water
1 chicken bouillon cube

1 cup water
2 cups half and half cream
Salt and pepper, to taste
1 cup shredded Swiss cheese

Combine butter, cabbage, potatoes and water in a pot. Cover and cook until tender, about 45 minutes. Add bouillon cube, water, half and half cream, salt, pepper, and cheese. Heat through but do not boil.

Preparation: 15 minutes
Cooking: 50 minutes

Serves: 6
Can do ahead

Beef Barley Vegetable Soup

½ pound ground beef
½ cup each: carrots, onion,
  celery, zucchini, potatoes
  (peeled), diced
1 cup canned tomatoes
1 teaspoon chopped parsley
½ cup pearl barley

1 cup water
5 cups beef stock (fresh, canned
  or bouillon)
1 bay leaf
Dash of garlic powder
Salt and pepper, to taste

In a small skillet, brown ground beef, breaking it into small pieces as it cooks. Drain fat and set meat aside. Place remaining ingredients except salt and pepper into a 4-quart pot. Cover and simmer on low heat for

½ hour. Add meat. Cover and simmer for 1 hour, stirring occasionally. Season to taste with salt and pepper.

Preparation: 20 minutes **Serves:** 6
Cooking: 1½ hours Can do ahead

Cheddar Chowder
A delicious, hearty soup that's perfect for Sunday suppers

2 cups diced potatoes ¼ cup butter
½ cup sliced carrots ¼ cup all-purpose flour
½ cup sliced celery 2 cups milk
¼ cup chopped onion 2 cups shredded sharp
¾ teaspoon salt   Cheddar cheese
¼ teaspoon pepper 1 cup cooked ham, cubed
2 cups boiling water

In a pot, combine potatoes, carrots, celery, onion, salt, and pepper. Add water. Cover and simmer for 10 minutes. Do not drain. In a separate saucepan, combine butter, flour, and milk to make a white sauce. Add cheese to white sauce. Stir until melted. Add ham and undrained vegetables. Heat but do not boil.

Preparation: 30 minutes **Serves:** 6-8
Cooking: 15 minutes Can do ahead

Mock Oyster Soup
Mushrooms take the place of oysters

½ cup minced onion 4½ teaspoons all-purpose flour
½ cup finely chopped celery 1 teaspoon salt
⅛ teaspoon oregano Dash of each: black pepper,
⅛ teaspoon thyme   red pepper
4 tablespoons butter 2 cups half and half cream
½ pound mushrooms Snipped parsley, to garnish

In a 2-quart saucepan, sauté onion, celery, oregano, and thyme in butter for 5 minutes or until onion is tender. Add mushrooms and continue to sauté for 5 minutes or until mushrooms are tender. Stir in flour, salt, and pepper until completely mixed. Slowly stir in cream. Heat and stir until thick and creamy. Correct seasoning. Garnish with parsley. Serve hot.

Preparation: 30 minutes **Serves:** 4
Cooking: 30 minutes Serve immediately

Clam Chowder

2 (10 ounce) cans minced clams
6 ounces bacon, raw, diced
1 large onion, coarsely chopped
1 medium-sized leek, sliced
  (optional)
2 medium-sized potatoes, peeled
  and chopped
1 bay leaf

1 stalk celery, chopped
½ teaspoon dried thyme leaves
1 (28 ounce) can whole tomatoes,
  coarsely chopped, with liquid
5 cups water
1 (8 ounce) can tomato sauce
2 teaspoons salt
Dash of pepper

Drain clams and reserve clams and liquid. Place diced bacon in a 5-quart Dutch oven. Cook bacon over moderately low heat until cooked but not crisp. Add onion and leek and cook until tender. Add clam liquid, potatoes, bay leaf, celery, thyme, tomatoes, water, tomato sauce, salt, and pepper. Stir well. Bring to a boil over moderate heat. Cover and reduce to simmer. Cook for approximately 30 minutes or until vegetables are tender. Add clams and cook for 5 minutes.

Preparation: 20 minutes
Cooking: 45 minutes

Yields: 6-8 servings
Can do ahead

Very Best New England Clam Chowder

2 dozen cherrystone clams
2 tablespoons olive oil
2 tablespoons butter
2 small onions, chopped
6 medium potatoes, peeled
1 bottle of clam juice
1 cup milk

1 cup heavy cream
½ cup sour cream
Garlic powder, salt, and pepper,
  to taste
2 teaspoons all-purpose flour
2 tablespoons chopped parsley,
  garnish

Scrub cherrystone clams to clean off the sand. Add the olive oil and butter to a large pot, put in the clams, cover and cook over medium heat until clams are opened. Reserve clam juice. Mince the clams and set aside. In another pot, sauté onions until wilted. Cube the raw potatoes and add to onions along with the reserved clam juice. The potatoes should be barely covered; if not, add a little bottled clam juice. Cook potatoes in clam juice until tender. Remove from heat. Mash up potatoes slightly with a potato masher. Add milk, heavy cream, sour cream, and seasonings. Return to heat. Add flour and allow to thicken. Add the minced clams. Top with chopped parsley for garnish.

Preparation: 30 minutes
Cooking: 45 minutes

Serves: 4-6
Serve immediately

Hot Shrimp Soup
A meal in itself

½ cup thinly sliced green onions
¼ cup butter
½ pound fresh mushrooms, sliced
3 tablespoons all-purpose flour
1 cup half and half cream
1½ cups milk

¼ cup white wine
1 teaspoon salt
¼ teaspoon pepper
1½ pounds fresh shrimp, cooked
2 tablespoons parsley, to garnish

In a 2-quart pan, sauté onions in melted butter until limp. Add mushrooms and sauté for 5 minutes. Add flour, stirring thoroughly. Add half and half cream and stir until heated. Gradually add milk. Stir thoroughly while heating. Add wine, salt, pepper, and cooked shrimp. Stir over low heat until shrimp is heated through. Serve immediately with parsley sprinkled over top.

Preparation: 45 minutes
Cooking: 15 minutes

Serves: 4 servings
Serve immediately

Bluefish-Oyster Stew

2 tablespoons butter
½ pound onions, chopped
1 pint shucked oysters with
   their liquid
¾-1 cup water
1 pound potatoes, peeled and cut
   into ¼-inch cubes
Salt and pepper, to taste

1 bay leaf
2 cups milk
1 cup heavy cream
1½ pounds skinless, boneless
   bluefish fillets, cut into
   1-inch cubes
Cayenne pepper

In a large saucepan, melt butter and sauté onions until wilted. Add oyster liquid and water. Add potatoes. Bring to a boil. Add salt, pepper, and bay leaf. Cover and simmer until potatoes are done, about 12 minutes. Add milk, heavy cream, and bluefish. Bring just to boil, stirring gently. Add oysters and remove from heat. When ready to serve, reheat thoroughly but do not overcook. Sprinkle cayenne pepper on top of each serving.

Preparation: 30 minutes
Cooking: 15-20 minutes

Serves: 4
Can do ahead

Chilled Curried Zucchini Soup

2 pounds zucchini, scrubbed, trimmed and chopped
1 cup minced scallions
6 tablespoons butter
1 tablespoon curry powder
1 tablespoon ground cumin (optional)

2 cups canned (or fresh) chicken broth
3 cups buttermilk
Salt and pepper, to taste

FOR GARNISH (optional):
½ carrot, trimmed, peeled and sliced on the diagonal
½ zucchini, scrubbed, trimmed and sliced on the diagonal

2 radishes, cleaned and thinly sliced

In a large heavy saucepan, steam zucchini and scallions in butter over moderate heat. (Make certain to cover this with a buttered round of wax paper and the lid.) Cook for 15 minutes or until zucchini are soft. Add curry powder and cumin. Stir in chicken broth. In a blender, purée mixture in batches. Transfer the puréed mixture to a large bowl and stir in buttermilk. Add salt and pepper to taste. Chill for 4 hours or more. Thin the soup with chicken broth or buttermilk to taste, if desired.
Garnishes should be chilled in ice water for at least 1 hour. Drain and pat dry.

Preparation: 15 minutes
Cooking: 15 minutes

Serves: 6 servings
Can do ahead

Gazpacho Andaluz

1 cup finely chopped tomatoes
½ cup finely chopped each: green pepper, celery, cucumber
¼ cup finely chopped onion
2 teaspoons chopped parsley
1-2 garlic cloves, minced
3 tablespoons red wine vinegar
2 tablespoons olive oil

1 teaspoon salt
¼ teaspoon freshly ground pepper
½ teaspoon Worcestershire sauce
1 (32 ounce) bottle or can tomato juice
Cucumber slices, or parsley sprigs, to garnish

Place all ingredients in a blender or food processor. Blend or process until vegetables are finely chopped, but not puréed. Refrigerate. Serve cold, garnished with sliced cucumber or parsley sprigs.

Preparation: 30 minutes

Serves: 4-6
Must do ahead

Cold Broccoli Soup

1 small onion, chopped
1 stalk celery, chopped
1 carrot, chopped
2 tablespoons butter
1 pound (or 3 large stalks)
    broccoli

3 cups chicken broth
1½ cups half and half cream
Salt
Pepper

In a large pot, sauté the vegetables in butter over medium heat for 5 minutes or until golden, stirring occasionally. Wash the broccoli thoroughly. Cut off the buds. Peel the stalks and coarsely chop them. Place chopped stalks in the pot and add chicken broth. Bring to a boil. Reduce heat and simmer for 15 minutes. Add the broccoli buds. Cook for 5 minutes or until buds are tender. With a slotted spoon, remove 4 buds and set them aside. Purée soup in a blender. Cool, uncovered. Add cream. Chill for at least 4 hours. Season with salt and pepper. Serve garnished with a broccoli bud in each serving bowl.

NOTE: This may also be served hot.

Preparation: 30 minutes
Cooking: 30 minutes

Serves: 4 servings
Must do ahead

Cream of Green Bean Soup
Delicious hot or cold

½ pound green beans, ends
    snipped off
2 small potatoes, peeled and
    quartered
1 medium onion, quartered
3 cups chicken broth

¼ cup butter
2 small garlic cloves, crushed
1 tablespoon dill
Salt and pepper, to taste
1 tablespoon lemon juice
¼ cup sour cream

In a large saucepan, combine beans, potatoes, onion, chicken broth, butter, garlic, and dill. Bring to a boil. Reduce heat. Cover and simmer 30 minutes. Season with salt and pepper. Purée soup in food processor or blender in batches until smooth. Return soup to saucepan. Stir in lemon juice and sour cream. Heat to serve or chill before serving.

Preparation: 10 minutes
Cooking: 30 minutes

Serves: 4-6
Serve immediately

Chilled Squash Soup

2 tablespoons butter
1 medium onion, thinly sliced
½ lemon, thinly sliced
¼ cup all-purpose flour
6 cups chicken broth

1½ pounds summer, yellow
  squash, sliced
¼ teaspoon white pepper
1 cup heavy cream

In a large saucepan, melt the butter and sauté the onion and lemon for about 10 minutes. Sprinkle the flour in the saucepan and cook, stirring until the flour is absorbed. Add the chicken broth, squash, and pepper and simmer for 1 hour. Place in a food processor or blender and purée. Stir in the cream. Chill several hours or overnight.

Preparation: 15 minutes
Cooking: 1 hour

Serves: 6-8
Must do ahead

Summertime Olive Soup
Similar to gazpacho, without the tomatoes

1 pint plain yogurt
1 (10½ ounce) can chicken broth
1 (16 ounce) can pitted black
  olives, thinly sliced
½ cup peeled, chopped
  cucumbers

¼ cup diced scallions
¼ cup diced green pepper
1 tablespoon parsley flakes

In a large bowl, combine all ingredients. Stir until yogurt is well blended. Chill thoroughly for 6 hours.

Preparation: 15 minutes

Yield: 1 quart
Must do ahead

Strawberry Champagne "Soup"

1 pint fresh ripe strawberries
1 bottle champagne, chilled

Mint sprigs, if available

Purée strawberries by pushing them through a sieve to remove the seeds and skin. Chill puréed strawberries.

TO SERVE: Pour purée into 4 soup bowls or champagne glasses. Open chilled champagne at the table to avoid it becoming flat. Pour champagne into purée. Garnish with a sprig of mint.

Preparation: 20 minutes

Serves: 4
Serve immediately

SALADS

The Shakers

The flowering of the Shakers in 18th and 19th century America was due in large part to their uncommon industry and inventiveness in agriculture. The people who gave us the clothespin, the match, and the broom also improved upon the plow, the rake, and countless other farm implements—all of which were used to raise bountiful crops and well-fed livestock. The sowing of seeds was both a labor of love and a spiritual inspiration: "Seed sown in the unseen soil of the heart," they said, "will germinate, blossom and bring forth fruit according to its kind."

In 1790, Joseph Turner, a Shaker from Watervliet, just up the river from Albany, had a surplus of seeds in his garden and decided to offer them for sale. From these small beginnings, the seed industry grew, and Shaker know-how was scattered over all parts of the United States and beyond. After seed sales came herbs, which the Shakers packaged in neatly printed envelopes or sacks, advertised in almanacs, and distributed through peddlers or city agents. Because of the Shakers' love of the land, the quality of food in America was greatly improved.

The Shakers themselves set a simple and plentiful table, though they were somewhat averse to meat. During one Thanksgiving celebration, a Shaker poet proclaimed, "Our tables groan under the burden of cake, cream and curd, of candies and nuts and such apples! But no murdered bird." The Shakers were among the first to advocate the greater use of vegetables and fruit in the diet, and their beliefs had an important impact on the eating habits of those living outside of their communities. It is clear from the recipes in this section that their spirit lives on. Follow the Shakers' example: Waste nothing and eat plenty of lettuce, and you will "reap a rich harvest of true felicity."

Bean Salad

SALAD:

2 (16 ounce) cans whole green
   beans, drained
1 large onion, sliced

3 tablespoons oil
3 tablespoons wine vinegar

DRESSING:

½ cup mayonnaise
1 tablespoon lemon juice
1 teaspoon horseradish
1 cup sour cream

¼ teaspoon dry mustard
¼ teaspoon onion salt
Paprika

SALAD: Place drained beans in rectangular covered container. Add sliced onion. Pour oil and vinegar on top. Cover and marinate overnight.

DRESSING: Combine all ingredients and mix well. Cover and chill.

TO SERVE: Drain the beans and place on a bed of lettuce. Pour dressing on top. Sprinkle with paprika.

NOTE: Serve individually or on a large tray. Garnish with onions and tomato wedges.

Preparation: 20 minutes

Serves: 4-6
Must do ahead

Marinated Carrots

5 cups carrots, peeled and sliced
Water
1 medium onion, peeled
1 small green pepper, cored and
   seeded
1 (10¾ ounce) can tomato soup

½ cup salad oil (not olive)
1 cup sugar
¾ cup vinegar
1 teaspoon each: prepared
   mustard, Worcestershire sauce,
   salt, and pepper.

Cover carrots with water and cook until crisply tender in a large sauce-pan or Dutch oven. Drain and cool. Slice onion and peppers in rings and mix with carrots. Mix tomato soup, salad oil, sugar, vinegar, mustard, Worcestershire sauce, salt, and pepper together and pour over vegetables. Cover, chill and marinate at least 12 hours or up to 2 days. To serve, drain and place in a dish.

NOTE: Carrots get better the longer they marinate. Garnish with additional pepper rings.

Preparation: 15 minutes
Cooking: 20 minutes
Marinating: At least 12 hours

Serves: 8
Must do ahead

Celery Root Remoulade

1 large celery root, peeled and
   shredded
1 cup mayonnaise
¼ cup Dijon mustard
¼ cup chopped parsley

2 teaspoons lemon juice
2 tablespoons heavy cream
2 scallions, chopped (white and
   green parts)
Black pepper

Mix together the mayonnaise, mustard, parsley, lemon juice, cream, and pepper. Toss this dressing with the shredded celery root and scallions.

NOTE: May be made 1-2 days ahead of time and refrigerated until ready to serve.

Preparation: 25 minutes

Serves: 14-16
Can make ahead

Cucumbers in Sour Cream

1 large or 2 small cucumbers
1 cup sour cream
1 tablespoon vinegar

1 tablespoon sugar
Salt and pepper, to taste
Paprika

Peel cucumbers and slice very thin. Mix sour cream, vinegar, sugar, salt, and pepper. Pour over cucumbers. Be sure each slice is covered. Refrigerate for 30 minutes. Sprinkle paprika over top and serve.

Preparation: 10 minutes

Serves: 4
Must do ahead

Endive Salad with Walnuts and Grapes

2-3 bunches endive
1 cup sweet, ripe seedless grapes,
   remove stems
¼ cup coarsely broken walnut
   meats
4 tablespoons olive oil

2 tablespoons imported French
   walnut oil
2 tablespoons wine vinegar
Salt
Pepper

Wash and chill endive. Break endive into small pieces and place in bowl with grapes and walnuts. Combine olive oil, walnut oil, wine vinegar, salt, and pepper. Mix well. Pour over endive mixture and toss until well coated.

Preparation: 10 minutes

Serves: 4
Serve immediately

Layered Salad
A festive looking salad

SALAD:
1 head lettuce, shredded
½ cup chopped celery
½ cup chopped green pepper

¼ cup chopped onion
1 (16 ounce) package frozen peas,
   defrosted

DRESSING:
1½ cups mayonnaise
2 tablespoons sugar

½ cup sour cream

TOPPING:
½ pound shredded Cheddar
   cheese

10 slices crisp-cooked bacon,
   crumbled

SALAD: In a clear, glass, high-sided bowl (at least 7 inches in diameter), layer all of the salad ingredients as listed.

DRESSING: Mix mayonnaise, sugar, and sour cream. Spread over layered salad. Refrigerate for 24 hours.

TOPPING: Sprinkle cheese and bacon on top of dressing just before serving.

Preparation: ½ hour

Serves: 6-8
Must do ahead

Three Green Salad with Warm Brie

Romaine lettuce
Endive lettuce
Red leaf lettuce
⅔ cup olive oil
⅓ cup fresh lemon juice

Salt
White pepper
8 wedges brie (4 inches long
   and 1 inch wide)

Wash, rinse, chill, and tear lettuce into large bowl. Combine oil, lemon juice, salt, and pepper and whisk to blend well. Let stand 1 hour at room temperature. Whisk dressing over greens and toss well. Divide among serving plates. Arrange brie on baking sheet and bake at 350°F. until warm but not runny (about 1 minute). Top each salad with a wedge of brie.

Preparation: 15 minutes
Cooking: 1 minute

Serves: 8
Serve immediately

Salade Facile
The capers make this dressing special

DRESSING:

1 teaspoon salt	½ teaspoon basil
4 cloves garlic, crushed	¼ cup parsley
1 teaspoon dry mustard	⅓ cup olive oil
¼ teaspoon black pepper	3 tablespoons wine vinegar
½ teaspoon oregano	2 tablespoons capers

GREENS:

3 tablespoons minced scallions	2 tomatoes
3 heads bib lettuce	3 tablespoons walnuts
1 Belgian endive	

DRESSING: Mix ingredients in order.

SALAD: Prepare greens. Toss dressing with greens at least 5 minutes.

NOTE: Dressing should be very thick.

Preparation: 30 minutes   **Serves:** 4-6
                                     Can do ahead

Mushrooms and Artichokes Vinaigrette

2 (9 ounce) packages frozen artichoke hearts	½ cup salad oil
1 pound mushrooms, washed and trimmed	2 tablespoons cider vinegar
	2 tablespoons lemon juice
	1 tablespoon prepared mustard
2 (4 ounce) jars pimientos, drained	⅛ teaspoon salt
	⅛ teaspoon pepper

Prepare artichokes according to package directions, omitting salt. Slice mushrooms thinly. Cut pimiento in strips. With a wire whisk, combine oil, vinegar, lemon juice, mustard, salt, and pepper in a large bowl. Add artichokes, mushrooms, and pimiento and toss to coat with dressing. Cover and chill at least one hour, stirring occasionally.

NOTE: Serve on lettuce leaves. Canned artichokes (14 ounce size) may be substituted for frozen artichokes but there may be more and they may be larger. If using canned artichokes, drain and follow remaining instructions.

Preparation: 20 minutes   **Serves:** 6-8
                                     Must do ahead

Alsatian and Sophisticated Potato Salad
Gives your cookout a real lift

2 pounds small, new red-skinned
   potatoes
Water
Salt, to taste
6 slices lean bacon
4 tablespoons finely chopped
   onion

3 tablespoons finely chopped
   parsley
Salt and pepper, to taste
1 tablespoon wine vinegar
5 tablespoons vegetable, peanut
   or corn oil
Lettuce leaves, for garnish

Cover potatoes with salted water in a large saucepan or Dutch oven. Bring
to a boil and cook until tender about 15-20 minutes. Remove from heat
and cool enough to peel. Cut potatoes into ¼-inch slices, put into bowl
and keep warm. Cook bacon until crisp. Drain, chop coarsely and set
aside. Add the onion and parsley to the potatoes and season to taste. Add
vinegar, oil, and ½ the bacon and toss. Spoon into a serving bowl and
garnish with the remaining bacon and lettuce.

Preparation: 10 minutes
Cooking: 20 minutes

Serves: 6-8
Can do ahead

Sour Cream Potato Salad

7 cups cubed cooked potatoes
   (about 3 pounds)
⅓ cup Italian salad dressing
   (prepared or your own)
4 hard-cooked eggs
⅔ cup mayonnaise
¾ cup sour cream

1½ teaspoons prepared mustard
⅓ cup chopped green onion
1 teaspoon salt
¼ teaspoon celery seed
½ pound bacon, cooked and
   crumbled (optional)

While potatoes are still warm, combine them with the Italian salad dressing. Cool. Separate egg yolks from whites. Mash the yolks. Chop the egg
whites and add them and the remaining ingredients to the yolks. Fold
into potato mixture and chill thoroughly.

Preparation: 1 hour
Cooking: 30 minutes

Serves: 8
Must do ahead

Spanish Slaw
A nice change from "mayonnaise slaw"

SALAD:

3 pounds cabbage	1 red pepper, cored and seeded or
1 onion, peeled	2 ounces pimiento
1 green pepper, cored and seeded	½ cup green olives, chopped
1 cup cauliflower florets	1 cup sugar
1 cup peeled, sliced carrots	

DRESSING:

¾ cup salad oil	1 teaspoon celery seed
¾ cup white vinegar	2 teaspoons salt
2 teaspoons sugar	

SALAD: Shred all vegetables. Mix with chopped olives and sugar. Let stand.

DRESSING: Mix ingredients in saucepan and bring to a boil. Pour over vegetables. Refrigerate at least 6 hours.

Preparation: 20 minutes   **Serves:** 8-10
Cooking: 10 minutes   Must do ahead

Spinach Salad
The dressing adds a springtime, lemony flavor to spinach salad

SALAD:

2 quarts fresh spinach	½ pound cooked bacon, crumbled
2 hard-cooked eggs, sliced	¾ cup croutons
5 scallions, sliced	

DRESSING:

½ cup mayonnaise	½ cup olive oil
2 teaspoons Dijon mustard	1 tablespoon tarragon vinegar
¼ cup lemon juice	½ teaspoon sugar

SALAD: Clean spinach, break into bite-size pieces and place in salad bowl. Arrange scallions, eggs, bacon, and croutons over spinach.

DRESSING: Combine all ingredients until well blended. Pour over salad and toss.

NOTE: Dressing can be made up to 1 week ahead and refrigerated until ready to use.

Preparation: 30 minutes   **Serves:** 8-12
                                        Can do ahead

Spinach and Bean Sprout Salad

SALAD:

1 package fresh spinach
1 cup bean sprouts

1 (8 ounce) can water chestnuts,
   thinly sliced

DRESSING:

½ cup salad oil
¼ cup soy sauce or tamari
3 tablespoons lemon juice
¾ tablespoon grated onion
1½ tablespoons toasted sesame
   seeds

½ teaspoon sugar
Black pepper, freshly ground
¼ teaspoon garlic powder

SALAD: Wash spinach in cold water and remove stems. Wrap in dry towel and place in refrigerator to crispen for 4-6 hours. Combine with bean sprouts and water chestnuts and toss. (If using canned bean sprouts, drain well and rinse with cool water and chill).

DRESSING: Combine all ingredients. Let stand 1 hour at room temperature to blend flavors. Toss salad with dressing at serving time.

NOTE: To toast sesame seeds, place in dry flat pan over medium heat until browned. Watch carefully as they brown quickly.

Preparation: 15 minutes

Serves: 6-8
Can do ahead

Tomato Feta Salad
A great compliment to a Greek dinner

⅓ cup plain yogurt
⅓ cup mayonnaise
½ teaspoon lemon juice
½ teaspoon each: salt, oregano,
   basil, thyme

1 large clove garlic, minced
1½ cups crumbled Feta cheese
4 large ripe tomatoes, cubed

Mix yogurt, mayonnaise, lemon juice, seasonings, and garlic. Gently stir in Feta cheese. Pour over tomatoes and chill.

NOTE: Garnish with fresh parsley.

Preparation: 15 minutes

Serves: 6
Must do ahead

Armenian Salad

4 cups tomatoes
⅔-1 cup green pepper
½ cup parsley
½ cup scallions

2 sliced cucumbers
¼ cup lemon juice
2 teaspoons salt

Mix together in salad bowl, toss and serve immediately. Serves 6.

George Deukmejian

George Deukmejian
Governor of California

Tomato Emince
A refreshing summertime salad

SALAD:
7 large ripe tomatoes, peeled
  and chopped
1 small onion, grated
1½ teaspoon salt

¼ teaspoon black pepper,
  freshly ground
Lettuce leaves

DRESSING:
1 teaspoon curry powder
5 tablespoons mayonnaise

1 tablespoon parsley flakes

SALAD: Mix all ingredients except lettuce leaves together and chill.

DRESSING: Mix all ingredients together and chill. Serve tomatoes on lettuce leaves topped with a dollop of dressing.

NOTE: Tomatoes may be easily skinned by dipping into boiling water for 30 seconds.

Preparation: 20 minutes

Serves: 6-8
Can do ahead

Avocados Stuffed with Scallops

½ cup dry white wine
½ cup water
¼ pound bay scallops
2 ripe avocados
½ cup sour cream

2-4 teaspoons lemon juice
Salt and pepper, to taste
4 tablespoons red caviar
4-6 tablespoons finely chopped
   chives

Bring wine and water to a simmer in a skillet. Add scallops and cook over lowest heat for 2-3 minutes. Drain and refrigerate for 1 hour. Keep uncut avocados in refrigerator until last moment. Mix sour cream with 1-2 teaspoons lemon juice and 2-3 grinds of pepper. Carefully stir in caviar trying not to smash grains. Refrigerate. When ready to serve, cut avocados in half lengthwise and discard pits. Sprinkle hollow of each avocado half with a bit of lemon juice, a little salt and pepper to taste. Fill hollows with scallops, top with caviar mixture, sprinkle with chives, and serve.

Preparation: 20 minutes
Cooking: 2-3 minutes

Serves: 4
Can do ahead

Bahamian Chicken Salad
The chutney and curry create a tangy taste

2 whole chicken breasts, or
   4 halves, cooked
⅓ (9 ounce) jar chutney
1 (8 ounce) can pineapple
   chunks, reserve juice
1 (11 ounce) can mandarin
   orange segments

2 bananas (optional)
½ cup mayonnaise
¼ cup sour cream or yogurt
1 teaspoon curry powder
Salt and pepper, to taste
1 avocado (optional)

Cut cooked chicken meat into bite-size pieces. Mix chicken with chutney and fruits. In a small bowl, blend mayonnaise and sour cream or yogurt. Add 2-3 tablespoons pineapple juice, curry powder, salt, and pepper. Toss chicken, chutney, and fruits with mayonnaise mixture. Chill until ready to serve. A diced avocado may be added just before serving.

Preparation: 30 minutes
Cooking: 25 minutes

Serves: 6
Can do ahead

Chicken Salad Almondine

4-5 cooked chicken breasts, cut into bite-size pieces
1 (20 ounce) can sliced water chestnuts, drained
2 pounds seedless grapes
2 cups sliced celery

2 cups toasted slivered almonds
3 cups mayonnaise
1 tablespoon curry powder
2 tablespoons soy sauce
2 tablespoons lemon juice
Lettuce

Combine chicken, water chestnuts, grapes, celery, and 1½ cups of the toasted almonds. Mix mayonnaise with curry powder, soy sauce, and lemon juice. Combine this mixture with chicken. Chill for several hours. Spoon onto lettuce. Sprinkle with remaining almonds.

VARIATION: Add 1 cup cubed pineapple chunks to chicken mixture and/or substitute turkey meat for the chicken.

Preparation: 45 minutes

Serves: 12
Must do ahead

Chicken Strawberry Salad

3½ cups cooked cubed chicken
1 cup seedless grapes
¾ cup sliced celery
¼ cup sliced green onion
¾ cup mayonnaise
½ teaspoon salt
¼ teaspoon tarragon, snipped and fresh

2 tablespoons lime or lemon juice
1 medium avocado
1 pint strawberries, hulled and rinsed
⅓ cup sliced almonds
Lettuce
3 cantalopes, halved and seeded

Combine chicken, grapes, celery, and green onion in bowl. Combine mayonnaise, salt, tarragon, and lime or lemon juice in small bowl. Pour over chicken, toss to mix well. Peel and pit avocado, cut into cubes, and add to salad. Halve strawberries and add to salad. Sprinkle with almonds. Serve on lettuce in a half of a cantalope.

Preparation: 45 minutes

Serves: 6
Serve immediately

Minnesota Wild Rice and Lobster
A lovely luncheon dish

SALAD:

3½-4 cups cooked wild rice

2 cups cooked lobster, cut in
  bite-size pieces

2 perfectly ripe large avocados

1 tablespoon lemon juice

½ cup coarsely chopped red
  onion

DRESSING:

1 tablespoon Dijon mustard

2½ tablespoons red wine vinegar

½ cup vegetable oil

½ teaspoon minced garlic

Freshly ground pepper, to taste

2 tablespoons chopped parsley

Lettuce leaves

SALAD: Combine cool rice and lobster. Peel avocados and cut into cubes; sprinkle with lemon juice. Add to rice and sprinkle with onion.

DRESSING: Put mustard and vinegar in a mixing bowl and beat lightly. Gradually add the oil, beating briskly. Add garlic, pepper and parsley.

TO SERVE: You may toss salad with dressing or simply drizzle dressing on top of salad when it is served over crisp lettuce leaves.

NOTE: 2 cups crabmeat may be substituted for the lobster.

Preparation: 30 minutes

Serves: 4-6
Serve immediately

Taco Salad
This recipe is a "snap" when a food processor is used

1 head Iceberg lettuce, shredded

1 onion, chopped

1 tomato, chopped

1 green pepper, chopped or sliced

1 (16 ounce) can drained
  Mexi-beans

1 pound sautéed ground beef

1 avocado, sliced

¾ pound Colby cheese, shredded

1 small bag crushed corn chips

Catalina salad dressing

In a large bowl, preferably glass to show the layers, layer lettuce, onion, tomato, green pepper, Mexi-beans, ground beef, avocado, and cheese. Sprinkle with corn chips just before serving. Serve with a pitcher of catalina dressing.

Preparation: 20 minutes

Serves: 4-6
Serve immediately

Dan's Lobster Salad

6 ounces lobster meat, diced
2 ribs celery, diced
1 small onion, minced
1 carrot, sliced
4-5 radishes, diced (optional)
1 clove garlic, minced

Pepper, celery salt, and celery
   seed, to taste
2 teaspoons curry powder
Mayonnaise, to moisten
3 drops Tabasco sauce

Combine lobster meat, celery, onion, carrot, and radishes. Season with garlic, pepper, celery salt, celery seed, and curry powder. Add mayonnaise and mix. Add Tabasco sauce to taste. Chill until ready to serve.

Preparation: 20 minutes

Serves: 2
Can do ahead

Tossed Taco Salad

TORTILLAS:
4 corn tortillas

Deep frying oil

SALAD:
1 (15¼ ounce) can red kidney
   beans, drained and rinsed
2 medium tomatoes, peeled,
   chopped and drained
1 small cucumber, peeled, seeded
   and chopped

1 small red onion, cut in thin
   rings
1 small green pepper, chopped
2 cups shredded lettuce

SPICY DRESSING:
½ avocado, cut in chunks
¼ cup sour cream
¼ cup canned enchilada sauce

1 small clove garlic, minced
2 teaspoons lemon juice
Pepper, freshly ground

TORTILLAS: Cut tortillas in half. Cut again in ½-inch strips. Fry in deep oil until crisp. Drain and set aside.

SALAD: Combine kidney beans, tomatoes, cucumber, onion, green pepper, and lettuce. Toss with dressing and serve topped with tortilla strips.

SPICY DRESSING: Place avocado and sour cream in blender. Purée. Add enchilada sauce, garlic, lemon juice, and pepper to taste. Blend until smooth and creamy. Chill.

Preparation: 25 minutes
Cooking: 10 minutes

Serves: 4-6
Can do ahead

Avocado Mousse Picante

2 (¼ ounce) envelopes unflavored
   gelatin
2 cups cold chicken broth
¼ cup lemon juice
2 tablespoons red wine vinegar
2 tablespoons minced onion

2 very ripe, large avocados,
   peeled and pitted
2 teaspoons salt
⅓ cup mayonnaise
¼ teaspoon Tabasco
1 cup heavy cream, whipped

Sprinkle gelatin over cold broth and stir over low heat until melted. Add lemon juice, vinegar, and onion. Chill until cold but in liquid form. Mash avocados and beat until creamy (there should be about two cups). Blend avocados into cold aspic mixture. Add salt and blend in mayonnaise. Season with Tabasco and more salt to taste. Chill until thick but not set. Fold in whipped cream. Pour into a 6-cup mold and chill until set. Unmold by dipping mold in hot water, for 30 seconds, just prior to serving.

Preparation: 1 hour

Serves: 8-10
Can do ahead

Lime-Cucumber Salad
Nice for summer buffet

1 (6 ounce) package lime-flavored
   gelatin
2 teaspoons salt
2 cups boiling water
2 tablespoons cider vinegar
2 teaspoons grated onion
⅛ teaspoon pepper

2 cups sour cream
½ cup mayonnaise
2 cups cucumbers, peeled,
   seeded, shredded, and
   well-drained
Lettuce leaves

Combine gelatin and salt in a bowl. Add boiling water and stir until gelatin is dissolved. Add vinegar, onion, and pepper. Chill mixture until it reaches the consistency of unbeaten egg whites. Add sour cream and mayonnaise and beat with a rotary beater to blend thoroughly. Fold in cucumber. Pour into a 2-quart mold. Chill until firm. Unmold onto crisp lettuce.

Preparation: 1½ hours

Serves: 10
Must do ahead

Tomato Soup Salad

SALAD:

1 (8 ounce) package cream
  cheese
2 tablespoons unflavored gelatin,
  softened in ½ cup water
1 (10¾ ounce) can tomato soup

1 cup mayonnaise
1 cup chopped celery
½ cup chopped green pepper
1 tablespoon grated onion
1 tablespoon grated cucumber

DRESSING:

½ cup sour cream
½ cup mayonnaise

2 tablespoons lemon juice

SALAD: Melt the cream cheese and softened gelatin in the tomato soup in a double boiler over boiling water. When melted, stir in mayonnaise, celery, pepper, onion, and cucumber. Pour into a 9 x 9 x 2-inch pan. Refrigerate to set.

DRESSING: Combine sour cream, mayonnaise, and lemon juice.

Cut set salad into squares and serve with sour cream dressing.

NOTE: For variation add 1 cup chopped walnuts to mayonnaise before setting.

Preparation: 30 minutes
Cooking: 30 minutes

Serves: 8
Must do ahead

Cherries Jubilee Fruit Salad
The sherry adds a very nice, unusual flavor

1 (16 ounce) can pitted dark
  sweet cherries, drained,
  reserve juice
1 (16 ounce) can pear halves,
  drained, reserve juice
Water

1 (3 ounce) package cherry-
  flavored gelatin
½ cup cream sherry
1 (3 ounce) package cream
  cheese, diced
¼ cup chopped pecans

Combine fruit syrups and water to make 1½ cups liquid. In a medium saucepan, heat fruit syrup liquid and gelatin until gelatin dissolves. Remove from heat. Add sherry. Chill until partially set. Chop all but 2 pear halves. Fold pears, cherries, cream cheese, and nuts into gelatin. Turn into a 4½-cup mold. Chill until firm. Unmold. Serve garnished with slices of the reserved 2 pear halves.

Preparation: 45 minutes
Cooking: 4 minutes

Serves: 6-8
Must do ahead

Tuna and Crab Molded Salad
This salad can be served as an appetizer also

1 (7 ounce) can white meat tuna, drained well
1 (6½ ounce) can crabmeat, drained well
1 hard boiled egg, chopped
¼ cup chopped stuffed olives

1 tablespoon minced chives or onions
1 package unflavored gelatin
¼ cup water
1¼ cups mayonnaise

Mince tuna and crab with egg, olives, and chives. Soften gelatin in cold water for 15 minutes. Dissolve over hot water. Add mayonnaise gradually, stirring constantly. Fold into mold and chill until firm. Unmold on lettuce and garnish with parsley or serve with crackers.

Preparation: 15 minutes

Serves: 4-5
Can do ahead

Molded Tuna Salad
A pleasant change from regular tuna salad

1 cup water
1 (3 ounce) package lemon-flavored gelatin
1 (7 ounce) can tuna fish
½ cup chopped celery

½ cup chopped pimiento-stuffed olives
1½ teaspoons vinegar
½ cup mayonnaise

Boil water and combine with lemon gelatin. Cool to room temperature. Combine tuna fish, celery, olives, vinegar, and mayonnaise. Chill. When gelatin is at room temperature, combine with tuna mixture. Pour into 1-quart mold. Chill until firm.

Preparation: 20 minutes
Cooking: 5 minutes

Serves: 4
Can do ahead

Frozen Cranberry Mold

1 pint sour cream
1 (16 ounce) can whole cranberry sauce

1 (20 ounce) can crushed pineapple
¼-½ cup sugar

Mix and pour into a 6-cup mold. Freeze until ready to unmold and serve.

Preparation: 10 minutes

Serves: 6-8
Can do ahead

Apricot Gelatin Mold
Nobody but you will know the secret to this delicious dish

1 (16 ounce) can apricots in heavy syrup, pitted and halved
1 (6 ounce) package apricot-flavored gelatin
1 (7½ ounce) jar and 1 (4½ ounce) jar apricot baby food
1 pint sour cream

Drain and reserve syrup from apricots. Add enough water to apricot syrup to make 2 cups liquid. Heat liquid to just before boiling. Add gelatin. Let mixture cool about 15 minutes (do not refrigerate). Add baby food and sour cream. Mix with beater until it's foamy. Pour into a 6-cup mold. Add apricots to mold. Chill until set, about 3 hours.

Preparation: 15 minutes

Serves: 8
Must do ahead

Frosted Cherry Salad Squares

SALAD:
1 (3 ounce) package cherry-flavored gelatin
1 (3 ounce) package orange-flavored gelatin
1½ cups boiling water
1 (1 pound) can pitted tart red cherries

1 (1 pound) package frozen strawberries, thawed
1 cup chopped celery
½ cup pecans

TOPPING:
1 (3 ounce) package cream cheese
¼ cup mayonnaise

½-1 cup heavy cream, whipped or whipped topping (commercial)
¼ cup shredded orange rind

SALAD: In a large bowl, dissolve both gelatins in boiling water. Add cherries with liquid, strawberries, celery, and pecans. Chill until partially set. Pour into a 9 x 9 x 2-inch pan and chill until firm.

TOPPING: Blend cream cheese and mayonnaise. Fold in whipped cream or topping. Spread atop gelatin layer. Chill. Garnish with shredded orange rind. Cut into squares to serve.

Preparation: 30 minutes

Serves: 12
Must do ahead

Strawberry Gelatin Mold

2 (3 ounce) packages strawberry-
flavored gelatin
1½ cups boiling water
1 (10 ounce) package frozen
strawberries, defrosted, not
drained

1 cup crushed pineapple, drained
1 cup mashed bananas
1 cup sour cream

In a large bowl, dissolve gelatin in boiling water. Add strawberries, pineapple, and bananas. Pour ½ of mixture into a lightly greased 6½-cup ring
mold. Let set 1 hour. Spread sour cream on top of partially set gelatin.
Pour remaining half of strawberry mixture on top of the sour cream layer.
Chill in refrigerator until ready to serve. Unmold (dip sides of mold in
warm water) and serve.

Preparation: 15 minutes

Serves: 8
Must do ahead

Sour Cream Fruit Mold
The creamy lime flavor goes nicely with ham

2 (3 ounce) packages lime-
flavored gelatin
1½ cups boiling water
1½ cups cold water
⅔ cup juice saved from
canned fruit

1 cup sour cream
1 (8 ounce) can pears
1 (8 ounce) can crushed
pineapple

Dissolve gelatin in boiling water. When dissolved, add cold water. Add
juice saved from drained canned fruit. Refrigerate. When mixture starts
to gel, mix with sour cream. Add pears and pineapple and mix well. Put
in a large ring mold and refrigerate until completely set.

NOTE: You can cut up the pears or not, depending on how you are serving this. If it is to be cut into individual servings, you may want to use
pear halves and pour the rest of the mixture around them in the mold.
If using a ring mold, you may want to cut them into bite-size pieces.

Preparation: 15 minutes

Serves: 8
Must do ahead

Italian Pasta Summer Salad

This salad could go with just about anything

1 (16 ounce) box of macaroni
   twists
1 (16 ounce) bottle of zesty
   Italian salad dressing
1 (6 ounce) can pitted black
   olives, drained
1 (16 ounce) can chick peas,
   drained
½ pound fresh mushrooms, sliced
1 (7 ounce) jar artichokes, drained

3 green peppers, chopped
1 bunch green scallions, chopped
¼ head medium Iceberg lettuce,
   shredded
1 pint cherry tomatoes, sliced
3 stalks celery, chopped
1 (8 ounce) package shredded
   Cheddar cheese
Parmesan cheese, to garnish

24 hours before serving cook macaroni twists according to direction on box. Drain, rinse, and cool. Put in large bowl and marinate overnight in Italian dressing. The following day, combine all other ingredients except Parmesan cheese. Chill until ready to serve. Sprinkle Parmesan cheese over top just before serving.

Preparation: ½ hour
Cooking: 10 minutes

Serves: 16
Must do ahead

Artichoke and Rice Salad

Makes a nice contribution to a potluck dinner or picnic

2 cups uncooked rice
4 chicken bouillon cubes
8 scallions, sliced
24 green olives, sliced
1 green bell pepper, chopped
2 (6 ounce) jars marinated
   artichoke hearts, diced

Reserve marinade from artichoke
   hearts
2 cups mayonnaise
1 teaspoon curry powder

Cook rice in water with bouillon cubes according to package directions. Cool. Add scallions, green olives, bell pepper, and artichoke hearts. Mix reserved artichoke marinade with mayonnaise and curry powder. Toss with rice mixture and chill.

Preparation: 20 minutes
Cooking: 20 minutes

Yield: 6 cups
Can do ahead

Curried Rice Salad
This is a nice change from macaroni and potato salad

1 cup rice
1 cup mayonnaise
½ cup finely chopped chutney
1 teaspoon curry powder
1 cup sliced celery

1 cup frozen peas, cooked and
  chilled
4 green onions, sliced
¼ teaspoon salt

Cook rice according to package directions. Put in bowl; cover and re-frigerate until well chilled. Stir in mayonnaise, chutney, and curry pow-der. Mix well and chill for an hour. Stir celery, peas, onions, and salt. Chill again. May be served in half a pineapple or melon.

Preparation: 20 minutes
Cooking: 20 minutes

Serves: 10
Must do ahead

Rice Tuna Salad Supreme
It's best when made 24 hours before serving

SALAD:
1 (7 ounce) can albacore tuna,
  drained and flaked
3 cups cooked rice, cold (not
  minute rice)
6 pimiento-stuffed olives, sliced
½ cup chopped sweet pickles
2 tablespoons minced green
  pepper

1½ cups finely chopped celery
½ cup mayonnaise
2 tablespoons minced parsley
2 tablespoons lemon juice
½ teaspoon salt
½ teaspoon pepper
Dash of cayenne

TOPPING:
½ cup sour cream
½ cup mayonnaise

2 hard-cooked eggs, finely
  chopped

SALAD: Combine all ingredients in order listed. Chill thoroughly in 2½ or 3-quart mold for several hours or up to 2 days. Unmold, shortly before serving, to add topping.

TOPPING: Mix sour cream and mayonnaise. Spread over the unmolded salad. Cover with finely chopped eggs.

Preparation: 30 minutes

Serves: 8
Can do ahead

Vegetable Rice Ring

2 cups cooked rice
½ cup Italian salad dressing
  (bottled or your own)
½ cup mayonnaise
1 cup sliced radishes
1 medium cucumber, seeded and
  chopped

2 small tomatoes, peeled, seeded,
  and chopped
1 medium green pepper, chopped
½ cup chopped celery
¼ cup chopped green onion
1 pint cherry tomatoes
Leaf lettuce

Combine rice and Italian dressing. Cover and chill several hours or over-night. Add mayonnaise to undrained rice mixture and stir until com-bined. Fold in radishes, cucumbers, tomatoes, green pepper, celery, and green onion. Press into 5½-cup ring mold. Cover and refrigerate at least 2-3 hours. Fill center of ring with cherry tomatoes. Serve on leaf lettuce.

Preparation: 30 minutes

Serves: 8-10
Must do ahead

Tabbouleh
This is an old family recipe handed down for generations

1½ pounds <u>fine</u> cracked wheat
4 large tomatoes, peeled and
  minced
1 bunch scallions (discard green
  part), minced
1 bunch parsley, minced

½ tablespoon salt
¼ teaspoon allspice
½ cup lemon juice
¼ cup olive oil
Lettuce leaves

Cover cracked wheat with water and soak for 10 minutes. Drain and set aside. Put tomatoes, scallions, and parsley in a large bowl. Add cracked wheat. Mix. Add salt, allspice, lemon juice, and olive oil and mix well. Refrigerate for at least 6 hours or overnight.

TO SERVE: Line serving bowl with lettuce leaves and mound Tabbouleh in middle.*

VARIATION: Add cucumber, celery, and/or other vegetables.

Preparation: 30 minutes

Serves: 8-10
Must do ahead

*In the Middle East, the Tabbouleh is eaten by scooping it out with lettuce leaves.

Bacon and Rice Salad

8 slices of bacon, cooked and
    crumbled
3 cups cooked rice, cooled
1 cup frozen peas, thawed but
    not cooked
¼ cup chopped green onion

1 cup thinly sliced celery
2 medium carrots, shredded
¼ cup chopped pimientos
½ teaspoon salt
¼ teaspoon pepper
½ cup mayonnaise

Combine all ingredients in a large bowl. Serve cold. Can be made the day before.

Preparation: 45 minutes

Yield: 8 servings
Can do ahead

Mandarin Salad

SALAD:
¼ cup sliced almonds
1 tablespoon plus 1 teaspoon
    sugar
⅓ head Iceberg lettuce, torn into
    bite-size pieces
⅓ head Romaine lettuce, torn into
    bite-size pieces

1 cup chopped celery, thinly
    sliced
2 green onions with tops, thinly
    sliced
1 (11 ounce) can mandarin
    oranges, drained

DRESSING:
½ teaspoon salt
Dash of pepper
2 tablespoons sugar

2 tablespoons vinegar
¼ cup salad oil
Dash of red pepper sauce
1 tablespoon chopped parsley

SALAD: Cook almonds and sugar over low heat in saucepan. Stir constantly until sugar is melted and almonds are coated, about 20 minutes. Cool and break apart. Store at room temperature. Place torn lettuce greens (about 4-6 cups), celery and onions in a large plastic bag. Fasten bag securely and refrigerate.

DRESSING: Mix all ingredients. Place in tightly covered jar, shake well, and refrigerate.

TO SERVE: Just before serving, pour dressing into bag of greens. Add mandarin orange segments. Fasten bag securely and shake until greens and oranges are well coated. Add almonds and shake to mix. Arrange on chilled salad plates.

Preparation: 30 minutes
Cooking: 20 minutes

Serves: 6-8
Must do ahead

Orange Cream Fruit Salad

1 (20 ounce) can pineapple
pieces, drained
1 (16 ounce) can peach slices,
drained
1 (11 ounce) can mandarin
oranges, drained
3 medium bananas, sliced

1 (3⅝ ounce) package instant
French vanilla pudding mix
1½ cups milk
3 ounces frozen orange juice
concentrate, thawed
¾ cup sour cream

In a large bowl, mix fruits and set aside. In medium bowl, mix together pudding, milk, and orange juice concentrate. Add sour cream. Fold into fruit and chill at least 4 hours.

NOTE: Substitute fresh fruit when in season.

Preparation: 10 minutes

Serves: 6
Must do ahead

24 Hour Salad
This custard-cream fruit salad MUST be made a day ahead

1 (20½ ounce) can pineapple
tidbits, drained, reserve 2
tablespoons syrup
3 egg yolks
2 tablespoons sugar
2 tablespoons vinegar
1 tablespoon butter or margarine
Dash of salt

1 (16 ounce) can pitted, light
sweet cherries, drained
2 oranges, peeled, diced and
drained or 2 (6 ounce) cans
mandarin oranges
2 cups miniature marshmallows
1 cup heavy cream

In top of double boiler, beat egg yolks slightly. Add reserved pineapple syrup, sugar, vinegar, butter and salt. Cook, stirring constantly, until mixture thickens slightly and barely coats a spoon, about 12 minutes. Cool to room temperature. In a large bowl combine cherries, oranges, pineapple, and marshmallows. Pour egg custard over fruit and mix gently. Whip cream and fold into fruit mixture. Turn into your favorite serving bowl, cover and chill for 24 hours. It cannot be moved.

Preparation: 30 minutes
Cooking: 12 minutes

Serves: 6-8
Must do ahead

Bonnie's Bleu Cheese Dressing
It can also be used as an appetizer dip

2 cups sour cream
4 ounces crumbled Bleu cheese
½ cup mayonnaise

1½ tablespoons white vinegar
½ teaspoon each: salt, pepper,
   paprika, garlic salt, celery salt

Mix all ingredients thoroughly. Chill several hours before serving.

Preparation: 15 minutes

Yield: 3 cups
Can do ahead

"Sooper Dooper" Salad Dressing
A Bleu cheese-flavored sweet and sour dressing

2 cups salad oil
1 cup cider vinegar
1 teaspoon salt
8-9 teaspoons sugar

1-2 teaspoons paprika
½ clove garlic
Bleu cheese

Put oil, vinegar, salt, sugar, paprika, and garlic in a food processor or blender. Blend thoroughly. Store in refrigerator in a glass jar. When ready to use, toss salad with dressing. Sprinkle salad with Bleu cheese.

Preparation: 10 minutes

Yield: 3 cups
Must do ahead

Lime-Walnut Riverside Dressing

Juice of 3 large fresh limes
½ cup oil, olive or walnut
3 teaspoons sugar
½ cup fresh chopped parsley

Salt, to taste
Freshly ground pepper, to taste
6-8 walnuts, halved

Combine lime juice, oil, sugar, parsley, salt, and pepper into blender or food processor. Blend until well mixed. Add mixture to salad and sprinkle walnut halves on top.

NOTE: It's best with Romaine lettuce, onions, croutons, green peppers, and cheese chunks.

Preparation: 5 minutes

Yield: ¾ cup
Can do ahead

Celery Seed Salad Dressing

¾ cup sugar
1 teaspoon paprika
1 teaspoon dry mustard
1 teaspoon salt

¾ cup vinegar
½ cup vegetable oil
2 teaspoons celery seed
1 small onion, minced

SALAD:
Salad greens
1 orange, peeled and sectioned

1 grapefruit, peeled and sectioned
1 avocado, peeled and cut up

In a small saucepan, combine sugar, paprika, mustard, salt, and vinegar. Bring to a rapid boil. Let cool. Add the oil, celery seed, and onion. Shake vigorously. Before using, pour through a fine strainer to eliminate onion and celery seed.

NOTE: Excellent over vegetable or fruit salads. Toss salad greens, add orange and grapefruit sections, add avocado, and toss with dressing.

Preparation: 15 minutes
Cooking: 15 minutes

Yield: 1½ cups
Can do ahead

Vegetable and Salad Seasoning
Try this as a change of pace on vegetables or leafy greens

¾ cup grated Parmesan cheese
¼ cup parsley flakes
1 teaspoon garlic powder
½ teaspoon pepper
1 teaspoon chives

1 teaspoon green pepper flakes
1 teaspoon basil
1 teaspoon tarragon
½ teaspoon salt

Combine ingredients and store in a closed glass jar in a cool place. Use on tossed green salads, cucumbers, sliced tomatoes, zucchini, and sliced summer squash.

Preparation: 5 minutes

Yield: 1 cup
Can do ahead

Mom's French Dressing

½ teaspoon salt
3 tablespoons sugar
½ teaspoon paprika
½ teaspoon dry mustard

¼ cup vinegar or lemon juice
1 cup salad oil
1 clove garlic, minced

Mix together the salt, sugar, paprika, and mustard. Add the vinegar (or lemon juice), oil, and garlic. Shake well.

Preparation: 10 minutes

Yield: 1¼ cups
Can do ahead

Aunt Kate's French Dressing

2 tablespoons sugar
½ cup salad oil
¼ cup cider vinegar

⅓ cup catsup
1 teaspoon salt
⅓ medium onion, grated

Mix sugar, oil, vinegar, catsup, and salt with a whisk until well blended. Add onion and mix again. Store, covered, in refrigerator.

Preparation: 5 minutes

Yield: 1 cup
Can do ahead

Diet Salad Dressing

1 clove garlic
½ cup plain yogurt
1 tablespoon lemon juice
Dash of cayenne pepper

Salt and pepper, to taste
Any fresh herb: chive, dill, basil
 (optional)

Mince or press garlic and add to yogurt. Add lemon juice, cayenne pepper, and salt and pepper. Chill at least 2 hours. Before serving, add fresh herbs.

Preparation: 5 minutes

Yield: 4 servings
Must do ahead

Tangy Salad Dressing

2 tablespoons vinegar
⅓ cup vegetable oil
⅛ teaspoon freshly ground
   pepper
¼ teaspoon sugar
¼ teaspoon paprika

½ teaspoon salt
¼ teaspoon dry mustard
¼ teaspoon tarragon
1 clove garlic, crushed, or ⅛
   teaspoon garlic powder
½ teaspoon Worcestershire sauce

Combine ingredients in a jar in the order given. Cover jar tightly. Shake vigorously to combine thoroughly. Let stand at room temperature at least 1 hour before using or refrigerating.

Preparation: 5 minutes

Yield: ½ cup
Can do ahead

Russian Dressing
Another dressing that can double as a vegetable dip

½ cup chili sauce
¾ cup mayonnaise
10 capers, finely chopped

⅛ teaspoon each: dry mustard,
   onion powder, pepper
Dash of garlic powder

Combine all ingredients and stir to blend well. Refrigerate overnight or until well chilled.

Preparation: 10 minutes

Yield: 1¼ cups
Can do ahead

Mustard Vinaigrette Dressing

¾ cup vegetable oil
¼ cup wine vinegar
1 tablespoon Dijon mustard

½ teaspoon salt
¼ teaspoon pepper

In a screw-top jar, mix all ingredients. Shake well to blend, just before adding to salad.

Preparation: 5 minutes

Yield: 1 cup

VEGETABLES

Native Americans

Vegetables held a prominent place in the American diet long before European settlement. American Indians are responsible for domesticating over fifty percent of the world's plant foods. They were widely cultivated and consumed, since many of these crops are complimentary both in their growing requirements and in their nutritional benefits. For example, one acre of Indian corn interplanted with beans and squash offered five times the nutritional value as one acre of wheat. So revered were vegetables that the Iroquois Indians dedicated a summer festival to the "three sisters"—corn, beans and squash.

European settlers continued to grow the native American crops. Corn (known as maize), beans, squash, white potatoes, cranberries, tomatoes (once people were convinced that they were not poisonous), and Jerusalem aritchokes quickly found their place on colonial tables. Numerous sources recount that abundant pumpkins saved many early colonists from starvation.

New World vegetables were easily incorporated into colonial recipes and menus. Green corn (unripe maize) was roasted at clam bakes; ground corn and maple syrup were combined to make "Indian pudding"; and succotash, a mixture of lima beans and corn, was borrowed directly from the Indians. Johnnycakes or journey cakes were tough corn cakes which, because they transported well, supplied many travellers and hunters with food along the way. Pease porridge, a thick gruel of peas and beans, also provided a long-term source of food. Early in the winter, great cauldrons of this soup were cooked and then frozen. Hunks of the frozen soup were chopped off with an axe and reheated as needed. Contrary to the old nursery rhyme, pease porridge, hot or cold, was often many more than nine days old!

Throughout the colonies, various renditions of corn bread appeared, sweet in the South and unsweetened, but served with maple syrup, in the North. Pumpkin and squash pies, also sweetened with the native American sap, were great favorites. Colonial children topped off their meal with a treat which made its debut on the first Thanksgiving—popcorn.

Today, our choice of vegetables is much more varied than it was in colonial times. The recipes presented here give a wide selection of ingredients and preparations. But remember the Iroquois attitude that vegetables provide harmony within a meal, the harmony of the "three sisters"—corn, beans and squash.

Asparagus with Almonds
A dressy way to serve asparagus

2 pounds fresh asparagus spears,
  washed thoroughly
⅓ cup butter, melted
1 tablespoon finely chopped
  onion

⅓ cup sliced almonds
⅓ cup bread crumbs
Salt and pepper, to taste

Cook asparagus in a small amount of boiling salted water until tender, about 10-15 minutes. Place cooked asparagus in a buttered, ovenproof dish. Sprinkle with onion, almonds, and bread crumbs. Add salt and pepper. Pour butter over top. Broil 2-3 minutes until lightly browned.

NOTE: This dish can be prepared a few hours ahead of time and then broiled just before serving.

Preparation: 25 minutes
Cooking: 2-3 minutes

Serves: 6-8
Can do ahead

The Original Baked Bean Recipe

2 pounds great northern dried
  beans
1 teaspoon baking soda
½ pound salt pork
1 teaspoon salt

½ teaspoon pepper
½ cup brown sugar
¼ cup granulated sugar
1 medium onion, finely chopped

Thoroughly wash beans and soak overnight in a 4-quart pot. Next day, rinse the beans, add fresh water to cover and simmer for 45 minutes. Add baking soda and let beans boil for 3-4 minutes. Rinse beans thoroughly and return to pot. Add water to cover the beans, salt pork, salt, pepper, sugar, and onion. Simmer for 45 minutes. Bake, uncovered, at 300°F. for 2 hours.

NOTE: Additional water may be added while baking if beans appear to be too dry.

Preparation: 2 hours
Cooking: 2 hours

Serves: 25
Can be frozen

Calico Beans

Great accompaniment at barbecues

1 pound ground beef
1 cup chopped onion
½ cup catsup
¾ cup brown sugar,
   firmly packed
4 tablespoons prepared mustard

2 tablespoons vinegar
1 (20 ounce) can kidney beans
1 (20 ounce) can baked beans
   and pork
1 (20 ounce) can lima beans

Sauté ground beef and onions. Place in a 1½-quart casserole. Add remaining ingredients and mix. Bake at 350°F. for 40 minutes.

Preparation: 15 minutes
Cooking: 40 minutes

Serves: 6-8
Can do ahead

New England Harvest Baked Beans

2 (28 ounce) cans baked beans
¼ cup catsup or barbecue sauce
½ cup cider vinegar
½ cup maple syrup

¼ cup brown sugar
3 teaspoons dry mustard
2 cups diced tart apples
¼-½ pound sliced thick bacon

In a large mixing bowl, combine baked beans, catsup, cider vinegar, maple syrup, brown sugar, and apples. Pour into a 2-quart baking dish. Arrange strips of bacon across top. Bake, uncovered, at 350°F. for 45 minutes or until bacon is cooked and the beans and liquid are bubbling.

Preparation: 10 minutes
Cooking: 45 minutes

Serves: 6-8
Can do ahead

Corn Pudding

1 (16 ounce) can cream-style corn
3 eggs
3 tablespoons milk
3 tablespoons melted butter

1 tablespoon all-purpose flour
1 tablespoon sugar
¼ teaspoon salt
¼ teaspoon pepper

Combine all ingredients. Pour into greased 2-quart casserole. Bake at 350°F. for 1 hour or until firm and brown on top.

Preparation: 10 minutes
Cooking: 1 hour

Serves: 5
Can do ahead

Italian Broccoli Casserole

2 (10 ounce) packages frozen cut
   broccoli
2 eggs, beaten
1 (11 ounce) can condensed
   Cheddar cheese soup

½ teaspoon oregano
1 (8 ounce) can stewed tomatoes,
   cut up
3 tablespoons grated Parmesan
   cheese

Cook broccoli in unsalted water for 5-7 minutes, or until tender. Drain
well. In a large mixing bowl, combine eggs, Cheddar cheese soup, and
oregano. Stir in tomatoes and broccoli. Turn mixture into a 10 x 6 x 2-
inch baking dish. Sprinkle with Parmesan cheese. Bake, uncovered, at
350°F. for 30 minutes.

Preparation: 20 minutes
Cooking: 30 minutes

Serves: 6
Can do ahead

Blue Cheese and Broccoli Casserole
An unusual combination with great flavor

2 (10 ounce) packages broccoli
   spears or 2 (20 ounce) bags
   broccoli cuts
2 tablespoons butter
2 tablespoons all-purpose flour
1 (3 ounce) package cream
   cheese, softened

¼ cup Blue cheese, crumbled
1 cup sour cream
⅓ cup crushed buttery-rich
   crackers

Prepare broccoli according to package directions. If using broccoli spears,
cut into bite-size pieces. While broccoli is cooking, melt butter in a
saucepan over low heat. Blend flour into melted butter. Add cream cheese
and Blue cheese, stir until smooth. Next add the sour cream, increase
heat to medium, and stir until mixture starts to boil. Add sauce to broccoli and stir well. Place in 1-quart casserole and top with crushed crackers. Bake at 350°F. for 30 minutes.

VARIATION: Omit cracker crumbs and serve as an appetizer spread on
party rye bread or crackers.

Preparation: 25 minutes
Cooking: 30 minutes

Serves: 6-8
Can do ahead

Barbara's Broccoli Soufflé
An elegant variation for broccoli

2 (10 ounce) packages frozen
  chopped broccoli
1 tablespoon vinegar
1 teaspoon Dijon mustard
6 eggs, separated

2 tablespoons all-purpose flour
½ teaspoon salt
½ pound Monterey Jack cheese,
  shredded
½ cup grated Parmesan cheese

Prepare broccoli according to package directions. Drain well. Add vinegar and Dijon mustard to the broccoli. Set aside to cool. In a large bowl, beat egg whites until soft peaks form. Using a small bowl, beat egg yolks with flour and salt until thick and lemon colored. Fold the egg yolk mixture into the egg whites. Spoon ⅓ egg mixture into a 2-quart greased soufflé dish. Top with ½ broccoli mixture, ¼ cup each Monterey Jack cheese and Parmesan cheese. Cover with another ⅓ egg mixture, remaining broccoli, and Monterey Jack cheese. Top with remaining egg mixture and Parmesan cheese. Bake at 350°F. for 25 minutes or until center is set.

NOTE: Timing is important. This dish must be served immediately.

Preparation: 15 minutes
Cooking: 25 minutes

Serves: 6-8
Serve immediately

Green Beans in Sour Cream
Lemon adds a special zing to the green beans

2 pounds fresh or frozen green
  beans
1 onion, sliced
2 tablespoons minced parsley
2 tablespoons butter
1 teaspoon salt

¼ teaspoon pepper
2 teaspoons grated lemon rind
2 tablespoons all-purpose flour
1 cup thick sour cream
1 cup buttered bread crumbs

Fresh green beans can be left whole, frenched, or cut into 1-inch pieces. Cook until tender-crisp by steaming or boiling. If using frozen green beans, cook according to package directions. Drain beans well. Sauté onion and parsley in butter. Add salt, pepper, lemon rind, flour, and sour cream. Heat until just hot and then spoon over beans. Place the entire mixture in a 2-quart casserole and top with buttered bread crumbs. Bake, uncovered, at 350°F. for 20 minutes.

Preparation: 25 minutes
Cooking: 20 minutes

Serves: 6
Can do ahead

Lima Bean Casserole

1 pound dry lima beans	⅔ cup brown sugar, firmly packed
Water	1 tablespoon molasses
2 teaspoons salt	1 cup sour cream
½ cup butter	Salt, to taste
1 teaspoon dry mustard	

Soak beans overnight in warm water. Rinse with fresh water and drain well. In a large pot, add water and salt to the beans. Bring to a boil over medium heat. Simmer until almost tender, about 20 minutes. Drain and rinse gently. Place the beans in a casserole dish and dot with butter. Add dry mustard, brown sugar, molasses, sour cream, and salt. Blend gently. Bake, uncovered, at 350°F. for 1 hour.

NOTE: Add additional water, if needed.

Preparation: 30 minutes	**Serves:** 8-10
Cooking: 1 hour	Must do ahead

Cabbage Pie

1 medium cabbage, shredded	30 soda crackers, crumbed

SAUCE:

½ cup butter	½ teaspoon celery seed
4 tablespoons all-purpose flour	1 teaspoon salt
½ teaspoon pepper	2 cups milk

In an 8-inch square baking dish, alternate layers of cabbage and crumbs, ending with a crumb layer.

SAUCE: Melt butter in double boiler and stir in flour. Add pepper, celery seed, and salt. Slowly, add milk. Continue to stir until sauce is thick and smooth. Pour sauce over cabbage. Bake at 350°F. for 1 hour.

NOTE: Unsalted saltines or similar crackers can be substituted for the soda crackers.

Preparation: 30 minutes	**Serves:** 8
Cooking: 1 hour	Serve immediately

Red Cabbage

1 medium red cabbage, shredded
3 tablespoons shortening
1 large onion, sliced
1 large apple, peeled and sliced

½ cup vinegar
½ cup granulated sugar
1 cup water
¼ teaspoon salt (optional)

In a 4-6 quart pan, melt shortening. Add cabbage, cover and cook over medium heat for 15 minutes, stirring occasionally. Add apple, vinegar, sugar, water, and salt. Turn heat to low and cook for 1 hour, stirring occasionally. Serve immediately or, chill and reheat before serving.

Preparation: 30 minutes
Cooking: 1¼ hours

Serves: 8-12
Can do ahead

Easy Carrot Casserole

1 cup water
8 medium carrots, pared and cut
   into 1-inch pieces

1 (16 ounce) can pie-sliced apples
½ cup sugar
2 tablespoons butter

Boil water and cook carrots for 15-20 minutes. Mix carrots and apples. Turn into a 9-inch pie plate and sprinkle with sugar. Dot with butter. Bake at 375°F. for 1 hour.

VARIATION: Add ½ cup raisins.

Preparation: 10 minutes
Cooking: 1 hour

Serves: 8
Can do ahead

Holiday Carrots
The olives make a colorful contrast

5 cups sliced carrots
3 tablespoons butter
1 medium onion, sliced thin

12 stuffed green olives, sliced
Parsley or dill weed, to garnish

Cook the carrots either by steaming or quick-frying them. Meanwhile, melt the butter and sauté the onions until they appear translucent. Next, add the olives. Put the cooked carrots in a serving dish and stir in onions and olives. Sprinkle with parsley or dill weed and serve.

NOTE: Whole baby carrots can be substituted for sliced carrots.

Preparation: 15 minutes
Cooking: 20 minutes

Serves: 6
Can do ahead

Moroccan Carrots
The taste of cumin gives this dish a unique delicious flavor

2½ pound carrots, peeled
   and sliced
½ cup olive oil
½ cup red wine vinegar
½ bunch fresh parsley, snipped

2 cloves garlic, minced
2 teaspoons cumin
2 teaspoons paprika
Salt and pepper, to taste

In a large pot over medium heat, cover and cook carrots in a small amount of boiling water until tender but firm, approximately 10 minutes. Meanwhile, mix all other ingredients. Drain carrots and toss with the seasonings while carrots are still warm.

NOTE: May be made ahead and then reheated in an ovenproof dish at 300°F. until hot.

Preparation: 15 minutes
Cooking: 10 minutes

Serves: 8-10
Can do ahead

Celery Casserole
A crunchy side-dish

4 cups celery, cut in ¼-½ inch
   slices
2 (10¾ ounce) cans cream of
   chicken soup
¼ cup pimiento, chopped
1 (8 ounce) can sliced water
   chestnuts

4 tablespoons butter
½ cup bread crumbs
½ cup Parmesan cheese
¼ cup sliced almonds

Lightly sauté celery in a skillet over low heat. Mix celery, cream of chicken soup, water chestnuts, and pimiento. Place in a buttered 8-inch square baking dish. Melt butter and add bread crumbs, Parmesan cheese, and almonds. Sprinkle crumb mixture on top of celery mixture. Bake at 350°F. for 30 minutes. Serve hot.

Preparation: 30 minutes
Cooking: 30 minutes

Serves: 6
Can do ahead

Cauliflower-Cheese Pie
The pie crust is potato!

CRUST:

2 cups grated raw potato,
   firmly packed
½ teaspoon salt

1 egg beaten
¼ cup grated onion
Vegetable oil

FILLING:

3 tablespoons butter
1 cup chopped onion
1 clove garlic, minced
½ teaspoon salt (optional)
½ teaspoon basil
Dash of each: thyme, pepper,
   rosemary

1 medium cauliflower, broken
   into florets
1¼ cup grated Cheddar cheese,
   firmly packed
2 eggs
¼ cup milk
Paprika

CRUST: Set freshly grated potato in a colander over bowl and sprinkle with salt. Set aside for 10 minutes. Then squeeze out excess water and mix potato with egg and onion. Pat mixture into a greased 9-inch pie pan, carefully building up the sides with lightly floured fingers. Bake at 400°F. for 30 minutes. Brush the crust with vegetable oil and continue baking for 10-15 minutes.

FILLING: In melted butter, sauté onions and garlic until lightly brown. Add salt if desired. Next add basil, thyme, pepper, rosemary, and cauliflower. Cover and cook over medium heat for 10 minutes, stirring occasionally. Spread half of the Cheddar cheese into baked crust. Add cauliflower mixture and top with the remaining cheese. Beat together eggs and milk. Pour over top of pie. Sprinkle with paprika. Bake at 375°F. for 35-40 minutes or until set.

Preparation: 40 minutes
Cooking: 1½ hours

Serves: 6-8
Can do ahead

Maple Corn Casserole

1 (10 ounce) package frozen corn
   or 2½ cups fresh or canned
   corn, drained
¾ cup heavy cream

3 eggs, beaten
½ cup maple syrup
Salt and pepper, to taste
4 tablespoons butter, cut-up

Mix 1½ cups corn with cream in a blender until the corn is coarsely ground. Pour into 9 x 9-inch baking dish. Add remaining corn, maple syrup, eggs, salt, and pepper. Mix thoroughly. Stir butter cuts into mixture. Bake at 350°F. for 50 minutes.

Preparation: 10 minutes
Cooking: 50 minutes

Serves: 6-8
Can do ahead

Cheesy Corn Casserole

1 (8 ounce) can cream-style corn
2 tablespoons all-purpose flour
1 (3 ounce) package cream
   cheese, cubed
¼ teaspoon garlic salt
1 (8 ounce) can whole kernel
   corn, drained

1 (4 ounce) can sliced
   mushrooms, drained
½ cup grated Swiss cheese
2 tablespoons butter
¾ cup bread crumbs

In a medium saucepan over low heat, mix cream-style corn and flour. Add cubed cream cheese and garlic salt. Stir until cheese melts. Add whole kernel corn and mushrooms. Stir in Swiss cheese. Place mixture in a 1-quart casserole. Melt butter over low heat in a small saucepan. Add bread crumbs and toss. Top corn mixture with buttered bread crumbs. Bake at 400°F. for 30 minutes.

NOTE: Recipe is easily doubled

Preparation: 10 minutes
Cooking: 30 minutes

Serves: 4-6
Can do ahead

Creamed Onions and Green Bean Casserole
When doubled, it's an elegant buffet-sized vegetable dish

3 tablespoons butter
2 tablespoons all-purpose flour
1 teaspoon dry mustard
1 teaspoon salt
¼ teaspoon pepper
1 cup half and half cream
1 (16 ounce) package frozen small
  onions, thawed and drained

1½ (9 ounce) package frozen
  French-style green beans,
  thawed and drained
½ (9 ounce) package baby carrots,
  thawed and drained
8 slices American cheese
½ cup chopped nuts, walnuts
  or pecans

Melt butter in a large saucepan over low heat. Add flour, mustard, salt, and pepper. Add cream. Stir constantly until thickened. Combine the sauce and vegetables. Put ½ mixture in an 8-inch square baking dish. Top with 4 slices cheese. Layer with remaining mixture and cheese. Top with chopped nuts. Bake at 350°F. for 45 minutes.

Preparation: 30 minutes
Cooking: 45 minutes

Serves: 8-10
Can do ahead

Sherried Onion Casserole

4 cups sliced onions
3 tablespoons butter
2 tablespoons all-purpose flour
½ teaspoon salt
⅛ teaspoon white pepper
Pinch of nutmeg

⅔ cup chicken broth
¼ cup dry sherry
1½ cups bread cubes
½ cup grated Swiss cheese
2 tablespoons grated Parmesan
  cheese

In a skillet over medium-low heat, cook onions in butter until soft, but not browned, about 10-15 minutes. Blend in flour, salt, pepper, and nutmeg. Add chicken broth and sherry. Cook, stirring constantly, until thickened, about 5 minutes. Put mixture into a shallow 5-cup baking dish. Top with bread cubes, Swiss cheese, and Parmesan cheese. Bake at 425°F. for 15 minutes or until crusty and lightly browned.

Preparation: 25 minutes
Cooking: 15 minutes

Serves: 4
Can do ahead

Mushrooms and Onions in Sherry

1 pound fresh mushrooms, cleaned
16 fresh pearl onions, or ½ pound frozen pearl onions, cooked according to directions

¼ cup butter
2 tablespoons all-purpose flour
4 tablespoons parsley flakes
⅓ cup chicken stock
¼ cup dry sherry

In a large sauté pan, lightly brown mushrooms and onions in butter. Sprinkle with flour and stir gently until coated. Add parsley and chicken stock. Bring to a slow boil and simmer for 15 minutes. Add dry sherry. Heat thoroughly before serving.

Preparation: 10 minutes
Cooking: 15 minutes

Serves: 4
Serve immediately

Parsley Peas
The Romaine lettuce adds an unusual touch

3 tablespoons butter
¼ cup chopped onion
1 (10 ounce) package frozen peas
1 tablespoon chopped fresh parsley

½ teaspoon salt
1½ cups sliced Romaine lettuce, sliced into long strips
3 tablespoons chicken broth

In a large saucepan, melt butter and sauté onions until tender, about 10 minutes. Add peas, parsley, and salt. Cover and steam, stirring frequently, about 3 minutes. Stir in lettuce and chicken broth. Reduce heat and simmer about 2 minutes, or until heated through.

Preparation: 15 minutes
Cooking: 5 minutes

Serves: 4
Serve immediately

Peas and Celery

2 beef bouillon cubes
¼ cup water
4 stalks celery, diagonally sliced

⅛ teaspoon thyme
⅛ teaspoon salt
2 (10 ounce) packages frozen peas

In a 10-inch skillet, dissolve bouillon cubes in water. Add celery, thyme, and salt. Cook until celery is slightly tender, but still crisp. Add peas. Cook until peas are tender and crisp, about 3-5 minutes.

Preparation: 10 minutes
Cooking: 10 minutes

Serves: 6
Serve immediately

Peas and Potatoes

A spicy variation of two traditional vegetables cooked in the
Indian style

2 tablespoons butter or margarine
2 tablespoons oil
1½ teaspoons cumin seed
1 medium onion, finely chopped
¼ teaspon turmeric
1 (2 x 1 inch) piece ginger root,
  peeled and coarsely chopped
½ teaspoon paprika

1 cup crushed tomatoes or 2 fresh
  tomatoes, chopped
3 medium potatoes, pared and
  cubed
1 cup water
¾ cup chopped fresh coriander
1 pound frozen peas
Salt, to taste

Heat butter and oil in a large skillet. Add cumin seed and onions. Cook
and stir until onions are lightly browned. Add turmeric, ginger, paprika,
and tomatoes. Stir over medium heat for 5 minutes. Add potatoes, water,
and ½ cup of the coriander. Cover and cook for 15 minutes, stirring frequently. Add the peas and cook for an additional 10-15 minutes. Add
salt. Garnish with remaining coriander before serving.

NOTE: Add additional water with the peas if mixture seems dry.

Preparation: 20 minutes
Cooking: 30 minutes

Serves: 6
Serve immediately

"Calories Don't Count" Potatoes

6 large baking potatoes with
  unblemished skins, baked
  and warm
7 tablespoons butter
½-¾ cup milk or cream

½ cup sour cream
¾ cup grated Cheddar cheese
10 pieces sliced bacon, cooked
  and crumbled

While potatoes are still very warm, cut in half lengthwise and carefully
scoop out insides. Set empty skins aside. Heat 4 tablespoons butter, milk,
sour cream, and ½ cup cheese. Whip mixture and potatoes to a soft and
fluffy consistency. Stir in bacon. Pile mixture back into potato skins,
mounding a bit on top. Dot with remaining 3 tablespoons butter and
remaining cheese. Bake at 400°F. for 15 minutes.

Preparation: 20 minutes
Cooking: 15 minutes

Serves: 6-10
Can do ahead

Mediterranean Potatoes
Serve with lamb or Greek-style dishes

2 lemons
½ cup butter
2 tablespoons olive oil
3 tablespoons chopped parsley
2 tablespoons chopped chives
¼ teaspoon nutmeg

½ teaspoon all-purpose flour
¼ teaspoon pepper
½ teaspoon salt
1 clove garlic, crushed
10-12 new potatoes, boiled

Grate lemon rinds and set aside. Squeeze juice from lemons and also set aside. In a small saucepan over low heat, melt butter. Add olive oil, lemon rind, parsley, chives, nutmeg, flour, salt, pepper, and garlic. Simmer for 10 minutes. Just before serving, add lemon juice and pour sauce over boiled new potatoes.

Preparation: 15 minutes
Cooking: 10 minutes

Serves: 6
Serve immediately

Party Potatoes
A special way to serve mashed potatoes

8-10 medium potatoes, peeled
1 (8 ounce) package cream
  cheese, softened
1 pint sour cream
¼ cup butter
¼ cup chopped chives

¼ teaspoon nutmeg
Salt and pepper, to taste
Paprika, to garnish
Grated Parmesan cheese,
  to garnish

Boil peeled potatoes until tender. Combine cream cheese with sour cream and set aside. Mash potatoes with hand masher or electric beater. Add butter to potatoes and continue beating until well blended. Beat potatoes and cream cheese mixture together. Add chives, nutmeg, salt, and pepper. Mix thoroughly. Pour into a greased 2-quart casserole. Sprinkle with paprika and grated cheese. Bake, uncovered, at 350°F. for 25 minutes.

NOTE: For an extra light texture, process all ingredients in a food processor.

Preparation: 25 minutes
Cooking: 25 minutes

Serves: 8-10
Can do ahead

Oven Fried Potatoes
These potatoes will be browned, crispy wedges

8-9 medium baking potatoes, washed
½ cup oil
2 tablespoons Parmesan cheese

1 teaspoon salt
½ teaspoon garlic powder
½ teaspoon paprika
¼ teaspoon pepper

Cut each potato into 8 wedges. Place skin side down in a shallow un-greaed baking pan. Mix all other ingredients and pour over the potatoes. Bake at 375°F. for 45 minutes, or until brown.

NOTE: Potatoes can be cut ahead of time, and kept in cold water until ready for use.

Preparation: 15 minutes
Cooking: 45 minutes

Serves: 6-8
Serve immediately

Potatoes Margaret

3 tablespoons butter
1 teaspoon salt

3 large potatoes, peeled and cut into ¼-inch slices
1 cup grated Cheddar cheese

In a greased 8-inch pie plate, arrange potato slices so that they overlap. Melt butter in a small saucepan over low heat. Add salt to butter. Drizzle butter over potato slices. Cover tightly with foil. Bake at 425°F. for 20 minutes. Remove foil and bake for 30 minutes more. Sprinkle cheese over potatoes and bake another 30 minutes. After removing potatoes from oven, let stand for 5 minutes. Loosen pie edges with a spatula and cut into wedges to serve.

Preparation: 15 minutes
Cooking: 1 hour 20 minutes

Serves: 4
Serve immediately

Brandied Sweet Potatoes

Wonderful on Thanksgiving when you need dishes that can be made ahead of time

2½ cups cooked sweet potatoes
2 tablespoons butter, or 1-3
   tablespoons of syrup from
   canned sweet potatoes

¼-½ teaspoon cloves
½ teaspoon nutmeg
½ teaspoon allspice

SAUCE:
1 cup brown sugar, firmly packed
½ cup butter

1 egg
¼ cup brandy

Cream potatoes, butter (or syrup), and spices until smooth using a food processor, blender, or beater. Place in a greased 1½-quart casserole. Make a well in the center for the sauce. Bake at 350°F. for 45 minutes.

SAUCE: Mix brown sugar, butter, and egg in a saucepan. Heat until slightly thick. Add brandy. Remove from heat and pour over sweet potatoes, in well and on top.

NOTE: The sweet potatoes can be mixed up to 2 days before being cooked and served. Add the brandy sauce just before serving.

Preparation: 10 minutes
Cooking: 45 minutes

Serves: 6
Can do ahead

Sweet Potato Date Puffs

A Christmas favorite

2 (17 ounce) cans sweet potatoes,
   drained
1½ cups chopped dates
½ cup butter
½ cup brown sugar, firmly packed

¼ cup honey
¼ cup reserved pineapple syrup
8 slices canned pineapple,
   drained

Mash sweet potatoes. Stir in ½ cup dates. Melt butter in a large skillet and stir in brown sugar, honey, reserved pineapple syrup, and remaining dates. Heat until sugar is dissolved. Place 8 slices of pineapple in skillet. Top each with a scoop (use ice cream scoop) of sweet potato mixture. Cover and simmer over low heat 10-12 minutes. Baste potatoes with syrup several times while cooking.

Preparation: 15 minutes
Cooking: 10-15 minutes

Serves: 8
Can do ahead

Spinach Ring

2 (10 ounce) packages frozen
    chopped spinach
Grated Parmesan cheese
½ cup chopped onion
4 tablespoons butter
1 cup light cream
1 teaspoon salt
½ teaspoon sugar
Dash of pepper
Dash of nutmeg
4 eggs
½ cup bread crumbs
⅓ cup grated Swiss or Gruyère
    cheese
Boiling water

Cook spinach, drain well, and set aside. Grease a 4½-cup mold and dust with Parmesan cheese. In a large saucepan, sauté onion in melted butter, until tender. Add spinach, cream, salt, sugar, pepper, and nutmeg. Heat until boiling. Remove from heat and set aside. In a large mixing bowl, beat eggs slightly. Add bread crumbs and Swiss or Gruyère cheese. Stir spinach mixture into egg mixture. Turn into mold. Set mold in a baking pan on oven rack. Pour boiling water into baking pan to a depth of 1½ inches around mold. Place wax paper over top of mold. Bake at 350°F. for 30-35 minutes or until knife comes clean.

Preparation: 20 minutes
Cooking: 30-35 minutes

Serves: 6-8
Serve immediately

Spinach au Gratin

1 pound mushrooms, fresh or
    canned, sliced
5 (10 ounce) packages frozen
    chopped spinach, thawed
¼ teaspoon each: salt, pepper,
    garlic salt
2 cups chopped onion
¼ cup butter, melted plus 2
    tablespoons if using fresh
    mushrooms
2 cups each: grated "orange"
    Cheddar cheese, grated "white"
    Cheddar cheese, grated
    Mozzarella cheese
½-1 pound sausage, cooked,
    cooled and sliced

If using fresh mushrooms, sauté them in 2 tablespoons butter. Drain canned mushrooms if not using fresh mushrooms. Thoroughly press out water from spinach. Spread spinach in 9 x 12-inch pan. Sprinkle with salt, garlic salt, pepper, and onions. Pour butter over top. Arrange 1 cup of each cheese over spinach. Add mushrooms, sausage, and then remaining cheese. Bake at 350°F. for 45 minutes until cheese is bubbly and brown.

Preparation: 30 minutes
Cooking: 45 minutes

Serves: 6
Can do ahead

Spinach and Mushrooms

1 pound fresh mushrooms,
  washed and dried
2 (10 ounce) packages frozen
  chopped spinach, cooked
  and drained
1 teaspoon salt

¼ cup chopped onion
¼ cup butter, melted
1 cup freshly grated sharp
  Cheddar cheese
Garlic salt

Slice stems off mushrooms. Beginning with the cap side of the mushroom, sauté stems and caps until brown. Set aside. Mix spinach with salt, onion, and melted butter. Line a shallow, 1½-2-quart casserole with spinach. Sprinkle with half of the cheese and arrange mushrooms, caps and stems, on top. Season with garlic salt, and cover with the remaining cheese. Bake at 350°F. for 20 minutes or until cheese is melted and browned.

NOTE: To double recipe, add extra cheese and mushrooms to fill a 9 x 13-inch dish.

Preparation: 15 minutes
Cooking: 20 minutes

Serves: 4-6
Can do ahead

Greek Cheese-Spinach Pie (Beuruk)
The two cheeses give this spinach dish a wonderful, rich flavor

1 (10 ounce) package chopped
  spinach, thawed
1½ pounds Monterey Jack cheese
½ pound Feta cheese, crumbled
4 eggs
1 bunch scallions, or 1 medium
  onion, chopped

½ teaspoon crushed oregano
½-¾ cup butter, melted
1 pound fresh mushrooms,
  sliced
1 pound phyllo pastry

Squeeze water out of spinach and set aside. In a large bowl, combine Monterey Jack cheese, Feta cheese, eggs, onions, and oregano. Set aside. Butter the bottom and sides of an 11 x 14-inch baking pan. Following directions on phyllo package, begin to layer ⅓ of the phyllo sheets into pan, buttering every other one with a pastry brush. Top with cheese mixture, spinach, and mushrooms. Continue to layer and butter the remaining phyllo dough. Tuck all edges into sides of pan. Bake at 375°F. for 30-35 minutes. Cut into squares to serve.

Preparation: 30 minutes
Cooking: 30-35 minutes

Yield: 12-15 squares
Can be frozen

Fried Stuffed Tomatoes
This makes a good brunch dish as well as a dinner vegetable

2 cloves garlic, minced
1 tablespoon parsley
¼ teaspoon celery salt
1 (8 ounce) package cream cheese
12 thick slices tomato
½ cup all-purpose flour

2 tablespoons milk
1 egg
1 cup bread crumbs
1 teaspoon basil
6 tablespoons oil

Blend garlic, parsley, celery salt, and cream cheese with electric mixer until smooth. Spread mixture on 6 tomato slices and top with remaining slices. Beat milk and egg together. Combine bread crumbs and basil. Coat the tomatoes with flour, dip in egg-milk mixture, and then coat with bread crumb-basil mixture. Heat oil in a large skillet and fry tomatoes over medium high heat for 10-15 minutes on each side. Serve hot.

Preparation: 15 minutes
Cooking: 25 minutes

Serves: 6
Serve immediately

Baked Tomatoes Stuffed with Spinach

6 large firm tomatoes
2 (10 ounce) packages frozen
  spinach
¼ cup minced onion
¼ cup butter or margarine
¼ cup all-purpose flour
1 teaspoon salt

¼ teaspoon pepper
½ teaspoon nutmeg
¼ cup heavy cream
6 tablespoons buttered bread
  crumbs, Parmesan cheese,
  or grated Cheddar cheese,
  to garnish

Cut a thin slice from the top of each tomato. Scoop out pulp and set aside. Sprinkle inside of tomatoes with salt and invert to drain. Cook spinach according to package directions. Drain, squeeze out all water, and chop very fine. In a large skillet, sauté onion in melted butter for 5 minutes. Stir in flour, salt, pepper, nutmeg, spinach, tomato pulp, and cream. Stir lightly, simmering until creamy. Fill the tomatoes with spinach mixture. Top with bread crumbs or cheese. Place in a foil-lined pan. Bake at 350°F. for 20 minutes or until tender and top is brown.

Preparation: 25 minutes
Cooking: 20 minutes

Serves: 6
Serve immediately

Spinach Topped Tomatoes

2 (10 ounce) packages frozen
   chopped spinach
¼ cup bread crumbs
¼ cup chopped scallions
2 eggs
½ cup grated Parmesan cheese
1 clove garlic, minced

¼ cup butter, melted
½ teaspoon thyme
⅛ teaspoon salt
⅛ teaspoon pepper
8 tomato slices, ¼-inch thick
1 teaspoon garlic salt

Cook spinach according to package directions and drain well using paper towels to remove excess moisture. In a medium bowl, combine spinach, bread crumbs, scallions, eggs, cheese, garlic, melted butter, thyme, salt, and pepper. Arrange tomato slices in a 2-quart shallow baking pan or cookie sheet. Sprinkle the slices with garlic salt and top each with about ¼ cup of the spinach mixture. Bake at 350°F. for 15 minutes.

Preparation: 15 minutes
Cooking: 15 minutes

Serves: 4
Serve immediately

Tomato Casserole
This was the outstanding favorite at a recipe-tasting luncheon

3 tablespoons butter
1 medium onion, diced
2 slices bread, cubed
3½ cups peeled, seeded,
   juiced tomatoes

⅓ cup brown sugar, firmly packed
¼ teaspoon pepper
½ teaspoon salt
1 teaspoon basil

In a large skillet, sauté onions gently in butter and toss in bread cubes. Mash or slice the tomatoes and add to onion-bread mixture. Mix in remaining ingredients. Pour into 2-quart rectangular baking dish. Bake at 350°F. for 1½-2 hours or until thickened.

NOTE: This mixture bakes down considerably.

Preparation: 20 minutes
Cooking: 1½-2 hours

Serves: 4
Can do ahead

Summer Squash Casserole

3 medium yellow summer squash
3 tablespoons butter or margarine
¼ cup finely chopped onion
1 small clove garlic, chopped, or
    ½ teaspoon garlic powder
½ cup chopped mushrooms
Salt and pepper, to taste

2 tablespoons chopped parsley, or
    1 teaspoon dried parsley flakes
¼ cup grated Swiss or Gruyère
    cheese
¾ cup fine bread crumbs
½ cup sour cream

Wash squash and chop into ¼-½-inch cubes. Do not peel squash. Melt butter in large skillet. Add squash, onions, and garlic. Cover and cook 5 minutes. Add mushrooms, salt, and pepper. Cook, covered, 5 minutes more. Add parsley, cheese, and bread crumbs. Mix well. Stir in sour cream. Pour into greased 2-quart casserole. Bake at 350°F. for 20 minutes.

Preparation: 20 minutes
Cooking: 20 minutes

Serve: 6
Can be frozen

Zucchini Patties
Serve these in place of a potato

1½ cups unpeeled grated
    zucchini, pressed dry
    between paper towels to
    remove extra moisture
2 eggs, lightly beaten
¼ cup all-purpose flour
¼ cup grated Parmesan cheese

2 tablespoons finely chopped
    onion
2 tablespoons mayonnaise
¼ teaspoon oregano
Salt and pepper, to taste
2 tablespoons butter (or more)
Sour cream and chives (optional)

Combine all ingredients except the butter and blend thoroughly. Melt butter in skillet. For each patty, spoon 1 heaping tablespoon batter into skillet and spread with back of spoon to flatten a bit. Cook over medium heat until browned, about 4-5 minutes on each side.

NOTE: Serve patties plain or topped with sour cream and chives.

Preparation: 10 minutes
Cooking: 10 minutes

Serves: 4
Serve immediately

Zucchini Cheese Bake
A great way to use the zucchini that grew just a bit too big!

1 pound mushrooms, chopped
2 tablespoons butter
1 teaspoon salt
¼ teaspoon pepper
1 clove garlic, minced
2½-3 pounds zucchini, sliced
1 (4 ounce) can chili peppers
1 medium onion, chopped

2 tablespoons butter
1 cup grated Cheddar cheese
2 eggs, beaten
2 cups cottage cheese or
   Ricotta cheese
2 teaspoons chopped parsley
4 tablespoons Parmesan cheese

Sauté mushrooms in butter and drain. Add salt, pepper, and garlic. Spread in a 2-quart baking dish. Cook the zucchini until tender, drain, and mash. Add the chili peppers, onion, and butter. Spread over the mushroom layer. Sprinkle with Cheddar cheese. To the eggs, fold in cottage cheese, parsley, and 2 tablespoons Parmesan cheese. Spread over the zucchini layer. Sprinkle with the remaining parmesan cheese. Bake at 350°F. for 45 minutes.

Preparation: 20 minutes
Cooking: 45 minutes

Serves: 8
Can do ahead

Zucchini Puff

6 medium zucchini, cut in
   bite-size chunks
1 cup cottage cheese
1 cup Cheddar cheese

2 eggs, beaten
¾ teaspoon dill weed
¾ teaspoon salt
½ cup bread crumbs

Simmer zucchini for 5 minutes in salted water and drain well. Combine with all remaining ingredients except 2 tablespoons Cheddar cheese. Pour in 1½-quart casserole. Bake, uncovered, at 350°F. for 20 minutes. Sprinkle with reserved cheese and bread crumbs. Bake 20 minutes longer.

NOTE: Cook and freeze extra zucchini in the summer. In the winter, defrost the zucchini and proceed with this recipe.

Preparation: 20 minutes
Cooking: 40 minutes

Serves: 6
Can do ahead

Broccoli Sauce
Good for asparagus, cauliflower, and tomatoes too!

½ cup mayonnaise
⅓ cup milk

¼ teaspoon salt
1 tablespoon lemon juice

Blend all ingredients in a bowl. Serve immediately or chill and serve later.

Preparation: 2 minutes

Serves: 6
Can do ahead

Cheese Sauce
Delicious sauce for vegetables or crêpes

¼ cup sweet butter
¼ cup all-purpose flour
1½ cups milk
½ cup heavy cream
1 tablespoon Dijon mustard

¾ cup extra sharp grated
   Cheddar cheese
¼ cup grated Romano or
   Parmesan cheese

Heat butter over medium heat in a heavy 2½-quart saucepan. With a wire whisk, gradually stir in flour, milk and cream, mustard, and both cheeses. Whisk until smooth and thick.

NOTE: To reheat, add ⅛-¼ cup milk and stir well.

Preparation: 10 minutes
Cooking: 10 minutes

Yield: 2½ cups
Can do ahead

Never-Fail Blender Hollandaise Sauce

3 egg yolks
1 tablespoon lemon juice
¼ teaspoon salt

Dash of cayenne pepper
½ cup butter

Place egg yolks, lemon juice, salt, and cayenne pepper into a blender. Heat butter until hot and bubbly but not browned. Turn on blender and pour in the hot butter in a slow, continuous stream. Blend for 10 seconds. Serve warm.

Preparation: 5 minutes
Serve immediately

Serves: 4

POULTRY

Stove Industry

Turkey, chicken, Christmas geese,
Pass no holiday in peace.

To roast that Christmas goose, and cook all the trimmings, you depend on your stove. Some of its ornate ancestors had their origins in the Albany-Troy area. The earliest stove factories, the Eagle Furnace in Albany and the James and Cornell Stove Factory in Troy, were founded in the early 1800's. Rensselaer Polytechnic Institute of Troy aided the local industry by providing updated technical knowledge. By the middle of the 19th century, the industry had grown to the point where there were 32 foundries in operation. The exportation of stoves was facilitated by New York's extensive waterways. At one time, foreign trade became so important that Perry and Company published its stove catalogue in many foreign languages. After the Civil War, iron ore was discovered in the Midwest and it became less expensive to manufacture stoves near the ore. Thus, the stove industry in Albany began to decline and the last foundry closed here in 1936.

In the past 150 years, many improvements have made cooking stoves much more efficient, cleaner, faster, and safer. We have come a long way from the old black monster with its "eight boiling holes" fitted with matching kettles. No longer do we have to venture to the wood pile or coal bucket for our source of cooking energy. While our stoves may not warm our dishwater in a special reservoir, they can bake, roast, braise, sauté, and broil with ease and accuracy.

A good stove, good poultry, and a good recipe make a winning combination. Many of the following poultry selections come from families that have passed them down from generation to generation. Just like the old cast iron stoves, they are tried, true, and reliable. And just like our modern ranges, they are easy to use. Most of all, they are delicious!

Cashew Chicken Stir-Fry

2 whole chicken breasts, skinned
   and boned
6 scallions, white part only,
   chopped
3 tablespoons soy sauce
1 teaspoon Chinese sesame oil
1 tablespoon dry sherry

7 tablespoons peanut or
   vegetable oil
1-inch piece ginger root,
   thinly sliced
6 cloves garlic, finely chopped
1 tablespoon hoisin sauce
¾ cup cashews

Cut chicken into 1-inch pieces. Combine chicken, scallions, soy sauce, sesame oil, and sherry. Marinate at least ½ hour. Heat wok or skillet. Add 5 tablespoons oil and heat until bubbles form. Toss in ginger and garlic. Stir fry 1 minute. Stir in hoisin sauce and cook about 20 seconds. Add chicken mixture, stir fry about 5 minutes, or until done, remove, and keep warm. Wipe pan, then heat 2 tablespoons oil. Stir fry cashews 20 seconds. Sprinkle chicken with cashews and serve.

NOTE: Hoisin sauce and Chinese sesame oil can be purchased at Oriental grocery stores. They will keep indefinitely.

Preparation: 45 minutes
Cooking: 15 minutes

Serves: 4
Serve immediately

Chicken à L'Orange

8 whole chicken breasts, split,
   boned, and skinned
½ cup flour
1 teaspoon salt
1 teaspoon garlic powder
½ teaspoon paprika
2 teaspoons fresh grated
   orange peel

5 tablespoons butter
¼ cup white wine
1¼ cups orange juice
¼ teaspoon thyme
1 teaspoon marjoram
⅓ cup toasted sliced almonds
1 (11 ounce) can mandarin
   oranges, drained

Pound chicken breasts between sheets of wax paper to flatten slightly. Combine flour, salt, garlic powder, paprika, and orange peel in plastic bag. Shake chicken in bag to coat. Melt butter in skillet, brown chicken, and remove to shallow baking dish. Pour off all but 3 tablespoons fat from browning pan. Add wine, juice, thyme, and marjoram to pan and bring to boil. Pour over chicken. Bake at 350°F. for 15 minutes. Top with almonds and oranges. Bake for another 15 minutes.

Preparation: 20 minutes
Cooking: 30 minutes

Serves: 8
Serve immediately

Chicken Cordon Bleu

This version of a classic dish deserves the rave reviews it receives from adults and children alike

4 whole chicken breasts, skinned
  and boned
4 slices cooked ham
4 slices Swiss cheese
1 cup bread crumbs
2 tablespoons chopped parsley

1 egg, beaten
Oil for frying
4 slices bacon
½ cup dry white wine or
  vermouth

Spread out chicken breast and place a slice of ham and cheese on inside. Fold breast in half to enclose filling. Dip stuffed breast in egg and then in crumbs to coat completely. Fry in oil until golden. Place chicken in 9 x 13-inch baking dish and lay bacon strip over each piece. Pour wine into pan. Bake, covered, at 350°F. for about 45 minutes or until tender.

Preparation: 20 minutes
Cooking: 45 minutes

Serves: 4
Can do ahead

Breasts of Chicken 'Coq Au Vin'

This treasured recipe has been impressing dinner guests for over twenty years

3 tablespoons butter
3 tablespoons olive oil
½ pound minced salt pork
1½ cups chopped mild onion
2 medium carrots, finely chopped
6 shallots, minced
2 garlic cloves, peeled and
  quartered
6 whole chicken breasts, skinned,
  boned, and split
4 tablespoons brandy

2 tablespoons all-purpose flour
½ cup minced parsley
2 tablespoons dried marjoram
1 bay leaf
1 teaspoon thyme
2 teaspoons salt
¼ teaspoon freshly ground
  pepper
4 cups dry white wine
1 pound mushrooms, sliced

Melt butter and oil in large skillet over medium heat. Add pork, onion, carrots, shallots, and garlic. Cook 5-6 minutes until pork begins to brown. Strain, reserve salt pork on warm plate, and return fats to pan. Brown chicken in same pan 2 minutes on each side, or until done. Add additional butter if needed. When all breasts are cooked, return them to pan. Pour brandy over chicken, light it, and let fire burn out. Remove chicken to heated platter, cover, and keep warm in oven. Add flour, parsley, marjoram, bay leaf, thyme, salt, and pepper to juices remaining in pan. Add reserved salt pork mixture. Add wine, stir well to combine, and cook uncovered 30-60 minutes over medium-low heat, adding mushrooms during last ten minutes. Can hold at this point and reheat when ready to serve.

TO SERVE: Remove garlic pieces and spoon heated sauce over breasts on platter or place two halves on heated individual plates and add sauce. Serve immediately.

Preparation: 90 minutes
Cooking: 30-60 minutes

Serves: 6
Can be frozen

Chicken Fromage

This recipe is for all of you who like multi-purpose cooking—it halves beautifully and can also be used as an appetizer

4 pounds boned chicken breasts
1 egg, beaten
½ cup milk
2 cups bread crumbs

16 ounces Mozzarella cheese, cut in 1-inch cubes
1 cup butter
1 cup white wine

Pound chicken breasts thin. Cut into 2-inch strips. Combine egg and milk. Dip strips in egg-milk mixture, then roll in crumbs. Wrap chicken piece around cheese cube. Secure with toothpick. Arrange in large greased baking pan. Put pat of butter on slice. Pour wine over chicken. Bake at 350°F. for 40 minutes.

Preparation: 30 minutes
Cooking: 40 minutes

Serves: 8-10
Can do ahead

Herbed Chicken Breasts

1 cup fine bread crumbs
½ teaspoon each: salt, ground thyme, ground rosemary, pepper
Dash of marjoram

2 whole chicken breasts, boned, skinned, and split
1 egg, beaten
2 tablespoons oil
½ cup white wine

Combine bread crumbs and spices. Dip chicken in egg, then crumb mixture (may be refrigerated overnight at this point). Heat oil. Sauté chicken until lightly browned on each side. Add wine. Bring to a boil, reduce heat, and simmer for 10-15 minutes.

Preparation: 10 minutes
Cooking: 20 minutes

Serves: 2
Can do ahead

Chicken Kabobs
An elegant dinner from the grill

1 (10 ounce) can condensed
  onion soup
¼ cup apple jelly
2 tablespoons lemon juice
1 tablespoon cornstarch

1 teaspoon curry powder
2 whole chicken breasts, skinned
  and boned
16 (¼ inch thick) zucchini slices
16 cherry tomatoes

Combine soup, jelly, lemon juice, cornstarch, and curry in medium saucepan. Cook over medium heat until thickened. Cool. Cut chicken into 1-inch pieces. Marinate chicken and zucchini in sauce at least 6 hours. Place chicken, zucchini, and tomatoes alternately on skewers. Grill 4 inches above coals for 20 minutes; turn and baste with marinade at 5 minute intervals.

Preparation: 20 minutes
Cooking: 20 minutes

Serves: 4
Must do ahead

Chicken Marsala

2 eggs, beaten
6 whole chicken breasts, boned,
  skinned, and split
Salt and pepper
1 cup Italian bread crumbs
¼ cup olive oil
4 tablespoons butter or margarine
1 cup chicken stock or 2 chicken
  bouillon cubes dissolved in 1
  cup water

1 clove garlic, minced
⅛ teaspoon oregano
1 teaspoon chopped parsley
¼ cup lemon juice
¾ cup Marsala wine
1 tablespoon cornstarch
¼ cup cold water
1 cup mushrooms, sliced

Season eggs with salt and pepper. Dip chicken in egg mixture, then bread crumbs. Let stand for 30 minutes. Heat oil and 2 tablespoons butter in skillet. Cook chicken until golden; then remove to ovenproof baking dish. Pour stock into skillet; then add garlic, oregano and parsley. Cook 5 minutes, stirring and scraping pan constantly. Add lemon juice and wine. Continue cooking 5 minutes. Combine cornstarch and water. Add to skillet and stir until sauce thickens slightly. Pour sauce over chicken. Bake, uncovered, at 350°F. for 50 minutes. Sauté mushrooms in remaining 2 tablespoons butter. Place mushrooms over chicken and continue baking 5 minutes.

Preparation: 30 minutes
Cooking: 55 minutes

Serves: 6
Can be frozen

Maureen Stapleton's One Dish Meal

Chicken
Onions
Rice (if you wish)

Carrots (if you wish)
Lowry salt
Butter

In a large pot with a cover, pat bottom with butter. Cover butter with fairly thick slices of onions. Cover onions with cleaned, quartered chicken that has been spread with Lowry salt. Repeat the process, covering first layer with more butter and onions, then seasoned chicken, etc. Close the pot and cook for 2 hours on the top of the stove with a fairly low flame. In the last hour, you can add the carrots or rice or both.

Maureen Stapleton

Maureen Stapleton
Well-known actress and native of Troy, New York

Fritto Misto with Blue Cheese

FRITTO MISTO:

3 eggs, beaten
1 (12 ounce) can beer
1½ cups all-purpose flour
1 teaspoon salt
3 whole chicken breasts, skinned
   and boned

2 medium zucchini
1 small eggplant
½ pound mushroom caps
1 cup oil

SAUCE:

¾ cup mayonnaise
¼ cup crumbled Blue cheese
¼ cup milk

⅛ teaspoon garlic powder
⅛ teaspoon white pepper
½ teaspoon Worcestershire sauce

FRITTO MISTO: Mix eggs, beer, flour, and salt until smooth. Set aside. Cut chicken into 1-inch cubes. Cut zucchini in half and then in ¼-inch thick strips diagonally. Peel eggplant and cut into ¼-inch thick strips. Heat oil in wok. Coat chicken and vegetables with flour mixture. Cook until crisp and drain on paper towels. Transfer to brown paper-lined cookie sheet and keep warm in 200°F. oven. When all are cooked, arrange on platter and pass sauce separately for dipping.

SAUCE: Combine all ingredients and mix well. May be made ahead to allow flavors to mellow.

VARIATION: Use other raw or parboiled vegetables of your choice.

Preparation: 30 minutes
Cooking: 30 minutes

Serves: 6
Serve immediately

Hawaiian Chicken

CHICKEN:

1 pound boneless chicken breasts
2 tablespoons soy sauce
1 tablespoon dry sherry
1 clove garlic, minced
1 teasoon ginger
1 teaspoon sugar

1 egg white
2 teaspoons cornstarch
1 teaspoon all-purpose flour
1 cup peanut oil for frying
½ lemon, sliced thin

SAUCE:

½ cup chicken broth
⅓ cup sugar
2 tablespoons vinegar
Juice of 1½ lemons

2 teaspoons cornstarch
1 tablespoon water
2 drops yellow food coloring

CHICKEN: Cut chicken into pieces 1½ x 1-inch. Combine soy sauce, sherry, garlic, ginger, and sugar. Add chicken and marinate for 30 minutes. Heat oil to 375°F. in wok or electric frying pan. Drain chicken. Combine egg white, cornstarch, and flour. Coat chicken with mixture. Fry chicken until golden, turning as needed.

SAUCE: In saucepan combine broth, sugar, vinegar, and juice. Bring to boil. Combine cornstarch and water. Stir into pan, reduce heat, and cook until clear and thick. Remove from heat and stir in coloring. Place chicken on serving plate, top with lemon slices, and pour sauce over all.

Preparation: 90 minutes
Cooking: 40 minutes

Serves: 4
Serve immediately

Chicken with Artichokes and Mushrooms

2 tablespoons butter
1½ cups rice, uncooked
8 chicken breasts, split or thighs
   and breasts
1 (14 ounce) can artichokes,
   chopped

1 cup fresh mushrooms, sliced
1 (10 ounce) can cream of chicken
   soup
1½ cups yogurt or sour cream
1 cup white wine
½ cup grated Parmesan cheese

Melt butter in 11 x 14-inch casserole in oven. Spread rice over bottom of casserole. Place chicken pieces on rice. Combine artichokes, mushrooms, soup, yogurt, and wine. Pour over chicken. Sprinkle with cheese. Bake at 350°F. for 90 minutes or until chicken is done.

Preparation: 20 minutes
Cooking: 90 minutes

Serves: 4-6
Can be frozen

Chicken Florentine

2 (12 ounce) packages frozen chopped spinach, partially defrosted and separated
1 small onion, chopped
Dash of garlic powder
6 tablespoons butter
Salt and pepper

4 whole chicken breasts, cooked and boned
4 tablespoons all-purpose flour
1 cup plus 2 tablespoons heavy cream
¾ cup chicken stock
½ cup grated Parmesan cheese

In large skillet, sauté spinach, onion, and garlic powder in 2 tablespoons butter. Cover pan and cook until spinach is completely thawed. Uncover pan, season with salt and pepper; then continue cooking until most of the moisture is evaporated. In another pan, melt one tablespoon butter, add one tablespoon flour, and whisk in 6 tablespoons heavy cream. Stir and cook until thickened. Add to spinach. Place mixture on bottom of 9 x 13-inch dish. Arrange chicken on top. Melt 3 tablespoons butter, add 3 tablespoons flour; then whisk in ¾ cup heavy cream and chicken stock. Season with salt and pepper to taste. Stir mixture until thickened. Pour over chicken, and sprinkle with cheese. Bake, uncovered, at 400°F. for 20 minutes, or until brown on top.

Preparation: 25 minutes
Cooking: 20 minutes

Serves: 6
Can be frozen

Not "Just Plain Old Chicken" Chicken

4 whole chicken breasts, split
½ teaspoon paprika
Salt and pepper
½ cup butter
1 (14 ounce) can artichokes

½ pound mushrooms, sliced
¼ teaspoon tarragon
3 tablespoons all-purpose flour
⅓ cup sherry
1½ cups chicken broth

Season chicken with paprika, salt, and pepper. Sauté in 4 tablespoons butter until golden. Place in large casserole. Arrange artichokes over meat. Melt remaining butter in same skillet. Add mushrooms. Season with tarragon and sauté 5 minutes. Sprinkle with flour. Add sherry and broth. Simmer for 5 minutes. Pour into casserole. Bake, covered, at 375°F. for 45 minutes.

Preparation: 20 minutes
Cooking: 45 minutes

Serves: 4
Serve immediately

Chicken Piccata

4 whole chicken breasts, skinned,
  boned, and split
½ cup all-purpose flour
½ teaspoon pepper
2 tablespoons butter

2 tablespoons oil
3 tablespoons lemon juice
3 tablespoons chicken broth
1-2 lemons, thinly sliced
Parsley, for garnish

Place chicken pieces between wax paper and pound thin. Combine flour and pepper. Dredge chicken in mixture and shake off excess. Heat butter and oil in large skillet; then lightly brown chicken 3-4 minutes each side. Remove pieces to a heated platter when done. Lower heat to moderate; add lemon juice and broth to skillet. Stir 1 minute to loosen bits. Add lemon slices and cook 1-2 minutes longer. Pour sauce over chicken. Garnish with parsley.

Preparation: 15 minutes
Cooking: 15 minutes

Serves: 4-6
Serve immediately

Sausage Stuffed Chicken Breasts
You can use sweet or hot sausage, as you prefer

1 pound Italian sausage meat,
  casings removed
½ cup chopped walnuts
⅓ cup chopped celery
¼ cup chopped onion
½ cup bread crumbs
1 egg
4 large whole chicken breasts,
  boned and split

½ cup all-purpose flour
¾ teaspoon paprika
2 tablespoons oil
1 (10¾ ounce) can chicken broth
1 tablespoon cornstarch
2 tablespoons white wine

Cook sausage, nuts, celery, and onion slowly in a large pan about 30 minutes. Remove from heat. Stir in bread crumbs and egg. Pound breasts very thin. Divide sausage mixture evenly among breasts. Roll up and secure tightly with toothpicks. Combine flour and paprika. Coat chicken in mixture. Heat oil in same pan used to cook sausage. Brown chicken on all sides. Pour in broth. Reduce heat, cover, and simmer 30 minutes. Remove chicken to warm plate. Dissolve cornstarch in wine; then add to pot and stir until sauce thickens. Pour over chicken.

Preparation: 45 minutes
Cooking: 45 minutes

Serves: 4-8
Serve immediately

Honey Orange Chicken
The aroma of this dish will be a bonus

CHICKEN:

2 whole chicken breasts, boned
  and split
Curry powder

½ cup orange juice
3 tablespoons honey
3 tablespoons prepared mustard

SAUCE:

3 teaspoons cornstarch
2 tablespoons cold water

1 orange, peeled and sectioned

CHICKEN: Sprinkle chicken with curry powder to taste. Place in shallow 9 x 13-inch baking dish. Combine orange juice, honey, and mustard. Pour over chicken. Bake at 375°F. for 40 minutes, or until tender. Remove chicken to warm platter.

SAUCE: In a small pan, combine cornstarch and cold water. Stir in pan juices. Cook, stirring constantly, until sauce thickens. Add orange sections and cook 2 minutes longer. Pour sauce over chicken to serve.

Preparation: 10 minutes
Cooking: 40 minutes

Serves: 2-4
Serve immediately

Polly's Chicken
A rich, moist, and delicious chicken

1 cup sour cream
¼ cup lemon juice
2 teaspoons each: paprika, celery
  seed, Worcestershire sauce
1 teaspoon salt
1 teaspoon pepper

2 small cloves garlic, mashed
6 whole chicken breasts, skinned,
  boned, and split
Bread crumbs
4 ounces butter, melted

Combine sour cream, lemon juice, seasonings, and garlic. Dip chicken pieces in mixture. Arrange in non-metal container, pouring remaining cream mixure over chicken. Cover and refrigerate overnight. Coat pieces with crumbs. Place in greased, shallow baking pan. Pour ¼ cup butter over chicken. Bake at 350°F. for 45 minutes. Pour remaining butter over chicken. Continue to bake 15 minutes.

Preparation: 20 minutes
Cooking: 60 minutes

Serves: 6-8
Must do ahead

Barbecue Chicken Missouri-Style

1 chicken, quartered or cut-up	½ teaspoon sugar
Salt and pepper, to taste	1 tablespoon chili powder
2 tablespoons vegetable oil	1 teaspoon dry mustard
¾ cup cider vinegar	1 teaspoon paprika
1 teaspoon finely minced garlic	½ teaspoon ground cumin

Rub chicken pieces with salt, pepper, and oil. Combine remaining ingredients in small bowl and mix well. Place chicken skin side down on barbecue grill. Baste and cook 10 minutes. Turn chicken. Baste frequently until chicken is coated.

OPTION: To cook under broiler, turn chicken skin side up for first 10 minutes; then turn and continue cooking.

Preparation: 10 minutes   **Serves:** 4
Cooking: 30 minutes (for pieces)   Serve immediately
    60 minutes (for quarters)

Chicken en Croûte

6 chicken thighs (1½ pounds)	1 cup half and half cream
2 tablespoons butter	Salt and pepper, to taste
1 chicken bouillon cube	1 (6 ounce) can sliced mushrooms
½ cup hot water	¼ cup dry white wine
3 tablespoons all-purpose flour	6 precooked pork sausages
¼ teaspoon paprika	6 frozen patty shells, thawed

Brown chicken in butter. Dissolve bouillon cube in water; then add to chicken. Cover and simmer 20-30 minutes. Remove chicken. Bone carefully, keeping thigh in one piece, and cool. Measure broth from pan, add water to measure one cup of liquid. Return broth to skillet. Combine flour, paprika, and cream. Add to broth. Cook and stir until sauce is thick. Season to taste with salt and pepper. Remove from heat. Stir in mushrooms and wine. Place patty shell on floured surface and roll out thin. Place sausage in bone cavity of each thigh. Place thigh in center of shell. Put 2 tablespoons sauce on top. Fold and seal shut. Bake seam side down and brush with cream while baking. Bake at 400°F. about 30 minutes, or until golden. Serve with remaining sauce on top.

Preparation: 45 minutes   **Serves:** 6
Cooking: 30 minutes   Can do ahead

Poulet Marengo

2 broilers, cut up (about 5 pounds)
1 can sliced mushrooms, drained
1 cup dry white wine
1 tablespoon brandy
1 tablespoon tomato paste
1 (No. 1) can tomatoes

¼ cup olive oil
5 small white onions
1 small clove garlic
2 teaspoons minced parsley
Flour
Salt
Pepper

Dust the chicken lightly with seasoned flour and sauté in olive oil until evenly browned. Remove from skillet and keep warm. Now add the onions, chopped fine, the garlic, mushrooms, parsley, and if needed, more olive oil. When the onions are a light golden color, add the tomatoes, wine, brandy, tomato paste, and 1 tablespoon of flour. Blend this sauce thoroughly, and simmer for about 15 minutes. Return the chicken to the pan, cover, and cook until tender, about 30 minutes.

Mrs C. V. Whitney

Mrs. Cornelius Vanderbilt Whitney

Mrs. Whitney is famous for her annual summer theme party in Saratoga Springs.

Sesame Parmesan Chicken

¼ cup Italian salad dressing
1 (3-3½ pound) chicken, cut up
1 egg, beaten
2 tablespoons water
½ cup grated Parmesan cheese
⅓ cup bread crumbs

1 tablespoon parsley, chopped
¼ cup sesame seeds
½ teaspoon salt
½ teaspoon paprika
⅛ teaspoon pepper

Pour salad dressing into 9 x 13-inch baking pan. Add chicken, turning to coat on all sides. Cover and refrigerate 4 hours. Beat together egg and water. Combine remaining ingredients in a plastic bag. Dip chicken pieces, one at a time, into egg mixture; then place in bag shaking to coat well. Return to baking dish. Bake at 350°F. for 45 minutes or until tender.

Preparation: 10 minutes
Cooking: 45 minutes

Serves: 4
Must do ahead

Glazed Chicken Wings

3 tablespoons brown sugar
2 teaspoons cornstarch
½ teaspoon salt
¼ teaspoon ground ginger
⅛ teaspoon pepper

⅓ cup water
3 tablespoons lemon juice
2 tablespoons soy sauce
2 tablespoons Worcestershire
  sauce
8-10 chicken wings

Mix sugar, cornstarch, salt, ginger, and pepper in small saucepan. Stir in water, lemon juice, soy sauce, and Worcestershire sauce. Cook over moderate heat, stirring constantly, until mixture thickens. Simmer 3 minutes. Remove from heat. Cook wings on grill over slow fire about 20-30 minutes. Spread glaze on wings. Continue cooking, turning chicken and reapplying glaze for another 10 minutes.

VARIATION: Use other chicken parts and change cooking time accordingly.

Preparation: 10 minutes
Cooking: 20-30 minutes

Serves: 2-3
Serve immediately

Chicken and Stuffing Casserole

3 whole chicken breasts or 1 (3
  pound) whole chicken
2 (10¾ ounce) cans cream of
  chicken soup
1 pint sour cream
½ pound fresh or canned
  mushrooms, sliced

½ cup dry white wine
1 (14 ounce) package seasoned
  stuffing mix (or make your own
  stuffing)

Boil the chicken for 25 minutes or until cooked. Remove skin, bone, and put chicken meat chunks in bottom of buttered 3-quart casserole. Combine soup, sour cream, mushrooms, and wine. Pour over the chicken. Prepare stuffing according to package directions (or prepare your own stuffing). Put stuffing on top of chicken mixture. Cover with aluminum foil. Bake at 350°F. for 1 hour.

NOTE: Turkey may be substituted for the chicken. This dish can be made up to 2 days before serving, or it can be frozen.

Preparation: 45 minutes
Cooking: 1 hour

Serves: 10
Can be frozen

Italian Chicken Croquettes

6 eggs, beaten
2 cups (8 ounces) grated
    Parmesan cheese
½ cup bread crumbs
4 cups finely chopped cooked
    chicken
3 tablespoons butter
½ cup chopped green pepper
½ cup chopped onion
1 clove garlic, minced

1 tablespoon oil
½ cup water
2 (15 ounce) cans tomato sauce
1 teaspoon sugar
½ teaspoon oregano
½ teaspoon basil
⅛ teaspoon pepper
Salt
2 cups shredded Mozzarella
    cheese

Combine eggs, cheese, and crumbs. Stir in chicken and mix well. Shape into 16 patties, ¾-inch thick. Melt butter in large skillet over medium heat. Brown patties, 2-3 minutes on each side. Arrange patties in two 6 x 10 x 2-inch baking dishes. Sauté green pepper, onion, and garlic in oil until tender. Remove from heat. Add water, tomato sauce, sugar, oregano, basil, pepper, and salt to taste. Spoon sauce over patties and sprinkle with cheese. Bake, uncovered, at 350°F. for 25 minutes. May be frozen. If baked frozen, bake at 400°F. for 50 minutes.

Preparation: 30 minutes
Cooking: 25-50 minutes

Serves: 8-10
Can be frozen

Yoshiko's Chicken Teriyaki
Quick, easy, and elegant—a real plus when you're in a rush

1 (3 pound) chicken, cut in
    twenty pieces by butcher or
    with cleaver
¼ cup sugar

Sake
⅓ cup Japanese soy sauce
6 slices ginger root

Place chicken in large non-metallic bowl. Pour sugar into glass measuring cup. Pour Sake over sugar until level is at ⅓ cup. Add soy sauce to bring level to ⅔ cup. Squeeze ginger in garlic press over the measuring cup to extract juice. Mix thoroughly. Pour over chicken; then marinate for 36 hours, turning several times. Broil, turning once, until done.

NOTE: You may substitute legs and thighs for the whole chicken.

Preparation: 10 minutes
    (plus 36 hours)
Cooking: 20-25 minutes

Serves: 4-6 as entree,
    10 as appetizer
Must do ahead

Chicken Soufflé

8 slices white bread
2 cups diced cooked chicken
½ cup mayonnaise
1 medium onion, chopped
1 green pepper, chopped
1 cup chopped celery
½ cup chopped almonds

3 cups milk
4 eggs
1 (10¾ ounce) can cream of
　mushroom soup
Parmesan cheese, grated
Paprika
Parsley

Dice 4 bread slices and place in bottom of large 2-3-quart casserole. Mix chicken, mayonnaise, onion, green pepper, celery, and almonds. Spread on top of diced bread. Trim crusts off remaining 4 slices of bread and place on top of chicken mixture. Beat eggs and milk. Pour over all. Refrigerate overnight. The next day, bake at 325°F. for 15 minutes. (If using a glass casserole, be careful not to put a cold casserole directly into a preheated oven, as the glass will break). Pour soup over the top. Sprinkle with grated cheese and paprika. Bake at 325°F. for 1 hour more. Serve garnished with parsley.

NOTE: It can also be made with shrimp or crabmeat.

Preparation: 30 minutes
Cooking: 1¼ hours

Serves: 8-9
Must do ahead

Chicken of a Different Sort

1 large garlic clove, minced
1 medium onion, finely chopped
4 medium green peppers, sliced
　into thin strips
4 tablespoons oil

2½ pounds chicken pieces
1 cup chicken broth
1 large lemon, seeded and thinly
　sliced
Salt and pepper, to taste

In large skillet, sauté garlic, onion, and peppers in olive oil until barely tender but not brown. Remove from fat. Next, brown chicken in skillet. Place chicken in deep casserole and sprinkle with green pepper mixture. Add broth, lemon slices, and seasonings to taste. Cover. Bake at 350°F. about 45 minutes or until chicken is tender.

Preparation: 20 minutes
Cooking: 45 minutes

Serves: 4
Can do ahead

Mexican Chicken Tortilla

3 whole chicken breasts, split, or
   1 whole chicken, cut up
1 (10¾ ounce) can cream of
   mushroom soup
1 (10¾ ounce) can cream of
   chicken soup
1 cup sour cream

1 package (one dozen) corn
   tortillas
2 (4 ounce) cans chopped green
   chilies, drained
1 pound Monterey Jack cheese,
   grated
1 cup pitted black olives, sliced

Simmer chicken covered with water for 25 minutes. Skin and remove meat from bones, leaving chicken in large pieces. Combine soups and sour cream. Pour half of mixture into bottom of 9 x 13-inch pan. Cut tortillas in quarters and arrange half on top of soup mixture. Layer half the chilies, then half the chicken on the tortillas. Cover with half the cheese. Repeat layers. Bake, covered, at 350°F. for 45 minutes. Garnish with olives before serving.

Preparation: 45 minutes
Cooking: 45 minutes

Serves: 6
Can do ahead

Supreme Casserole
Don't be afraid of the pickle relish. It's great!

¾ cup mayonnaise
3 tablespoons Dijon mustard
2 tablepoons chopped pimiento
2 tablespoons pickle relish

1 tablespoon minced onion
2 tablespoons slivered almonds
3 cups cubed chicken or turkey
2 eggs, hardcooked, sliced

TOPPING:
½ cup grated sharp Cheddar
   cheese

½ cup bread crumbs
Paprika

Combine mayonnaise, mustard, pickle relish, onion and almonds. Add chicken or turkey. Mix well. Add sliced eggs and toss gently. Put into 2-quart baking dish.

TOPPING: Mix cheese with bread crumbs. Add to top of casserole. Sprinkle with paprika. Bake at 350°F. for 30 minutes.

TO SERVE COLD: Omit the topping. Simply refrigerate mixture at least 3 hours before serving.

Preparation: 30 minutes
Cooking: 30 minutes, optional

Serves: 6-8
Can do ahead

Curried Capon with Chutney Rice

1 (4 pound) capon	Pepper
1 small onion, chopped	Cayenne pepper
2 tablespoons butter	Salt
4 tablespoons curry powder	3 cups cooked rice
2 tablespoons all-purpose flour	4 ounces chutney, more or less, to
4-5 cups stock (from capon)	taste

Cut capon into pieces. Place in large pan. Cover with water and simmer until tender. Remove capon from pot reserving stock. Skin, bone, and cut meat into bite-sized pieces. Cook onion in butter until tender and lightly browned. Stir in curry powder, flour, and hot stock. Add capon to heat through. Season to taste with pepper, cayenne and salt. Combine hot rice with chutney. Pour sauce over rice and serve.

NOTE: Chicken may be substituted for capon.

Preparation: 2 hours   **Serves:** 6
Cooking: 30 minutes   Serve immediately

Lemon Butter Cornish

4 cornish hens	¾ cup butter, melted
Vodka	2 teaspoons grated lemon rind
8 thin slices lemon	1 tablespoon lemon juice
8 thin slices butter	1½ cups chicken broth
2 teaspoons salt	2 tablespoons heavy cream
1 teaspoon white pepper	½ cup sour cream
2 teaspoons crushed tarragon	1 tablespoon parsley, chopped

Coat hens with vodka inside and out. Let rest 15 minutes. Carefully loosen skin over breast, making a pocket. Place 2 slices lemon and 2 slices butter in the skin pocket of each hen. Season inside and out with salt, pepper, and tarragon. Combine butter with lemon rind and juice. Place hens in roasting pan. Baste with lemon butter mixture. Pour in chicken broth to cover bottom of pan. Bake at 450°F. for 15 minutes. Baste. Reduce heat to 375°F. and cook an additional 30-45 minutes or until done. Remove hens to heated platter. Reduce pan liquids by half. Stir in cream, sour cream, and parsley. Pour over hens and serve.

Preparation: 20 minutes   **Serves:** 4
Cooking: 1-1¼ hours   Serve immediately

Roast Duckling

1 (5-6) pound or 2(2½-3 pound)
  oven-ready ducks
Salt
Pepper
3 large cloves garlic
1 large apple cut into ½-inch
  cubes

1 large lemon, peel grated
1 small bunch celery with leafy
  tops, chopped
1 sprig fresh thyme (or
  ½ teaspoon dried)

Season cavity of duck with salt and pepper. Combine 2 finely chopped garlic cloves, apple, lemon peel, celery, and thyme. Loosely stuff duck with mixture. Use skewers and string to seal cavity opening, then tie the legs together. Bruise garlic clove. Cut lemon in half. Rub duck with garlic and lemon. Place duck on a rack in a shallow pan. Bake at 450°F. for 20 minutes. Reduce heat to 350°F. Baste with pan drippings every 15 minutes. Continue cooking 1-1¾ hours (time depends on duck size). Duck is done if juices run clear when thickest part of thigh is pierced with sharp knife point.

Preparation: 30 minutes
Cooking: 1½-2¼ hours

Serves: 4
Can do ahead

Ovenless Duck

1 Long Island duckling, quartered
1½ teaspoons salt
1 teaspoon pepper
2 teaspoons paprika
½ cup port
1 clove garlic, crushed
Pinch of each: nutmeg, thyme,
  allspice

¼ teaspoon grated orange rind
½ cup bottled brown sauce
½ cup currant jelly
½ cup pitted black cherries, may
  be canned
Juice of ½ orange
1 tablespoon butter

Rub duck with salt, pepper, and paprika. Place in dry skillet skin side down and cover tightly. Cook at 350°F. for electric skillet or over medium heat for 1 hour. Turn at 20 minute intervals. Do not pour fat off while cooking. Meanwhile combine port, spices and orange peel in saucepan. Cook over medium heat until volume is reduced by half. Add brown sauce and heat through. Add jelly, stirring until dissolved. Stir in cherries, juice, and butter. To serve, pour hot sauce over duckling on platter.

Preparation: 20 minutes
Cooking: 1 hour

Serves: 4
Serve immediately

Dramatic Duck with Cherry Sauce

2 (4-5) pound ducklings, thawed
  and quartered

Salt and pepper
2 tablespoons honey

SAUCE:

1 (17 ounce) can pitted dark
  sweet cherries
1 tablespoon cornstarch
½ cup Burgundy wine

1 teaspoon lemon juice
½ teaspoon salt
⅛ teaspoon marjoram
2 tablespoons duck fat

½ cup brandy, to flame duckling

Cook duckling on the day before serving. Prick ducklings' skin at intervals with a fork. Be careful not to prick the meat. Sprinkle cavity and skin with salt and pepper. Place duckling pieces in a shallow roasting pan on a rack. Roast, uncovered, at 275°F. for 2½-2¾ hours. Drain off fat reserving 2 tablespoons for cherry sauce. Cool duck and refrigerate overnight. 2 hours before serving, remove duckling from refrigerator, arrange on a shallow roasting pan, and brush with honey. Bake in a 400°F. oven for 30 minutes.

SAUCE: Drain cherries and reserve juice. Place cornstarch in saucepan and gradually blend in cherry juice and wine. Add lemon juice, salt, marjoram and duck fat. Cook over medium heat stirring constantly until thickened and smooth. Add the cherries. Keep sauce warm.

TO SERVE: Place duckling on a warm, heatproof serving dish. Warm brandy in a small saucepan. Pour brandy over duckling. Carefully ignite. Pour cherry sauce over duckling and serve.

Preparation: 30 minutes
Cooking: 3 hours

Serves: 8
Can do ahead

Tangy Chicken Marinade

½ cup oil
1 cup cider vinegar
2 teaspoons salt

1½ teaspoons poultry seasoning
¼ teaspoon pepper
1 egg, beaten

Combine all ingredients. Marinate overnight for best results. Grill, basting often.

Preparation: 5 minutes

Yield: Enough for 8-10 pieces of
        chicken

MAIN DISHES

Fur Trade

In the early days of Dutch settlement, the vast numbers of fur-bearing animals and game influenced the nature of life around Ft. Orange, as Albany was originally called. In 1652, Peter Stuyvesant apportioned a tract of land surrounding the fort and called it "Beverwyck" which was Dutch for "town where beavers gathered." With the establishment of Beverwyck, the beaver trade, formerly controlled exclusively by the Dutch West India Company, was thrown open to all citizens and rapidly flourished. Between June and September of 1657, no less than 41,000 beaver pelts were shipped to Holland.

A 17th century account of the abundance of game in the Albany area states that "there were so many turkeys and deer that they came to the house and hogpens to feed, and were taken by the Indians with so little trouble that deer was sold to the Dutch for a loaf of bread, or a knife, or even a tobacco pipe."

Dutch menus reflected this bounty of meat. It was said that the greatest pleasures of the Dutch were those of the table. Accounts of scant food supplies or starvation were never told. A typcial Dutch dinner included all these items:

> oysters, raw, roasted, and pickled
> roasted haunch of venison (purchased for 15¢)
> wild turkey
> wild goose
> breads and sweet cakes
> watermelon

While you will probably serve only one kind of meat at a meal, the following recipes will provide you with many selections from which to make your choice.

Broccoli Beef Roll-Up

1 pound ground beef
1 medium onion, minced
1 (10 ounce) package frozen
  broccoli, thawed and
  squeezed dry
½ cup shredded Mozzarella
  cheese

½ cup sour cream
¼ cup dried bread crumbs
½ teaspoon salt
¼ teaspoon black pepper
½ pound phyllo pastry
⅓-½ cup melted butter or
  margarine

In a large skillet over high heat, sauté beef and onion until all juices evaporate and meat is well browned. Stir, as needed, to prevent burning. Remove from heat. Stir in broccoli, cheese, sour cream, bread crumbs, salt, and pepper. Place a large sheet of wax paper (larger than dimensions of phyllo pastry) on a flat surface. Lightly brush paper with melted butter. Place a phyllo leaf on buttered wax paper and quickly brush with melted butter. Repeat with all of phyllo leaves, buttering each layer. Spoon beef mixture onto ½ of phyllo leaves' surface, starting at the short end of rectangle. Starting with the beef-covered end, roll up the phyllo jelly-roll fashion. Place phyllo roll, seam side down, on cookie sheet. Brush with remaining butter. Bake at 350°F. for 45 minutes or until golden brown. Cool 15 minutes before slicing. Serve warm.

NOTE: Filling can be made 1 day ahead or frozen until ready to use. Assemble the phyllo roll on the day to be served.

Preparation: 1 hour
Cooking: 45 minutes

Serves: 6-8
Can do ahead

Chili
Quick and easy, it won a prize among friends

2 pounds ground beef
1 (32 ounce) can crushed
  tomatoes
1 (16 ounce) can kidney beans
3 onions, coarsely chopped
1 green pepper, coarsely chopped

3 cloves garlic, crushed
2 tablespoons chili powder
1 teaspoon cumin
Salt and pepper, to taste
Hot pepper sauce, to taste

In a large skillet or saucepan, brown and drain beef. Add remaining ingredients. Mix well. Cover and cook on stove for 1-2 hours over low heat. Stir occasionally.

Preparation: 20 minutes
Cooking: 1-2 hours

Serves: 8
Can do ahead

Cider Pot Roast

3½-4½ pound beef pot roast
2 tablespoons all-purpose flour
3 tablespoons shortening
1 envelope dry onion soup mix
1½ cups apple cider
½ teaspoon celery seed

6 parsnips, cut in half lengthwise
6 carrots, cut in half lengthwise
Flour
Water
2 tablespoons chopped parsley

Dredge roast in flour. Melt shortening in Dutch oven and brown roast. Pour off drippings. Combine dry onion soup mix, apple cider, and celery seed. Stir to dissolve and add to meat in pan. Cover and cook slowly on top of stove for 2 hours or until meat is nearly done. Add parsnips and carrots. Continue cooking for 50 minutes, or until vegetables and meat are cooked. Remove meat and vegetables to platter. Garnish vegetables with 1 tablespoon parsley.

GRAVY: Thicken cooking juices in pan with a paste of 1 tablespoon flour and 1 tablespoon cold water for each cup of cooking juice. Boil at least 5 minutes to cook flour thoroughly. Sprinkle 1 tablespoon parsley in gravy. For a clearer sauce, substitute 1 tablespoon cornstarch for each tablespoon flour. Serve over noodles.

Preparation: 45 minutes
Cooking: 3 hours

Serves: 6
Serve immediately

Beef Curry

½ cup all-purpose flour
3 teaspoons curry powder
2½ pounds top sirloin, cut into
    bite-size pieces
¼ cup butter
2 cloves garlic, minced
2½ cups water

¾ cup white, seedless raisins
1 tart apple, peeled and chopped
½ cup chopped onion
Salt and pepper, to taste
1½ pounds mushrooms, sliced
4 tablespoons butter

Mix flour and curry powder. Dredge meat. Melt butter in Dutch oven and add meat and garlic. Stir often until meat is browned. Then add water, raisins, apple, and onion. Cover and cook over low heat for 45 minutes or until meat is tender. Season with salt and pepper. In a separate pan, melt butter and sauté mushrooms. Add mushrooms to meat. Simmer until ready to serve over noodles or rice.

NOTE: For curry lovers, add 1 teaspoon curry powder to simmering curry.

Preparation: 30 minutes
Cooking: 1 hour

Serves: 6-8
Can do ahead

Dill Flavored Meatballs

MEATBALLS:
1½ pounds ground beef
½ cup sour cream (commercial)
2 teaspoons salt

¼ teaspoon freshly ground black
  pepper
½ teaspoon garlic powder

GRAVY:
1 cup sour cream (commercial)
¼ teaspoon garlic powder

½ teaspoon granulated white
  sugar
2 teaspoons dried dill weed

MEATBALLS: Combine ground beef, ½ cup sour cream, salt, pepper, and garlic powder in a bowl. Stir well. Form into small (½-¾ inch) balls, about 35 of them. Chill for 15 minutes. Heat butter in 10-12 inch skillet. Sauté chilled meatballs over high heat, stirring to brown them quickly all over. When brown, drain any fat from the pan. Place pan in 200°F. oven for 10 minutes.

GRAVY: In a small saucepan, combine 1 cup sour cream, garlic powder, sugar, and dried dill weed. Stirring constantly, heat until just bubbling. Stir in juices accumulated from pan holding meatballs in the oven.

TO SERVE: Serve cooked meatballs in a warm bowl or platter with gravy poured over them. Serve as a main course or as an appetizer.

NOTE: The uncooked meatballs can be made ahead of time and chilled until ready to cook.

Preparation: 45 minutes
Cooking: 15 minutes

Serves: 5-6
Serve immediately

Polynesian Beef Ribs

4 pounds lean beef short ribs, cut
  into serving pieces
1 cup orange juice

½ cup soy sauce
¼ cup honey
1 tablespoon ginger

Trim excess fat from beef ribs. Place ribs in large 4-quart casserole dish. Mix together orange juice, soy sauce, honey, and ginger. Pour mixture over meat. Cover and refrigerate for 3-6 hours. Bake at 325°F. for 1-1½ hours until done. While cooking, turn ribs once to coat ribs with sauce on both sides.

VARIATION: You could substitute pork spareribs or chicken in place of the beef ribs.

Preparation: 20 minutes
Cooking: 1-1½ hours

Serves: 4
Must do ahead

Ranch-Style Short Ribs

2 pounds lean beef short ribs	1 tablespoon prepared mustard
1 (8 ounce) can tomato sauce	2 tablespoons minced onion
1 cup beer, at room temperature	2 tablespoons brown sugar
2 tablespoons lemon juice	1 teaspoon salt

Trim any excess fat off short ribs. Place on foil, in baking dish, large enough to enclose ribs. Fold up the sides of foil. Boil remaining ingredients in 2-quart saucepan. Then pour sauce over short ribs. Fold foil over meat to make a packet, leaving some room for steam to escape. Bake at 350°F. for at least 2 hours. Open foil packet and bake for 30 minutes longer.

NOTE: A day ahead, bake ribs for 2 hours, cool slightly, and then refrigerate. When cold, remove the congealed fat as even with lean ribs there is a surprising amount of fat. Thicken remaining sauce slightly using a paste of ½ tablespoon cornstarch mixed with 1 tablespoon cold water. Cook sauce until thickened and clear. Re-heat ribs while making sauce. Pour sauce over ribs and serve.

Preparation: 20 minutes   **Serves:** 4
Cooking: 2½ hours   Can do ahead

London Broil à la Bourguignon

2½ pounds boneless steak, flank
   steak or round steak

SAUCE:

10 tablespoons butter	½ teaspoon paprika
1 cup Burgundy wine	Salt and pepper, to taste

8 slices French bread, ½-inch
   thick

Broil steak until rare (or medium if preferred).

SAUCE: While steak is cooking, melt butter in a large skillet. Add wine, paprika, salt, and pepper. Let bubble slowly.

TO ASSEMBLE: Toast bread under a broiler. Arrange toast on a platter. Slice broiled steak and place in sauce momentarily to coat slices. Place steak slices on bread. Pour sauce over all and serve.

NOTE: A 4-ounce can of sliced mushrooms can be added to the sauce.

Preparation: 20 minutes   **Serves:** 4-6
Cooking: 15 minutes   Serve immediately

Lobster Stuffed Tenderloin of Beef

3-4 pounds whole beef tenderloin
2 (4 ounce) lobster tails, frozen
1 tablespoon butter, melted

1½ teaspoons lemon juice
6 slices bacon

SAUCE:
½ cup sliced green onions
½ cup butter

½ cup dry white wine
⅛ teaspoon garlic salt

Cut beef tenderloin lengthwise to within ½ inch of end to butterfly. Place frozen lobster tails in boiling salted water to cover. Return water to boiling,then reduce heat and simmer 5 minutes. Remove lobster from shells, cut in half lengthwise. Place lobster end-to-end inside beef. Combine 1 tablespoon melted butter with lemon juice and drizzle on lobster. Reassemble beef tenderloin and tie securely with string at 1 inch intervals. Refrigerate for several hours until ready to bake. Before baking, lay bacon strips on top. Place on rack in a shallow pan. Roast at 425°F. for 40 minutes for rare, 50 minutes for medium or until done to taste.

SAUCE: While meat is cooking, in a saucepan cook green onions in ½ cup butter over low heat until tender. Stir frequently. Add wine and garlic salt. Heat thoroughly.

TO SERVE: Slice roast and spoon on sauce.

Preparation: 35 minutes
Cooking: 50 minutes

Serves: 8
Can do ahead

Corned Beef Baked in Sherry

4 pounds corned brisket of beef,
    straight cut
1 tablespoon whole pickling
    spices
1 celery stalk with leaves

1 onion, peeled
1 carrot, peeled
⅓ cup brown sugar, firmly packed
1 teaspoon prepared mustard
½ cup cooking sherry

Wash corned beef. In a large kettle, place corned beef and cover with boiling water. Add pickling spices, celery, onion, and carrot. Cover and simmer 3-4 hours or until tender. Cool beef in broth. Remove corned beef and place in a shallow roasting pan. Score the fat layer. Save the broth. Mix brown sugar and mustard and pat on corned beef. Pour cooking sherry over beef. Bake at 300°F. for 1 hour basting every 15 minutes.

Preparation: 15 minutes
Cooking: 4-5 hours

Serves: 4-5
Serve immediately

Flank Steak, Marinated and Grilled

1½ pounds flank steak

MARINADE:

1 (8 ounce) can tomato sauce
¼ cup molasses
3 tablespoons water
2 tablespoons plus 1 teaspoon
   vinegar
1 tablespoon salad oil
1 tablespoon chopped onion

1 tablespoon Worcestershire
   sauce
1½ teaspoons dry mustard
½ teaspoon black pepper
Dash of cayenne pepper or
   Tabasco sauce, to taste

In a shallow dish, place flank steak in a marinade made by combining all the remaining ingredients. Marinate 6 hours or overnight in a refrigerator, turning several times. Drain steak, reserving marinade. Barbecue or broil steak until medium rare. In a saucepan, heat marinade. Slice hot steak very thinly on the diagonal and pour sauce over meat or use sauce as a dip.

Preparation: 10 minutes
Cooking: 12 minutes

Serves: 4
Must do ahead

Herbed Flank Steak Rolls

1 pound flank steak
1 tablespoon instant minced
   onion or ¼ cup minced onion
1 tablespoon water
½ teaspoon instant meat
   tenderizer

½ teaspoon crumbled rosemary
¼ teaspoon salt
4 strips bacon

Place flank steak on a cookie sheet in freezer for 15 minutes. Combine instant minced onion with water and set aside (omit if using fresh onion). With a sharp knife, butterfly partially frozen steak by slicing almost in half but without cutting all the way through. Open steak, press fold flat. Sprinkle meat with tenderizer, rosemary, salt, and onion. Roll up with grain running the length of the roll. Cut into 4 sections. Wrap each with a bacon slice and secure with a toothpick. Broil, cut side down, about 4 inches from heat, 5-8 minutes on each side.

Preparation: 15 minutes
Cooking: 10-16 minutes

Serves: 4
Serve immediately

Beef Stroganoff

½ pound fresh mushrooms, sliced
1 large onion, chopped
1 clove garlic, minced
4 tablespoons butter
2 pounds round steak, ½-inch
   thick
½ cup all-purpose flour

½ teaspoon salt
Dash of black pepper
1 (10½ ounce) can beef broth
⅔ cup water
¼ cup sherry or dry red wine
½ (6 ounce) can tomato paste
1 cup sour cream

In a heavy skillet, sauté mushrooms, onion and garlic in 2 tablespoons butter. Remove from pan. Trim off fat from steak. Slice steak into 2½ x ¾-inch strips. Dredge meat strips in flour seasoned with salt and pepper. Coat strips thoroughly. In same skillet, melt remaining 2 tablespoons butter and brown meat strips. Add beef broth and water. Cover and simmer, stirring occasionally, until meat is tender, about 1½ hours. Add sautéed mushrooms, onions, and garlic to meat. Add tomato paste and sherry or wine. Cover and simmer 5 minutes more. Stir sour cream into sauce. Heat through but do not boil. Serve over noodles or rice.

Preparation: 20 minutes   **Serves:** 6
Cooking: 1¾ hours   Serve immediately

Beef with Green Peppers
A fine recipe for the busy working person or to serve unexpected guests

1 pound beef, beef shoulder or
   London broil
4 tablespoons soy sauce
2 tablespoons cornstarch
⅛ teaspoon freshly ground black
   pepper

4 medium green peppers, seeded
   and slivered
6 tablespoons cooking oil,
   vegetable or peanut
Salt, to taste

Slice beef in slivers about 2½ inches long and ¼ inch thick. Combine cornstarch and 2 tablespoons soy sauce. Mix with beef slivers and set aside. Heat 3 tablespoons oil in cooking wok or heavy skillet. Stir-fry green peppers until crisp tender and remove. Add remaining oil and stir-fry beef, pushing meat up the sides as its redness disappears. Add peppers, pepper, salt, and remaining 2 tablespoons soy sauce to beef in wok. Heat thoroughly and serve.

Preparation: 30 minutes   **Serves:** 4
Cooking: 5 minutes   Serve immediately

"Blarney" Beef
This is a hearty, warming stew for a chilly day

2 tablespoons bacon drippings or
    cooking oil
1½ pounds stew beef, cubes
3 tablespoons all-purpose flour
1 clove garlic, minced
1 teaspoon dry mustard
2 (7 ounce) bottles or 1 (12 ounce)
    bottle stout

1 cup beef broth
1 bay leaf
⅛ teaspoon oregano
⅛ teaspoon marjoram
1 large onion, sliced
1 green pepper, sliced
¼ pound fresh mushrooms, sliced

Heat drippings or cooking oil in a large skillet or saucepan and brown meat. Then mix in flour. Add garlic, dry mustard, stout, broth, bay leaf, oregano, and marjoram. Bring slowly to a boil. Cover and simmer on low heat for 2½ hours. Add onion, green pepper, and mushrooms. Continue cooking for another ½ hour. Correct seasonings to taste.

NOTE: If made in a crockpot, brown meat in skillet and transfer to crock-pot. Cook all day on slow and turn to high temperature for last 30-45 minutes.

Preparation: 20 minutes   **Serves:** 4
Cooking: 3 hours   Can do ahead

Rachael's French Bread Meat Loaf
A fun way to serve meat loaf

1 (8 ounce) loaf French bread
1 pound ground chuck or ground
    round
1 cup cottage cheese

½ cup catsup
2 teaspoons Worcestershire sauce
¼ teaspoon salt
¼ teaspoon pepper

Cut a slit into underside of bread loaf and remove inside bread. Tear the removed bread into bits as if making stuffing. Mix bread with remaining ingredients. Stuff bread shell with meat loaf mixture. Wrap in foil and refrigerate until ready to bake. Bake, stuffed side up at 350°F. for 50 minutes. Slice and serve hot, warm, or cold.

NOTE: This can be served as an appetizer, a buffet dish, or an informal supper.

Preparation: 20 minutes   **Yield:** 10 slices
Cooking: 50 minutes   Can do ahead

Mexibeef

1 pound ground beef
⅓ cup catsup
1 tablespoon minced onion
2 tablespoons chili powder
1 clove garlic, minced
¼ teaspoon Tabasco sauce

Water
¾ cup thin egg noodles,
  uncooked
Tortilla chips
½ cup grated Cheddar cheese

In a large skillet, sauté ground beef. Drain off excess fat. In a measuring cup, combine catsup, onion, chili powder, garlic, and Tabasco sauce. Add enough water to make 2 cups of catsup mixture. Pour over meat in skillet. Add noodles. Simmer, uncovered, 20 minutes or until liquid is absorbed. Stir occasionally. Crush tortilla chips on each plate. Top with meat mixture. Sprinkle with grated cheese and serve.

Preparation: 30-40 minutes
Cooking: 20 minutes

Serves: 4
Serve immediately

Korean Barbecued Beef (Bul Go Gi)
An excellent light, but hot, summertime meal

1 pound sirloin tenderloin

MARINADE:
2 tablespoons sugar
5 tablespoons dark soy sauce
2 tablespoons sesame oil
1½ teaspoons ground sesame
  seeds

4 teaspoons chopped green onion
¾ teaspoon minced garlic
½ teaspoon black pepper

¼ cup butter

Slice beef in thin slices (if possible have this done by a butcher to get very thin strips). Mix sugar, soy sauce, sesame oil, sesame seeds, green onion, garlic, and black pepper for a marinade. Place beef strips in sauce and marinate overnight. Fry beef in butter for 2-3 minutes or grill over charcoal using aluminum foil to put beef on. Serve immediately.

Preparation: 10 minutes
Cooking: 2-3 minutes

Serves: 3-4
Must do ahead

Lamb Chops with Vegetables "En Papillote"
It is a quick way to prepare the meat and vegetables in a one-dish dinner

4 shoulder lamb chops
1 teaspoon celery salt
¼ teaspoon black pepper
2 medium yellow cooking onions, sliced thin
4 medium zucchini, quartered lengthwise

4 medium carrots, cut into 2-inch strips
1 teaspoon salt
Garlic powder and rosemary, sprinkle to taste

Place each chop on a piece of foil (about 12 x 12 inch). Sprinkle chop with celery salt and pepper. Add vegetables on top of chop. Sprinkle evenly with salt, garlic powder, and rosemary. Wrap tightly. Place on baking sheet or shallow roasting pan. Bake at 350°F. for 50-60 minutes. Serve in individual foil packets.

Preparation: 15 minutes
Cooking: 50-60 minutes

Serves: 4
Serve immediately

Rack of Lamb
A good company dish, the racks can be put in the oven when guests arrive

2 racks of lamb (6-7 chops each)
3 cloves garlic, sliced lengthwise into 4 pieces each

½ cup butter
Salt, black pepper, and marjoram, to taste

Cut racks of lamb so you can carve through the chops before serving (ask a butcher for help). Lay racks fat side down. With a sharp knife, make a slit into each chop. Stuff slit with ¼ clove garlic. Rub racks well with butter. Sprinkle with salt, black pepper, and marjoram. Turn racks over and rub fat side with butter. Then sprinkle with salt, black pepper, and marjoram. Place them on a rack in roasting pan. Roast at 375°F. for 1 hour. When done, remove fat from top of racks. Carve in 2 chop sections to serve.

NOTE: You can use a crown roast of lamb in place of the racks of lamb, if preferred.

Preparation: 15 minutes
Cooking: 1 hour

Serves: 4
Serve immediately

Indonesian Lamb Roast

6 racks of lamb (3-4 rib) or 6 thick
  lamb chops

MARINADE:

¾ cup vegetable oil
⅓ cup finely chopped celery
⅓ cup finely chopped onion
1 clove garlic, minced
¼ cup vinegar
2 teaspoons curry powder
2 dashes Tabasco sauce

3 tablespoons honey
1 teaspoon oregano
2 bay leaves
½ cup strong prepared mustard
1 large lemon, juice and zest
  (grated outer rind)

MARINADE: Heat the oil in a large saucepan over medium high heat. Sauté celery, onion, and garlic until onion is transparent. Stir in remaining ingredients. Simmer for 5 minutes. Remove from heat and cool. Marinate lamb in mixture in refrigerator about 4 hours, turning several times.

TO BAKE: Drain lamb and reserve marinade. Wrap exposed bones in foil. Place in greased shallow baking pan. Brush with marinade. Bake at 400°F. until done to taste or about 20 minutes per pound. Turn once while baking. Baste often with marinade. Carve and serve with heated marinade or a peanut sauce.

NOTE: For a summer variation, barbecue the ribs on an outside grill.

Preparation: 30 minutes
Cooking: 1 hour

Serves: 4-6
Must do ahead

Lamb Curry
The cooking aroma is sure to whet appetites

2 pounds lamb, cut in ¾-inch
  cubes
3 tablespoons oil
1 medium onion, chopped
1 clove garlic, minced
1 cup red wine, or enough to
  cover meat
1 beef bouillon cube

1 tablespoon curry powder, or to
  taste
1 teaspoon paprika
½ teaspoon ginger
½ teaspoon sugar
1 (6 ounce) can tomato paste
2 cups chopped apples
½ cup raisins

CONDIMENTS:
Peanuts, chopped
Coconut, grated

Tomatoes, chopped
Hard-boiled egg, chopped

In a large stew pot, brown lamb in oil. Add onion, garlic, wine (1 cup or
enough to cover meat), bouillon cube, and spices. Simmer, covered, about
1½ hours until meat is tender. Add tomato paste, apples, and raisins.
Simmer another 15 minutes. Serve over rice.

CONDIMENTS: Pass the condiments in separate bowls when lamb curry
is served.

NOTE: Beef can be substituted for lamb.

Preparation: 30 minutes   **Serves:** 4-6
Cooking: 1½ hours   Can do ahead

Yankee Pot Roast

5-6 pounds chuck or round beef
  roast
2 cups red (Zinfandel) wine
1 (2 pound) can crushed tomatoes
1 onion, chopped
4 carrots, sliced ¼-inch thick

2 cloves garlic, minced
⅓ cup brown sugar, firmly packed
2 bay leaves
½ teaspoon nutmeg
Salt and pepper, to taste

Place roast in a heavy roasting pan. Mix remaining ingredients together
and pour over meat. Bake, uncovered, at 250°F. for about 1 hour per pound.

SAUCE: If desired, you can thicken the gravy juices by mixing 4 tablespoons flour with ½ cup cold water until smooth. Pour flour mixture
into juices and bring to a boil.

Preparation: 15 minutes   **Serves:** 6-8
Cooking: 5-6 hours   Can do ahead

Lamb Navarin

6-8 pounds lamb, shoulder or leg,
 cut in 1½-inch pieces
2 tablespoons vegetable oil
2 tablespoons butter
2 cups chopped onion
2 cloves garlic
¼ cup flour
1 teaspoon salt
¼ teaspoon black pepper
2 cups dry white wine
2 (8 ounce) cans tomato sauce
2 (13¾ ounce) cans chicken broth

¼ cup chopped parsley, stems
 reserved
1 bay leaf
½ teaspoon leaf thyme, crumbled
2 cups fresh or frozen peas,
 cooked and drained
2 (1 pound) cans small carrots,
 drained
2 (1 pound) cans small white
 onions, drained
Parsley, chopped, to garnish

In a large skillet, brown lamb in oil and butter (add more oil to pan if needed) over medium heat. Transfer meat to large Dutch oven. Sauté onion in skillet for 2-3 minutes, stirring occasionally. Add garlic and cook 1 minute. Sprinkle onions and garlic with flour, salt, and pepper. Mix well. Add wine. Bring to a boil, stirring until all brown bits are dissolved. Add tomato sauce, chicken broth, parsley stems, bay leaf, and thyme. Bring to a boil again. Pour sauce over meat. Simmer, covered, for 1¼ hours or until meat is tender. Discard parsley stems and bay leaf. Add vegetables. Simmer until heated through. Garnish with chopped parsley.

Preparation: 30 minutes
Cooking: 1½ hours

Serves: 12
Can do ahead

Applefest Stew

1 onion, finely chopped
4 tablespoons oil
1½ pounds lean lamb, cut into
 1-inch cubes
¼ teaspoon salt
Dash of freshly ground black
 pepper

1 teaspoon cinnamon
1½ cups water
4 medium apples, peeled, cored,
 chopped
2 tablespoons lemon juice

In a Dutch oven, sauté onion until soft in 2 tablespoons oil. Add lamb cubes and brown on all sides. Add salt, pepper, cinnamon, and water. Bring mixture to a boil, immediately reduce heat, cover, and simmer for 45 minutes. In a frying pan, sauté chopped apples for 3 minutes in remaining 2 tablespoons oil. Add apples and lemon juice to the stew. Simmer for 30 minutes more.

Preparation: 20 minutes
Cooking: 1¼ hours

Serves: 4
Can do ahead

Baked Fresh Ham with Barbecue Sauce
This has a very "down home" barbecue taste

½ fresh ham, small, not cured

Salt and pepper, to rub

SAUCE:

5 tablespoons vinegar
2 tablespoons sugar
Salt, black pepper, paprika,
   Tabasco sauce, to taste

1 tablespoon Worcestershire
   sauce
2 tablespoons prepared mustard
½ cup catsup

Rub salt and pepper into ham from which the skin has been removed.

SAUCE: In a saucepan, combine all ingredients for the sauce. Stir and heat.

TO BAKE: Place ham in a roasting pan. Pour sauce over ham. Cover. Bake at 350°F. for 3-4 hours. Baking time depends on size of ham. During last 30 minutes, remove cover and baste frequently with sauce until brown. Serve on heated platter. Degrease "barbecue" sauce and pass sauce with meat.

NOTE: If any meat is leftover, chop into pieces, place on open hamburger buns, spred with sauce, and broil a few minutes to heat.

Preparation: 30 minutes
Cooking 3-4 hours

Serves: 4-6
Serve immediately

Liver with Tomatoes
An appetizing way to serve liver Italian-style

1½-2 pounds beef or calves liver,
   sliced and deveined
4 tablespoons all-purpose flour
Salt and pepper, to taste

2 tablespoons bacon fat or butter
½ cup chopped onion
1 (15 ounce) can stewed tomatoes

Cut liver into 1-inch slices. Coat liver with flour seasoned with salt and pepper. Set aside. In a large skillet, at medium to low heat, melt bacon fat. Brown onions in melted fat. Add the liver slices coated with flour. Stir until browned and all traces of flour disappear. Drain and save the juice from tomatoes. Add drained stewed tomatoes and about one-half of reserved tomato juice (add more if needed). Simmer for 15 minutes.

Preparation: 25 minutes
Cooking: 15 minutes

Serves: 4
Serve immediately

Chicken Livers in Wine and Tarragon Sauce

1 pound chicken livers
6 tablespoons butter
1 medium large onion, thinly
sliced
1 (8 ounce) can sliced
mushrooms, drained, or ½
pound fresh mushrooms, sliced

2 tablespoons all-purpose flour
1 (10½- ounce) can beef gravy
3 tablespoons dry white wine
½ teaspoon dried tarragon
Salt and pepper, to taste

Slice chicken livers in half and set aside. Melt butter in a large skillet. Sauté onions in butter slowly, about 15 minutes. Add mushrooms and continue cooking another 5 minutes. Put flour in a small paper bag. Add sliced livers to the bag and shake. Cook flour-coated livers in skillet for 7 minutes, turning them repeatedly. Add gravy, wine, and tarragon to skillet. Mix and heat over medium-low heat, about 15 minutes. Season to taste and serve.

Preparation: 15 minutes
Cooking: 45 minutes

Serves: 4-6
Serve immediately

Aunt Lilja's Liver Pancakes

1 pound liver, chicken, calf, or
beef
½ cup bread crumbs
¼ cup heavy cream
1 large egg
1 medium onion, minced

1 teaspoon salt
¼ teaspoon pepper
Nutmeg, to taste
2 tablespoons unsalted butter
Cranberry sauce, currant jelly, or
lingonberry sauce

Chop liver into <u>very fine</u> pieces. Combine liver, bread crumbs, heavy cream, egg, onion, salt, pepper, and nutmeg in a medium bowl. Mix well. Heat butter in a skillet. Shape liver mixture into pancakes using 2 tablespoons mixture per pancake. Brown pancakes 2 minutes or until done. Serve hot with a topping of cranberry sauce, currant jelly, or lingonberry sauce which is at room temperature or warmed.

SUGGESTION: Serve with wild rice and a dry wine, red or white.

Preparation: 10 minutes
Cooking: 10-15 minutes

Serves: 2
Serve immediately

Baked Stuffed Pork Chops

4 centercut pork chops, 2 inches
  thick
2 tablespoons butter
1 small onion, finely chopped
½ cup mushrooms, chopped
1 tablespoon parsley
½ cup bread crumbs
1 egg

½ teaspoon marjoram
½ teaspoon caraway seeds
Pinch of salt and pepper
2 tablespoons oil
½ cup chicken broth
¼ cup plus 2 tablespoons dry
  white wine
1 tablespoon cornstarch

Cut a pocket in pork chops. Melt butter in a large skillet. Sauté onion for about 3 minutes. Add mushrooms, parsley, and bread crumbs. Mix. Beat egg. Add marjoram, caraway seeds, salt, and pepper to egg. Mix. Combine egg mixture with bread-mushroom mixture. Stuff pork chops with bread mixture. Secure closed with toothpicks or small skewers. Heat oil in skillet and brown pork chops on both sides. Transfer pork chops to shallow casserole. Pour wine and chicken broth over chops. Cover. Bake at 375°F. for 1¼ hours. Remove chops. Keep warm. Mix 2 tablespoons wine and cornstarch until smooth. Add mixture to drippings in casserole. Heat to thicken. Pour over chops.

Preparation: 30 minutes
Cooking: 1½ hours

Serves: 4
Serve immediately

Savory Pork Chops
The simmered pork chops are surprisingly moist

4-6 porkchops, trim off fat
2 tablespoons vegetable oil
1 green pepper, chopped
2 tablespoons all-purpose flour
1 (10¼ ounce) can onion soup,
  undiluted

2 tablespoons Worcestershire
  sauce
1 teaspoon garlic powder
1 teaspoon salt
1 tomato, chopped

In a large skillet, brown pork chops in vegetable oil. Remove chops. Sauté green pepper in same skillet. Remove pepper. In the same skillet, stir in the flour, onion soup, Worcestershire sauce, garlic powder, salt, and chopped tomato. Over medium heat, stir 2-3 minutes to blend ingredients. Return pork chops to skillet. Spoon sauce over chops, cover, and simmer for 1 hour. Add the sautéed green pepper and simmer 5 minutes more.

Preparation: 10 minutes
Cooking: 1¼ hours

Serves: 4-6
Can do ahead

Deep Fried Pork Chops

With this novel Chinese recipe, the chops are as fun to
cook as they are good to eat

4 pork chops, sliced very thin
4 scallions, sliced in ½-inch
  pieces
1 (1 inch) piece ginger root, sliced
  in ⅛-inch matchstick pieces

3 tablespoons soy sauce
1 teaspoon sesame oil
1 teaspoon sugar
½ cup cornstarch
1 cup peanut oil

Trim fat from chops and pound until even thinner. In a large bowl, sprinkle meat with scallions and ginger. Combine soy sauce, sesame oil, and
sugar. Pour over meat and marinate for ½ hour, occasionally turning meat.
Remove ginger and scallions from chops. Coat chops with cornstarch.
Heat oil in wok or heavy skillet. Cook chops until golden, about 3 minutes, turning constantly. Drain on paper towels.

NOTE: The recipe is easily doubled, tripled, etc. Keep cooked chops
warm in 350°F. oven on paper until all are cooked.

Preparation: 30 minutes
Cooking: 5 minutes

Serves: 2
Serve immediately

Elegant Pork Chop Broil

6 pork loin or shoulder chops, cut
  ¼-½-inch thick

SAUCE:
½ cup brown sugar, firmly packed
¼ cup cider vinegar
3 teaspoons prepared brown
  mustard

1 teaspoon Worcestershire sauce
Dash of powdered cloves
  (optional)

Chopped parsley, to garnish

SAUCE: Mix ingredients for sauce. If time permits, marinate chops in
sauce for 2-3 hours. However, it will also serve well to baste chops while
cooking if time is too short to marinate. Broil about 4 inches from heat
for 15-20 minutes. Baste with sauce occasionally.

TO SERVE: Serve on a bed of rice. Pour drippings over meat and rice.
Sprinkle chopped parsley over all.

Preparation: 10 minutes
Cooking: 20 minutes

Serves: 4-6
Serve immediately

Pork Chops with Linguini

¾ cup (16 ounce) package
   linguini
2 tablespoons salad oil
8 centercut pork chops, thin-
   sliced
¼ cup minced onion

1 clove garlic, minced
1¼ cups catsup
⅓ cup cider vinegar
2 tablespoons brown sugar
½ teaspoon Worcestershire sauce
⅓ cup water

Cook linguini according to package directions. Drain and place in large roasting pan. In a large skillet, brown pork chops in salad oil. Remove chops and arrange on top of linguini. In skillet drippings, cook onion and garlic until tender. Stir in catsup, vinegar, brown sugar, Worcestershire sauce, and water. Simmer 15 minutes. Pour sauce over chops and cover pan with foil. Bake at 350°F. for 45 minutes. Remove foil and bake another 10 minutes. Mix sauce into linguini before serving.

Preparation: 30 minutes
Cooking: 55 minutes

Serves: 4
Can be frozen

Pork Casserole

1 pound ground pork
½ cup chopped onion
¼ cup water
1 (10¾ ounce) can cream of
   chicken soup

½ cup bread crumbs
½ teaspoon sage
¼ teaspoon pepper
2 medium zucchini, sliced
1 cup grated American cheese

Cook pork and onion in skillet about 10 minutes, stirring occasionally. Stir in water, soup, bread crumbs, sage, and pepper. Mix well. Layer half the zucchini on bottom of 10 x 6-inch greased baking dish. Spoon pork mixture over zucchini. Top with remaining zucchini. Cover with foil. Bake at 350°F. for 1 hour. Remove foil and sprinkle with cheese. Return to oven and bake until cheese melts.

Preparation: 15 minutes
Cooking: 1¼ hours

Serves: 6
Serve immediately

Pork Roast and Potato Dinner

Requires some careful preparation but it is worth it

5 pound pork rib roast	¼ teaspoon black pepper
1 clove garlic, slivered	½ cup chopped onion
1½ teaspoons salt	½ cup chopped carrots
1 teaspoon dried thyme leaves	2 sprigs of parsley
1 bay leaf, crumbled	

GRAVY:

2 tablespoons all-purpose flour	¾ cup water
1 (10¾ ounce) can chicken broth, undiluted	

VEGETABLE:

3 pounds medium potatoes, peeled and sliced thin	1 tablespoon salt
	⅛ teaspoon black pepper
1 cup chopped onion	¼ cup butter, melted
1 tablespoon chopped parsley	Chopped parsley, to garnish

Wipe pork with damp paper towel. Rub outside of pork with cut side of garlic slivers. Combine 1½ teaspoons salt, thyme, bay leaf, and ¼ teaspoon pepper. Rub these spices over pork to coat well. Insert garlic slivers in any crevices in the pork roast. In a large 13 x 9 x 2-inch shallow roasting pan, place ½ cup onion, ½ cup chopped carrots, and parsley sprigs. Place roast on top with meat thermometer in center of roast. Roast at 425°F., uncovered, for 1 hour. Remove roast from pan.

GRAVY: Remove all but 1 tablespoon fat from roasting pan. Add 2 tablespoons flour to pan. Over a low heat, stir 3-5 minutes to brown. Gradually blend in 1 cup chicken broth and ¾ cup water. Bring to a boil, reduce heat and simmer, constantly stirring, for 2 minutes or until gravy is thickened and nicely browned. Strain gravy into saucepan and discard vegetables. Set gravy aside to reheat later.

VEGETABLE: Gently toss sliced potatoes with 1 cup chopped onions, 1 tablespoon chopped parsley, salt, and pepper. Mix well. Return pork roast to roasting pan and arrange potatoes around roast. Boil remaining chicken broth and pour over potatoes. Brush potatoes with melted butter. Reduce oven to 400°F. and continue roasting pork ¾-1 hour or until meat thermometer reaches 170°F. Potatoes should be fork tender and nicely browned. Garnish potatoes with chopped parsley.

TO SERVE: Roasted pork and potatoes can be transferred to a serving platter or served in roasting pan. Serve with reheated gravy.

Preparation: 30-45 minutes
Cooking: 2 hours

Serves: 6-8
Serve immediately

Cranberry Roast of Pork

1½ cups cranberries,
   fresh or frozen
⅔ cup sugar
⅓ cup water
1 cup minced onion
1 cup dry red wine (hearty
   burgundy)

4 pounds pork loin, excess
   fat removed
Salt
Pepper
½ teaspoon dried thyme
1 cup beef bouillon

GRAVY:
Cornstarch

Water

Combine cranberries, sugar, and water. Bring to a boil and continue cooking for 5 minutes until berries pop and mixture is thick. Add onion and ½ cup wine. Rub pork with salt, pepper, and thyme. Place pork, bone side down, in roasting pan. Spread cranberry mixture over roast. Bake at 350°F. for 2½ hours or about 40 minutes per pound. Baste roasting pork every 20-30 minutes with a mixture of beef bouillon, ½ cup wine, and pan juices. When roast is done, transfer to board for carving.

GRAVY: After roast is removed, stir pan juices and season to taste. For each cup of juices, combine 1 tablespoon cornstarch with 1 tablespoon cold water. Mix this paste with pan juices and cook in a saucepan until thickened. Spread some sauce over carved meat and serve the remaining sauce at the table.

NOTE: Prepare roast in a deep pan which can just hold your roast so that the juices don't burn all to dust, leaving you with no sauce. Also, this dish can be prepared a day ahead, carved into bite-size pieces, reheated with meat and sauce together, and served as a buffet dish.

Preparation: 45 minutes
Cooking: 2½ hours

Serves: 6
Can do ahead

Roast Pork with Candied Ginger

3½ pound loin pork roast
3 tablespoons candied ginger,
   finely chopped

¼ cup soy sauce
¼ cup rice wine
   (optional)

Pierce 1-inch slits in fat side of roast, making 8 or more. Insert half the ginger in slits. Combine remaining ginger with soy sauce and rice wine and use for basting. Roast at 350°F. for 30-35 minutes per pound.

NOTE: Roast will become very brown because of soy sauce.

Preparation: 30 minutes
Cooking: 1¾-2 hours

Serves: 6
Serve immediately

Cousin Maddy's Spareribs
Serve with wipe-ettes, the ribs are delicious but messy!

RIBS:

Boiling salted water (enough to cover rack of ribs)

1 onion, studded with cloves

1 teaspoon each: thyme, marjoram, oregano

2 racks of pork ribs (not country-style)

MARINADE:

⅓ cup soy sauce

⅓ cup honey

3 tablespoons cider vinegar

2 tablespoons dry sherry

1 tablespoon sugar

1 teaspoon powdered ginger

1½ cups beef broth

2 cloves garlic, minced

2 teaspoons catsup

RIBS: Bring salted water to a boil. Add onion with cloves, rosemary, thyme, marjoram, oregano, and ribs. Boil for 45 minutes.

MARINADE: Combine all ingredients in a large bowl. Marinate ribs in mixture overnight or for at least 2 hours, turning them every half hour. Drain off marinade and reserve.

BROIL: Broil ribs 5-15 minutes turning frequently to prevent burning until desired crispness is attained. Baste with marinade if desired. DO NOT baste if cooking over charcoal flame. Basting is also not needed if ribs were marinated overnight.

Preparation: 2 hours

Cooking: 1 hour

Serves: 4

Can be frozen

Stuffed Creole Peppers

8 medium green bell peppers

2 small onions, chopped

1 (15 ounce) can tomatoes, mashed

2 cups Italian-style bread crumbs

3 tablespoons butter, melted

¾ cup cooked chopped ham

Salt and pepper, to taste

Grated Parmesan cheese, to garnish

Finely chop 2 peppers. Combine chopped peppers with onions, tomatoes, bread crumbs, butter, ham, and seasonings. Set aside. Core remaining 6 peppers and blanch in boiling water for 3 minutes. Stuff peppers with meat mixture. Sprinkle cheese on top. Bake at 350°F. for 40 minutes.

Preparation: 20 minutes

Cooking: 40 minutes

Serves: 6

Can do ahead

Honey 'N' Wine Ham

1 (8 pound) ham, preferably
    boneless
Whole cloves
1 (20 ounce) can pineapple slices,
    reserve juice

Water
1 cup honey
½ cup red wine, preferably a
    fruity type such as lambrusco

Line the bottom of a broiler pan or other large, shallow baking dish with heavy duty foil. Place ham on rack on foil. Remove any rind from ham but leave on fat. Score ham in diagonal, criss-cross pattern and place one whole clove in each resulting square. Pour pineapple juice over ham. Add 2 pineapple cans of water to the pan. Bake at 325°F. for 3 hours, basting every half hour. Arrange pineapple slices on ham using cloves to anchor. Combine honey and wine and pour over all. Continue to cook for another hour, basting every 20 minutes.

Preparation: 30 minutes
Cooking: 4 hours

Serves: 12
Serve immediately

Party Ham Casserole
A great way to use leftover ham

6 ounces flat noodles
1 (10½ ounce) can cream of
    mushroom soup
½ cup milk
1 teaspoon minced onion
2 teaspoons prepared yellow
    mustard
1 cup sour cream
2 cups leftover ham, cut in
    1-inch slivers

¼ cup packaged dry bread
    crumbs
1½ tablespoons butter, melted
1 tablespoon grated Parmesan
    cheese
1 (4 ounce) can sliced
    mushrooms, drained
    (optional)

Cook noodles as directed. Combine soup and milk in a small saucepan. Heat, stirring until smooth. Add onion, mustard, and sour cream to soup mixture. Stir until well mixed. In a greased 2-quart casserole, layer half of the noodles, ham, and sauce. Repeat. Sprinkle bread crumbs over casserole. Sprinkle cheese over bread crumbs. Drizzle melted butter over cheese. Top with mushrooms, if desired, or add mushrooms to soup mixture. Bake, covered, at 325°F. for 30 minutes. Remove cover to let brown a few minutes just before serving.

Preparation: 30 minutes
Cooking: 30 minutes

Serves: 6
Can do ahead

Veal Scallops with Asparagus

8-12 asparagus spears, peeled,
   trimmed and washed
4 veal scallops
Salt and pepper, to taste
¼ cup all-purpose flour

3 tablespoons butter
¼ pound mushrooms, thinly
   sliced
¼ pound Gruyere or Swiss
   cheese, cut into 4 slices

SAUCE:
¼ cup butter
Juice of ½ lemon

¼ cup dry sherry

Cook asparagus in boiling water for 4 minutes or until just tender. Drain. Set aside but keep warm. Pound veal to ¼-inch thickness. Season veal with salt and pepper. Dredge with flour. In heavy skillet, melt 2 tablespoons butter. Sauté veal 2 minutes on each side or until golden. Transfer veal to shallow baking dish, large enough to have veal all in one layer. In another skillet, sauté mushrooms in 1 tablespoon butter until lightly browned. Spoon mushrooms over each veal scallop. Top each scallop with 2-3 asparagus spears and 1 slice of cheese over asparagus. Place under preheated broiler 4 inches from heat for 2 minutes or until cheese is melted.

SAUCE: Melt ¼ cup butter in skillet in which veal was sautéed. Add lemon juice and sherry. Stir. Deglaze skillet of any browned bits. Cook 1-2 minutes over moderate high heat, until bubbly. Remove veal from broiler. Pour sauce over to serve.

Preparation: 20 minutes
Cooking: 15 minutes

Serves: 4
Serve immediately

Veal Scaloppine

1-1½ pounds veal round steak
½ cup all-purpose flour
2 tablespoons olive oil
2 tablespoons butter
Salt and pepper, to taste
4 green onions, chopped

2 cloves garlic
1 teaspoon rosemary
¼ cup chopped parsley
1 cup Sauterne wine
¼ pound sliced mushrooms

Pound veal thin. Cut into 2-inch pieces. Dredge in flour. Sauté veal in large skillet in hot olive oil and butter. Add salt and pepper. Add remaining ingredients except mushrooms. Simmer for 1 hour, adding more wine if necessary. Add mushrooms after 40 minutes.

Preparation: 20 minutes
Cooking: 1 hour

Serves: 4-6
Serve immediately

Veal Chops in White Wine

4 veal chops, about ¾ pound each
6 tablespoons butter, at room
  temperature
½ cup fresh bread crumbs
½ cup freshly grated Parmesan
  cheese

2 tablespoons finely chopped
  shallots
¼ cup dry white wine

Melt 2 tablespoons of butter in a heavy skillet. Using high heat, cook chops 2 minutes on each side or until golden brown. Transfer chops to a platter. Keep warm. Mix remaining butter, bread crumbs, and cheese by hand until thoroughly blended. Divide the mixture into 4 equal parts. Sprinkle shallots over the bottom of the skillet in which the chops were browned. Put chops back into skillet. Flatten the bread mixture to cover the top of each chop. Pour wine around the chops. Place skillet, uncovered, in oven. Bake at 400°F. for 10 minutes until tops are browned. Place a layer of foil loosely over the veal. Return to oven. Continue baking 20 minutes more. When ready to serve, spoon wine sauce <u>around</u> the veal.

Preparation: 30 minutes
Cooking: 30 minutes

Serves: 4
Serve immediately

Veal Scallops with Gorgonzola Sauce

6 (3 ounce) veal scallops
Flour for dredging

3 tablespoons olive oil

SAUCE:
½ cup brandy
½ cup unsalted butter, cut into
  bits

¼ pound Gorgonzola cheese,
  crumbled
½ cup heavy cream

Dredge veal scallops in flour, shaking off the excess. In a large skillet, sauté them in oil over moderately high heat for 30 seconds on each side. Transfer to warmed platter.

SAUCE: Add the brandy to skillet and deglaze. Reduce the mixture over moderately high heat by half. Reduce heat to low, whisk in butter until melted. Stir in the Gorgonzola and the cream. Cook the sauce, whisking until the cheese is melted. Top the veal with the sauce.

Preparation: 20 minutes
Cooking: 10 minutes

Serves: 4-6
Serve immediately

Veal Marsala with Mushrooms

1 pound veal scallops, ⅛-inch
    thick
Salt and pepper
¼ cup all-purpose flour
4 tablespoons butter
2 tablespoons olive oil
½ pound fresh mushrooms,
    thinly sliced

2 tablespoons minced scallions
1 teaspoon minced garlic
½ cup Marsala wine
⅓ cup beef broth
1 teaspoon lemon juice
Parsley, to garnish
Noodles, white or green, cooked

Flatten veal scallops between sheets of wax paper. Sprinkle with salt and pepper. Dredge in flour and shake off excess. In a medium skillet over high heat, sauté veal scallops in 2 tablespoons butter and olive oil until browned on both sides. Transfer to a platter. Add remaining 2 tablespoons butter to the skillet. Add mushrooms, scallions, and garlic. Cook over moderate heat for 3 minutes or until mushrooms are tender. Transfer mushroom mixture to a dish. Into the same skillet, add Marsala wine, beef broth, and lemon juice. Bring to a boil. Return veal scallops and mushroom mixture to the skillet and simmer 10 minutes. Garnish with minced parsley. Serve over cooked noodles.

Preparation: 15 minutes
Cooking: 15 minutes

Serves: 4
Serve immediately

Economy Saltimbocca

1 (10 ounce) package frozen
    chopped spinach, thawed
½ cup chopped onion
2 tablespoons butter or margarine
Pinch of each: salt, pepper,
    nutmeg

4 cubed veal patties
½ teaspoon sage
⅓ cup dry white wine
4 tissue thin pieces proscuitto
    ham
Lemon slices, to garnish

Press spinach dry in strainer. Sauté onion in 1 tablespoon of butter in a medium saucepan for 5 minutes. Mix in spinach, salt, pepper, and nutmeg. Cover. Cook on low while preparing veal. Sprinkle veal patties with sage and rub in. Brown quickly in a skillet in remaining butter. Remove to heated plate to keep warm. Add wine to skillet. Bring to boil. Add ham. Heat until ham ruffles. Place ham slice on each piece of veal. Boil wine mixture 1-2 minutes. Arrange spinach on platter. Top with veal. Drizzle wine mixture over veal. Garnish with lemon slices.

Preparation: 25 minutes
Cooking: 20 minutes

Servings: 3-4
Serve immediately

Veal Fillets

4 lean veal fillets   4 tablespoons butter
Salt and pepper, to taste

SAUCE:
5 shallots, minced   ½-1 cup heavy cream
¾ cup vermouth   1 tablespoon Dijon mustard

Pound veal slightly. Lightly salt and pepper both sides. Melt butter in large skillet. Brown veal slightly. Put in oven to keep warm.

SAUCE: In same skillet, sauté shallots until tender. Add vermouth to pan drippings. Boil and reduce by half. Add heavy cream to 1:1 proportion. Add mustard. Heat until warm. Spoon over veal.

Preparation: 20 minutes   **Serves:** 4
Cooking: 10 minutes   Serve immediately

Veal Julienne

1½ pounds veal steak, cut in   1 (15 ounce) can tomato sauce
   julienne strips   ½ cup canned, halved or chopped
4 tablespoons butter   water chestnuts
½ cup water   2 good splurts of Tabasco sauce or
1 teaspoon basil   other hot sauce
1 medium green pepper, diced   1 teaspoon Worcestershire sauce
1 cup thinly sliced onions   Salt and pepper, to taste
1 (6 ounce) can broiled sliced   ½ cup dry sherry
   mushrooms, drained   1 cup sour cream

Brown veal strips slowly in 2 tablespoons butter, stirring often to prevent burning. Add water and basil. Simmer 20 minutes with pan covered. Meanwhile, cook green pepper and onions in remaining butter until soft but not brown. Add green peppers and onion mixture to veal. Stir in mushrooms, tomato sauce, and water chestnuts. Mix well, then simmer, cover on, for 15 minutes. Stir in hot pepper sauce, Worcestershire sauce, salt, pepper, and sherry. Simmer 5 minutes. Lower heat to below simmer and add sour cream slowly. Stir to blend flavors.

NOTE: Fresh mushrooms can be substituted if sautéed in butter in advance and drained.

Preparation: 15 minutes   **Serves:** 6
Cooking: 1 hour   Can do ahead

Veal Paprika Casserole

3 pounds stewing veal, cut into
    bite-size pieces
⅓ cup all-purpose flour
2 teaspoons salt
¼ teaspoon pepper
⅓ cup salad oil
2½-3 tablespoons paprika
1 pound yellow onions, peeled
    and sliced

2 (10¾ ounce) cans beef broth,
    undiluted
½ teaspoon Worcestershire sauce
8 carrots, peeled, cut into chunks
½(8 ounce) package noodles
1 cup sour cream

Coat veal in a mixture of flour, salt, and pepper. Brown veal in a heavy skillet, a little at a time, in oil. Remove veal and set aside. Mix paprika with pan drippings. Sauté onion until transparent. Add broth, Worcestershire sauce, veal, and carrots. Place in a 4-quart casserole. Cover. Bake at 350°F. for 1½ hours. Cook noodles separately according to package directions. Add cooked noodles to veal. Bake ½ hour longer. After baking, stir a little of the hot liquid into sour cream. Stir the sour cream mixture, a little at a time, into veal casserole. Do not let boil.

Preparation: 30 minutes
Cooking: 1½ hours

Serves: 6-8
Can do ahead

Veal Cutlet Supreme

1 pound veal cutlets, thinly sliced
2 tablespoons all-purpose flour
¼ teaspoon salt
2 tablespoons butter or margarine
1 chicken bouillon cube

½ cup hot water
½ cup sour cream
½ teaspoon lemon juice
Parsley and lemon slices, to
    garnish

Pound veal cutlets between sheets of wax paper until thin. Sprinkle with 1 tablespoon of flour and the salt. Sauté in butter in large skillet until tender and golden brown on both sides. Remove from skillet and place on serving plate. Do not discard skillet drippings. Dissolve bouillon cube in water. Blend remaining 1 tablespoon of flour into pan drippings. Add bouillon. Bring mixture to boil over medium heat. Blend in sour cream and lemon juice. Reduce heat and simmer until slightly thickened, about 2-3 minutes. Strain mixture over veal cutlets. Garnish with chopped parsley and lemon slices.

Preparation: 45 minutes
Cooking: 10 minutes

Serves: 3-4
Serve immediately

Veal Gourmet
Delicious variation of "cordon bleu"

8 pieces veal scaloppine (about
    1½ pounds)
4 slices Swiss cheese
4 slices boiled ham
¼ pound mushrooms, sliced

4 egg yolks
1 cup all-purpose flour
2 cups bread crumbs
6 tablespoons butter
4 tablespoons dry white wine

Pound veal until very thin. Place one slice Swiss cheese and one slice of ham on four pieces of veal. Place mushrooms on top of ham. Put remaining four pieces of veal on top and secure with toothpicks. Beat egg yolks. Dip scaloppine in flour, then egg yolks, then bread crumbs. Melt butter in large skillet and sauté veal slowly for about 15 minutes on each side. Remove meat to heated platter and remove toothpicks. Add wine to the drippings in skillet and bring to a boil. Spoon over meat.

Preparation: 30 minutes
Cooking: 20 minutes

Serves: 4
Serve immediately

Swedish Beef Casserole
The allspice is an important ingredient in this dish

3 pounds stew beef
2 tablespoons butter
2 tablespoons oil
1 large onion, thinly sliced
1 tablespoon all-purpose flour

½ teaspoon allspice
1 bay leaf
1 (10¾ ounce) can beef broth
2 tablespoons sour cream
Salt and pepper, to taste

Put stew beef through food processor using slicing disk. In a large skillet, brown meat in butter and oil. Transfer meat to 4-quart stove-to-oven casserole. Cook onion in pan drippings for 10 minutes. Add onions and flour to meat. Toss lightly. Add allspice, bay leaf, and broth to skillet. Boil for 2 minutes loosening pan scrapings. Pour into casserole and bring to boil on top of stove. Cover. Bake at 325°F. for 1¼ hours.

TO SERVE: Remove meat with slotted spoon to platter and keep warm. Skim fat from liquid in casserole. Beat in sour cream with wire whisk and heat gently on stove. Season to taste with salt and pepper. Pour over meat and serve.

Preparation: 30 minutes
Cooking: 1½-1¾ hours

Serves: 6
Serve immediately

Hamburger-Cheese Casserole
Excellent for last minute meal preparation

4 ounces medium egg noodles,
  uncooked
1 pound ground beef
⅓ cup chopped onion
1 (8 ounce) can tomato sauce
1 teaspoon salt

½ cup creamed cottage cheese
1 (3 ounce) package cream
  cheese, softened
⅓ cup sour cream
1 medium tomato, sliced

Cook noodles as directed on package. Drain and set aside. In a large skillet, sauté ground beef and onion. Drain off excess fat. Stir in tomato sauce and salt. Heat to boiling, then reduce heat to simmer 1 minute. Remove from heat. Add cottage cheese, cream cheese, and sour cream. Mix thoroughly. Mix in noodles. Pour into ungreased 1½-quart casserole. Garnish with tomato slices. Bake at 350°F. for 30 minutes.

Preparation: 30 minutes
Cooking: 30 minutes

Serves: 4
Can do ahead

TAVA
Farmer's Vegetable Casserole

1 pound lean ground round beef
1 teaspoon salt
2 cups canned tomatoes
1½ cups water
⅛ teaspoon black pepper
½ teaspoon allspice
½ pound green string beans, cut
  in 2-3-inch pieces
1 pound zucchini, cut in
  1-inch cubes

1 or 2 green peppers, cut in
  1-inch squares
½-1 pound eggplant, cut in 1-inch
  cubes (optional)
½ pound okra, fresh or frozen
  (if frozen, remove stems)
3 tablespoons lemon juice

Brown ground round with salt. When completely brown, add tomatoes, water, black pepper, and allspice. Let simmer. Place green string beans, zucchini, green peppers, eggplant, and okra alternately in a 3-quart casserole with 2 tablespoons meat mixture each time. Bake covered at 400°F. for 1 hour. Add 3 tablespoons lemon juice and bake 45 minutes longer, or until vegetables are tender. Serves 6-8.

George Deukmejian

Governor George Deukmejian
Now Governor of California, he was born in Menands, New York and graduated from Siena College.

Eggplant Pie

1 pound eggplant, unpeeled, cut
   in ½-inch cubes
8 tablespoons butter
½ cup chopped onion
1 clove garlic, crushed
¾ pound ground round beef
1 tablespoon chopped fresh
   parsley
¼ cup chopped celery tops

1 teaspoon Worcestershire sauce
1 teaspoon salt
Dash of pepper
1 (8 ounce) can tomato sauce
1 (9 inch) deep dish pie crust,
   uncooked
6-8 ounces Mozzarella cheese,
   shredded

In a large skillet, sauté eggplant in 6 tablespoons butter until soft. Cover eggplant while cooking. Remove from pan and drain. Sauté onion and garlic in remaining butter until onion is tender. Add meat to pan and sauté until browned. Drain excess fat. Mix meat with other ingredients except cheese. Put into pie shell. Top with Mozzarella. Bake at 375°F. for 45-60 minutes. Cool 5 minutes before cutting and serving.

Preparation: 30 minutes
Cooking: 45-60 minutes

Serves: 6
Can do ahead

California Marinade for Beef

6 tablespoons soy sauce
6 tablespoons oil
1 tablespoon wine vinegar
1 tablespoon minced onion

1 teaspoon Worcestershire sauce
Few dashes of Tabasco sauce
1 clove garlic, crushed or minced

Mix all ingredients together in a glass or plastic shallow pan. Refrigerate, up to 2 days, until ready to use.

NOTE: Use as marinade for flank or round steak. Marinate meat for 5 hours, turning occasionally.

Preparation: 5 minutes

Yield: ½ cup
Can do ahead

Barbecue Sauce for Pork

½ cup butter or margarine
1 (14 ounce) bottle catsup
3 cloves garlic, crushed

1 tablespoon each: dry mustard,
   vinegar, Worcestershire sauce,
   brown sugar, grape jelly

Slowly melt butter in medium saucepan. Add remaining ingredients and mix thoroughly. Simmer slowly for ½ hour, stirring occasionally. Brush on spareribs, pork chops, or pork roast.

NOTE: Sauce keeps for 1 week in the refrigerator.

Preparation: 45 minutes
Cooking: 30 minutes

Yield: 1½ cups
Can do ahead

Barbecue Sauce for Pork Chops

¼ cup chopped or grated onion
2 tablespoons sugar
½ teaspoon pepper
1 teaspoon Worcestershire sauce

¼ cup catsup
3 tablespoons vinegar
2 tablespoons lemon juice

Mix all ingredients together. Refrigerate until ready to use. Use to baste chops on outdoor grill, basting frequently in the last 15 minutes.

NOTE: It's equally good on chicken.

Preparation: 5 minutes

Yield: 1 cup
Can do ahead

Dad's Special Barbecue Sauce

1 cup salad oil
⅓ cup lemon juice
3 tablespoons soy sauce
1 clove garlic, minced

1 teaspoon oregano
1 teaspoon MSG (optional)
½ teaspoon salt
¼ teaspoon pepper

Combine all ingredients. Use to baste frequently during last 20 minutes of cooking.

Preparation: 5 minutes

Yield: 1½ cups
Can do ahead

Raisin Sauce

½ cup brown sugar, firmly packed
1 teaspoon dry mustard
2 tablespoons each: cornstarch,
   vinegar, lemon juice

1½ cups water
½ cup raisins
2 tablespoons butter or ham fat,
   melted

Mix brown sugar, mustard, and cornstarch in a 1-quart saucepan. Slowly stir in vinegar, lemon juice, water, raisins, and butter or ham fat. Stir over low heat until thickened. Serve warm.

VARIATION: Add a dash of cinnamon or curry powder, to taste. Or, cook with 1 orange slice in it.

Preparation: 10 minutes
Cooking: 5 minutes

Yield: 2 cups
Can do ahead

Party Applesauce

6 tart apples, peeled and sliced
¼ cup brown sugar, firmly packed
½ cup water

¼-½ cup Amaretto liqueur
1 (2¾ ounce) package slivered
   almonds

Put apples, brown sugar, and water in a medium saucepan. Cover. Simmer for 15-20 minutes, stirring occasionally, until apples are tender. Cool. "Toast" almonds on a cookie sheet in 300°F. oven for 5-10 minutes.

TO SERVE: Put applesauce in serving dish. Pour liqueur over applesauce and sprinkle almonds on top.

Preparation: 30 minutes
Cooking: 15-20 minutes

Serves: 6
Can do ahead

FISH &
SEAFOOD

The Hudson River

Fish and seafood have always been important in the Albany area despite its location so far from the ocean. Named for the 17th century Dutch explorer, Henry Hudson, the river has produced fresh water clams, oysters, eels, shad, and two of the more prized food fish in the world—the striped bass and the sturgeon.

In the 1600's, Henry Hudson found the Algonkian Indians using nets to catch striped bass and sturgeon. The Indians took fresh water clams from the river bottom and used them for food and their shells for purple-colored wampum which served as money. Streams leading to the Hudson River supported large populations of trout and bass, both much sought after by Indians and early colonists.

In the 19th century, Albany became a prime sturgeon processing site, producing barrels of caviar and such vast quantities of the smoked fish that, for a time, sturgeon was nicknamed "Albany beef." It was said that a poor family could dine well on two pounds of sturgeon which cost them ten cents.

As years went by, and "civilization" encroached on the river, it supported fewer and fewer fish. There came a time when few of the original species could be found. Pollutants caused the State of New York to prohibit the eating of fish from the Hudson, but its many tributaries in the Capital District continued to support natural and stocked populations. Fishermen still find native trout in some areas. Even at its lowest point the Hudson supported one commercial fisher—goldfish was hit catch!

Recently, hundreds of millions of dollars have been spent on clean-up efforts. Fish are making a comeback. Almost any spring or summer day, at any junction of the river and its tributaries, one can see avid throngs angling for a piscine treat.

The long tradition of fondness for fish and seafood in Albany led to delectable and unique recipes. Whether you catch the fish yourself, or buy it in the market, you are sure to enjoy our suggestions for preparing the "denizens of the deep."

Skillet Sole à Bonne Femme

2 teaspoons butter
¾ cup dry white wine
4 ounces fresh or canned
   mushrooms, sliced
3 tablespoons minced onion
1 pound fillet of sole
Pepper
Dried tarragon

1 cup skim milk, or 2 percent
   milk
1½-2 tablespoons all-purpose
   flour
Paprika
2 tablespoons finely chopped
   parsley

Combine the butter with one tablespoon wine in a nonstick skillet. Add the mushrooms. Cook and stir over high heat until liquid evaporates and mushrooms begin to brown. Remove mushrooms and set aside. Put onion and remaining wine in skillet. Add the fish fillets in a single layer and sprinkle lightly with pepper and tarragon. Simmer over low heat about 5-8 minutes, depending on the thickness of fillets, until fish is opaque and most of the wine has evaporated (add more wine if it evaporates completely). Spoon wine over fish occasionally while it simmers. Stir milk and flour together and stir into simmering skillet, until it simmers and thickens. Sprinkle browned mushrooms on top with paprika and parsley. Heat through. Finished dish may be put under broiler for a minute to further brown.

Preparation: 30 minutes
Cooking: 15-20 minutes

Serves: 4
Serve immediately

Baked Fillet of Sole

6 fillets of sole
½ cup lemon juice
1 onion, finely chopped
1 pinch tarragon, basil or thyme
1 (10¾ ounce) can cream of
   mushroom soup

½ cup dry sherry
Salt
Pepper
Grated Parmesan cheese

Marinate fillets in lemon juice for 30 minutes. Place fillets in flat, buttered, 8 x 13-inch casserole. Sprinkle with onion and herb. Combine soup and sherry. Pour over fish. Season with salt and pepper. Cover the surface with a sprinkling of Parmesan cheese. Cook at 350°F. for 15-20 minutes until fish is opaque and starts to turn golden brown.

Preparation: 35 minutes
Cooking: 15-20 minutes

Serves: 4
Serve immediately

Paella Valenciana

Olive or vegetable oil to cover bottom of pan
2 cloves garlic, minced
½ teaspoon crushed peppercorns
Chicken breasts (½ per person)
1 quart chicken stock
½ cup dry vermouth or dry white wine
1 (19 ounce) can Italian plum tomatoes
2-3 bay leaves, crushed
1 teaspoon oregano

Lobster, pieces (tail, claws) 1 piece per person
2 capsules of powdered saffron, or a pinch of saffron thread
1 pound medium shrimp, cleaned with tails left on
2½ cups long-grain white rice
2-3 dozen clams, scrubbed
2-3 dozen mussels, scrubbed
Spanish sausage or pepperoni
1 green pepper
Spanish olives

Brown garlic in oil in paella pan. Add peppercorns and chicken breasts and brown. In separate pot, bring chicken stock to a simmer and add vermouth or wine. Bring to a boil for a few minutes. Add tomatoes, bay leaves and oregano. Drop the browned chicken into stock pot. Add all lobster pieces (pre-cook if using fresh lobster). Cover and simmer. Paella can be done ahead to this point.

Reheat oil in pan. Add saffron and stir. Add shrimp and sauté until translucent. Remove shrimp and set them aside. Add the rice to the oil and stir until the rice "puffs up." Add liquid from the stock pot to cover the rice. Arrange chicken, lobster, shrimp, clams, and mussels over the rice. Garnish with sausage or pepperoni, green peppers, and olives. Cover pan tightly. Bake at 350°F. until rice has absorbed all of the liquid and the clams and mussels have opened, about 45 minutes.

NOTE: If making for 10-12 people, just leave the extra chicken and seafood pieces in the stockpot until ready to serve.

Preparation: 1 hour
Cooking: 45 minutes

Serves: 8-10
Can be partially made ahead

Cioppino

3 tablespoons olive oil
1 cup chopped onion
½ cup chopped green pepper
1 carrot, peeled
½ cup chopped celery
3 cloves garlic, minced
1 (32 ounce) can tomatoes, peeled
   and crushed
1 (8 ounce) can tomato sauce

1 bay leaf
1 teaspoon salt
¼ teaspoon pepper
1½ cups dry white wine
1 pound haddock, cut in bite-size
   chunks
½ pound shrimp
½ pound scallops
1 dozen fresh clams

In a Dutch oven, heat olive oil and sauté onion, green pepper, carrot, celery, and garlic until soft. Add tomatoes, tomato sauce, bay leaf, salt, and pepper. Bring to a boil, lower heat and simmer 2 hours. Add wine, haddock, shrimp, and scallops. Simmer 10 minutes. Add clams. Simmer 10 more minutes or until clam shells open.

NOTE: Tomato-base stew can be prepared a day ahead. Add the wine and seafood to cook after your guests arrive.

Preparation: 30 minutes
Cooking: 2½ hours

Serves: 6-8
Can do ahead

Fish Fillets Parmesan

1½ pounds flounder, sole, or
   ocean fillets
¼ teaspoon salt
¼ teaspoon celery salt
Pepper, to taste
¾ cup mayonnaise
¼ cup grated Parmesan cheese

⅓ cup minced onion
½ teaspoon basil
1 tablespoon chopped parsley
4 tablespoons fine, dry bread
   crumbs
Paprika

Skin fish fillets and score lightly on the skin side. Sprinkle with salt, celery salt, and pepper. Place in a single layer in a well-buttered 8 x 13-inch baking dish. Mix mayonnaise, cheese, onion, and herbs and spread on the fish. Sprinkle with crumbs and paprika. Bake at 400°F. for 10-15 minutes until lightly browned.

Preparation: 10 minutes
Cooking: 10-15 minutes

Serves: 6
Serve immediately

Fillet of Sole Surprise

8 small fillets of sole
8 large cooked shrimp
Salt and pepper, to taste

¼ teaspoon tarragon
1 cup dry white wine

SAUCE:
¼ cup heavy cream
1 tablespoon butter
½ cup bread crumbs

1 tablespoon all-purpose flour
1 tablespoon butter

Wrap each fillet of sole around a shrimp and secure with a toothpick. Place fillets in a greased 3-quart casserole. Season with salt, pepper, and tarragon. Pour wine over fillets. Cover. Bake in a 350°F. oven for 10 minutes or until done.

SAUCE: In a saucepan, melt butter and blend in flour to make a roux. Add cream and stir over low heat until blended. Set aside. Remove liquid from casserole in the oven. In a small saucepan, simmer liquid for 5 minutes, stirring occasionally. Reduce liquid to ½ cup but add more white wine if needed. Add cream sauce to the reduced liquid.

TO ASSEMBLE: Pour cream sauce over fillets. Sprinkle with bread crumbs and dot with butter. Place under broiler until browned.

Preparation: 30 minutes
Cooking: 20 minutes

Serves: 4
Serve immediately

Fish Wenham

2 (10 ounce) packages frozen
   chopped spinach
¼ cup chopped onion
2 pounds fillet of sole
4 tablespoons butter, melted

Juice of ½ lemon
3 tablespoons sesame seeds
Salt and pepper, to taste
1 cup sour cream

Cook spinach according to package directions, drain completely and place in bottom of 8 x 13-inch baking dish. Sprinkle onion over spinach. Dip fish fillets in melted butter and place on bed of spinach. Sprinkle with lemon juice, 2 tablespoons sesame seeds, salt, and pepper to taste. Spread sourcream over the top. Sprinkle remaining 1 tablespoon sesame seeds over all. Cover. Bake at 350°F. for 30-45 minutes.

Preparation: 25 minutes
Cooking: 30-45 minutes

Serves: 4
Serve immediately

Fruits de Mer

This is a traditional Christmas Eve family dinner

1 pound shrimp, peeled and deveined
1 pound scallops
½ cup water
½ cup dry white wine
2½ slices bakery bread, crumbled
½ cup milk
½ cup butter

2 large onions, minced
1 teaspoon paprika
1 teaspoon salt
⅛ teaspoon dried ground chili peppers
1 cup light cream
¼ cup grated Parmesan cheese

Put shrimp, scallops, water, and wine in pan and bring to a boil. Then turn heat very low and cook 5 minutes. Remove from heat immediately. Strain and reserve liquid. Chop seafood coarsely and set aside. Soak bread crumbs in milk. Melt butter in pan in which seafood was cooked. Add onions, and paprika and cook slowly until onions are soft, not brown. Add moist bread crumbs to onions and slowly stir in reserved wine stock. Add fish, cream, salt, and peppers. Cover and cook over low heat for 10 minutes stirring occasionally. Serve in soup plates, garnished with Parmesan cheese.

NOTE: You may substitute equal amounts of oysters, mussels, clams or crabmeat in place of the shrimp and scallops. Total amount of seafood used should be 2 pounds.

Preparation: 30 minutes
Cooking: 20 minutes

Serves: 6
Serve immediately

Salmon Steaks Mayonnaise

4 salmon steaks
Juice of ½ lemon
1 egg, separated

½ cup mayonnaise
Paprika

Mix lemon juice, mayonnaise, and egg yolk. Beat egg white until stiff. Fold in mayonnaise mixture. Place salmon on aluminum foil on top of broiler pan. Broil 3 inches from heat about 8 minutes or until fish flakes. Swirl tops of salmon with mayonnaise mixture and a sprinkle of paprika. Broil 2 minutes more and serve.

Preparation: 10 minutes
Cooking: 10 minutes

Serves: 4
Serve immediately

Bouillabaisse

½ pound shrimp, shelled and
   deveined
6 ounces lobster or crabmeat
½ pound fresh mushrooms, sliced
2½ pounds fish fillet (any type),
   cut in bite-size pieces
¾ cup sliced onions
1 garlic clove, minced
1 stalk celery, diced
½ cup olive oil

¾ cup crushed cooked tomatoes
2 bay leaves
6 peppercorns
2 cloves
2 teaspoons lemon juice
1 teaspoon salt
1 dozen oysters in shell, scrubbed
1 dozen clams in shell, scrubbed
¾ cup dry white wine
2 tablespoons parsley

Boil shrimp, lobster or crabmeat, mushrooms, and 1 pound of fish fillet in 3 cups of water until cooked, approximately 5 minutes. Drain fish and mushrooms, reserve liquid, and set aside.

To liquid add water to make 4½ cups. Add remaining fish fillet and cook until fish flakes. Blender may be used to create a finely flaked fish broth. Set liquid aside. In a large pot sauté the onions, garlic and celery in ½ cup oil until softened. Add tomatoes, 4½ cups fish stock, bay leaves, peppercorns, cloves, lemon juice, and salt. Cover pot and simmer for ½ hour. Add fish and mushrooms and simmer for 10 minutes. Add oysters and clams and simmer 5 minutes more. Add wine and salt to taste. Serve immediately. Garnish servings with parsley.

NOTE: 1 pound shrimp in shell may be substituted for oysters or clams if you prefer.

Preparation: 1½ hours
Cooking: 1½ hours

Serves: 4 dinner-sized servings
Serve immediately

Chili—When It's Not

"The fish chili recipe is especially marvelous
when made with shrimp."

8 thick slices smoked bacon,
diced
2 large onions, finely chopped
5 large garlic cloves, minced
4 fresh or canned jalapeno
peppers, seeded and minced
⅓ cup pure chili powder (or 1
tablespoon regular chili
powder)
2 (28-32 ounce) cans whole
tomatoes, drained and coarsely
broken up
½ teaspoon sugar or 1-2
tablespoons grated carrot
1 heaping teaspoon oregano

2 teaspoons cumin
2 teaspoons sherry vinegar
1 (4 ounce) can whole mild green
chilies, cut into strips
2-3 pounds barely poached fish,
skinned, boned and broken into
large pieces (shark, bass,
halibut, swordfish or snapper)
OR use 1½-2 pounds peeled
shrimp or scallops or a
combination of both. Just tuck
the shrimp in the simmer
mixture for about 4 minutes.
The scallops only take a minute
to cook.

In a 10-inch shallow casserole, render bacon and remove with slotted
spoon to paper towel-lined plate and reserve. Pour off all but 3 tablespoons fat. In this fat, sauté onions and garlic until transparent. Add
jalapeno peppers and chili powder and cook for 3 minutes. Meanwhile,
in a 2½-quart saucepan, simmer tomatoes with sugar or carrots, oregano,
cumin, and sherry vinegar for 15 minutes. Transfer this mixture to the
shallow casserole containing onions and garlic. Add the reserved bacon
and simmer 15-20 minutes or until thick. You may now refrigerate this
mixture until you're ready to use it later. Just reheat mixture slightly in
microwave or on stovetop while fish is poaching. Add strips of mild
chilies and poached fish and sprinkle with cilantro or parsley or finely
chopped celery leaves just before serving. Serves 6-8.

NOTE: To poach fish, mix together half white wine and half water, a bay
leaf, several peppercorns, and some celery leaves. Bring this barely to a
simmer, add the fish and poach until fish is barely opaque. Poach 10
minutes per inch thickness of fish pieces measured at thickest part. Shrimp
takes 3-4 minutes, scallops 1 minute.

Cornelius

Cornelius O'Donnell

A native of Delmar, New York, he is the author of *Cooking with Cornelius*
and a regular contributor to a well-known gourmet food magazine.

Mini-Clambake

2 dozen littleneck clams,
  scrubbed
4 medium ears of corn, husked
4 lobster tails, uncooked
4 medium baking potatoes,
  cleaned

4 small onions, peeled
2 cups bottled clam juice
4 tablespoons vodka
1 lemon, halved
Melted butter

In a large piece of heavy duty foil, arrange 6 clams, 1 ear of corn, 1 lobster tail, 1 potato, and 1 small onion. Fold up edges of foil. Pour ½ cup clam juice and 1 ounce vodka in each packet. Fold and seal tightly. Repeat for remaining 3 packets. Grill packets 4 inches from charcoal coals about 1 hour. Open packets and squeeze lemon juice over each. Serve with melted butter.

NOTE: For additional guests, just assemble 1 extra foil packet per serving.

Preparation: 15 minutes
Cooking: 1 hour

Serves: 4
Serve immediately

Gingered Scallops
Gives a nice fresh taste to scallops

6 tablespoons unsalted butter
1½ pounds bay scallops
2 tablespoons finely sliced fresh
  ginger

Freshly ground pepper, to taste
2 tablespoons finely chopped
  parsley

In a large skillet, heat butter until sizzling. Sauté scallops and ginger for just a minute or so, just long enough to heat the scallops through and brown them lightly on the outside. Season with pepper. Sprinkle with parsley and serve.

Preparation: 5 minutes
Cooking: 5 minutes

Serves: 4
Serve immediately

Marin Seafood Quiche

It can be served for brunch or cold as an appetizer

2 (9 inch) unbaked pie shells
  (prepared or make your own)
2 (6 ounce) packages frozen king
  crabmeat, thawed and drained
2 cups shrimp, cooked and
  chopped

8 ounces Swiss cheese, chopped
½ cup finely chopped scallions
1 cup mayonnaise
2 tablespoons all-purpose flour
1 cup dry white wine
4 eggs, slightly beaten

Combine crab, shrimp, cheese, and scallions. Pour half into each pie shell. Mix mayonnaise, flour, wine, and eggs. Pour half over each seafood mixture. Bake at 350°F. for 35-40 minutes. Cool 10 minutes before cutting.

Preparation: 30 minutes
Cooking: 35-40 minutes

Serves: 12
Can be frozen

Baked Cod with Bacon

1½ pounds cod, cut into 4 serving
  portions
½ cup seasoned bread crumbs
1 tablespoon chopped fresh
  parsley

1 egg
Salt and pepper, to taste
2 strips bacon, cut in half

Rinse fish in cold water and pat dry. Place in buttered 8 x 13-inch baking dish. Mix bread crumbs, parsley and egg. Put mixture on fish. Season with salt and pepper. Place 1 piece of bacon on each portion. Bake at 350°F. for 20 minutes or until fish flakes with fork.

Preparation: 15 minutes
Cooking: 20 minutes

Serves: 4
Serve immediately

Fish au Gratin

An all-purpose recipe that is successful with nearly any kind of fish

1 pound fillet, sole, haddock,
scrod, etc.
⅓ cup mayonnaise

¼ cup grated Parmesan cheese
2 tablespoons bread crumbs

Brush each fillet with mayonnaise. Mix cheese and bread crumbs. Roll fillet in mixture. If fish won't roll, spread each side as you would toast. Lay fish in a single layer in a greased 9 x 13-inch baking pan. Bake at 375°F. for 15-20 minutes or until lightly brown and fish flakes easily when tested with a fork.

Preparation: 10 minutes
Cooking: 15-20 minutes

Serves: 4
Serve immediately

Crab Soufflé Imperial

¾ cup butter
¾ cup all-purpose flour
3 cups milk
12 egg yolks
⅔ cup mayonnaise
1½ teaspoons lemon juice
2 teaspoons horseradish

3 teaspoons Dijon mustard
3 teaspoons minced onion
6 tablespoons minced celery
3 cups crabmeat, washed and cut
in chunks
14 egg whites
1½ teaspoons salt

In a large saucepan, melt butter and blend in flour. Gradually stir in milk and cook over low heat, stirring constantly, until thick. Remove from heat and beat in egg yolks, one at a time. Fold in mayonnaise, lemon juice, horseradish, mustard, onion, celery, and crabmeat. Set aside to cool. Beat egg whites with salt until stiff but not dry and fold into crab mixture. Divide between two buttered 2-quart soufflé dishes. Bake at 325°F. for 55-60 minutes or until a knife inserted in the center comes out clean.

NOTE: The crab mixture may be made a few hours ahead and refrigerated until ½ hour before using. Then combine it with egg whites and continue cooking.

Preparation: 1 hour
Cooking: 1 hour

Serves: 8-10
Serve immediately

Stuffed Crabs Caribbean-Style

These "crabs farcis des iles" can be served as an
appetizer or the main course

5 green onions, minced
2 teaspoons garlic, minced
1 hot green chili pepper, minced
or use dried red pepper flakes,
to taste
½ cup butter
1 tablespoon curry powder

¾-1 pound crabmeat, finely
shredded, reserve liquid
2 tablespoons minced parsley
Salt and freshly ground black
pepper, to taste
2 cups bread crumbs
Lime wedges, to garnish

In a large skillet, sauté onions, garlic, and chili in melted butter. Mix in
curry powder. Add crabmeat, salt, pepper, and parsley. Add enough crabmeat liquid to moisten. Add bread crumbs and blend well. Heat through
and remove from heat. Fill clam or scallop shells with mixture. Bake at
400°F. for 15 minutes or until top is lightly brown. Garnish with lime
wedges.

NOTE: If you don't have shells, then put mixture in a 1½-quart casserole.

Preparation: 30 minutes
Cooking: 15 minutes

Serves: 2-3
Serve immediately

Hot Crabmeat Casserole

Unusual combination of textures

2 (6 ounce) cans Alaskan
King crab
2 cups crushed shredded wheat
(or stuffing mix, potato chips or
cracker crumbs)

1 (8 ounce) can water
chestnuts, sliced
2 cups cheese, grated or shredded
2 medium onions, sliced
2 cups sour cream

Mix all ingredients together. Spoon into a greased 2-quart casserole dish.
Bake at 350°F. for 30 minutes.

Preparation: 15 minutes
Cooking: 30 minutes

Serves: 6
Can be frozen

Broccoli and Crabmeat Casserole

6-8 broccoli spears, cooked al
   dente
6 ounces grated sharp Cheddar
   cheese
½ cup butter
2 tablespoons minced onion
2 tablespoons flour
⅛ teaspoon curry powder

½ teaspoon salt
1 cup milk
1 tablespoon lemon juice
8 ounces frozen king crabmeat,
   thawed and drained
2 tablespoons melted butter
½ cup seasoned bread crumbs

Arrange cooked broccoli in greased 1-quart shallow casserole. Sprinkle
with grated cheese. Melt ½ cup butter in saucepan, add onions and cook
until golden. Add flour, curry, and salt. Gradually add milk, stirring constantly over low heat until thickened. Add lemon juice and crabmeat.
Pour mixture over broccoli. Mix 2 tablespoons melted butter and bread
crumbs and sprinkle on top. Bake at 325°F. for 30-40 minutes. It will
brown on top.

Preparation: 30 minutes
Cooking: 30-40 minutes

Serves: 6
Serve immediately

Crab Delicious

1 cup light cream
1 cup cooked rice
Salt
Paprika or celery salt, to taste
1 cup flaked crabmeat

2 tablespoons melted butter or
   margarine
3 tablespoons catsup
4 patty shells

Heat cream and cooked rice together in top of a double boiler over hot
water. Season with salt and paprika or celery salt. When blended and
well heated, stir in crabmeat and butter. After heating through, stir in
catsup. Serve at once in patty shells.

Preparation: 10 minutes
Cooking: 10 minutes

Serves: 4
Serve immediately

Breaded Scallops

¾ pounds bay scallops, rinsed, drained, and dried
3 tablespoons butter, melted
½ teaspoon minced onion
½ teaspoon parsley

⅛ teaspoon tarragon
Pinch of garlic salt
Pinch of black pepper
1 teaspoon lemon juice
½ cup soft bread crumbs

Place scallops in a single layer in a shallow, 8-inch square baking dish. To the melted butter, add, in order, the remaining ingredients. Toss this bread mixture in with the scallops. Bake at 400°F. for 20 minutes.

Preparation: 15 minutes
Cooking: 20 minutes

Serves: 2
Serve immediately

Scallop Casserole, New England-Style

2 cups biscuit mix (prepared or make your own)
2 pounds sea scallops
1 (14½ ounce) can evaporated milk
1 (8 ounce) can tomato sauce with tomato bits
1 (16 ounce) can Italian plum tomatoes, drained, reserve juice

¼ teaspoon rosemary
¼ teaspoon savory
⅓ cup all-purpose flour
2 teaspoons salt
Dash of pepper and paprika
½ cup butter or margarine, melted
1 (12 ounce) can Mexican-style kernel corn

Make and bake enough small baking powder biscuits to circle rim of 11½ x 7-inch casserole. Remove biscuits from oven when light brown. Simmer scallops 5 minutes in water to cover. Drain and save ½ cup scallop broth. Combine scallop broth, evaporated milk, tomato sauce, juice from canned tomatoes, and herbs. Mix flour, salt, pepper and paprika. Combine with melted butter. Add broth mixture all at once, stirring constantly, and cook until thickened. Cover to cook 5 minutes over low heat. Add drained tomatoes, corn and scallops. Pour into greased casserole. Place biscuits around edge. Bake at 350°F. for 15 minutes or until bubbly.

Preparation: 30 minutes
Cooking: 15 minutes

Serves: 6
Can be frozen

Oysters and Wild Rice

3 cups wild rice
1 cup butter, melted
3 pints oysters, drained
Salt, pepper, and Tabasco sauce,
   to taste
1½ (10¾ ounce) cans cream of
   chicken soup

1½ cups half and half cream
1 tablespoon curry powder
¾ cup water
1 tablespoon onion powder
1½ teaspoons thyme

Cook and drain wild rice according to package directions. Toss in melted butter. Place ¼ of rice in each of two 9 x 3-inch shallow baking dishes. Season oysters with salt, pepper, and Tabasco sauce. Place ½ of oysters on top of rice in each dish. Evenly cover oysters with remaining rice. In a saucepan, heat cream of chicken soup and half and half cream. Dissolve curry powder in water. Add dissolved curry powder, onion powder, and thyme to soup-cream mixture. Pour over rice and oysters in pan. Bake at 300°F. for 45 minutes.

NOTE: To cut the expense of wild rice, substitute some brown rice for the wild rice.

Preparation: 1 hour
Cooking: 45 minutes

Serves: 24
Can do ahead

Creole Jambalaya

6 strips sliced bacon, cut into 2-
   inch pieces
1 medium onion, chopped
1 clove garlic, minced
1 (19 ounce) can whole tomatoes
   and liquid
½ teaspoon thyme
1 teaspoon salt
⅛ teaspoon freshly ground
   pepper

½ pound cooked, smoked ham
   (cut into 2-inch strips)
3 (4½ ounce) cans medium
   shrimp or 1 pound shrimp,
   cooked
1 tablespoon parsley
1 cup chicken stock
1 cup raw rice

In a large skillet, fry bacon moderately brown, but not crisp. Discard most of bacon drippings. Add onions, garlic and rest of ingredients, except rice. Bring to a boil. Add rice. Cover and simmer until tender – approximately 45 minutes.

Preparation: 10-15 minutes
Cooking: 45 minutes

Serves: 6
Serve immediately

Peking Shrimp

1 pound medium shrimp, shelled,
   cleaned, and deveined
2 tablespoons cornstarch
1 egg, beaten
3 tablespoons oil
1 small onion, thinly sliced
1 teaspoon garlic, chopped
1 tablespoon sliced ginger or 1
   teaspoon ginger powder

2 tablespoons soy sauce
2 tablespoons chicken broth
1 tablespoon cooking sherry
1 teaspoon red pepper
1 tablespoon vinegar
2 teaspoons sugar
1 cup cooked rice

Slice each shrimp in half, lengthwise. Mix cornstarch with beaten egg.
Add shrimp and coat evenly with mixture. In electric fry pan, heat oil
until very hot. Add shrimp, separate them and stir-fry for 3 minutes.
Remove shrimp. Add onions, garlic, and ginger to pan. Stir-fry for 2 minutes. Add remaining ingredients to pan except rice. Bring to a boil, stirring constantly. Return shrimp to pan. Add rice and simmer for about 5
minutes.

Preparation: 30-45 minutes
Cooking: 10 minutes

Serves: 4
Serve immediately

Scampi
A low-calorie variation

1 pound raw jumbo shrimp,
   shelled and deveined
1 cup olive oil
2 tablespoons minced parsley

1 clove garlic, crushed
1 teaspoon salt
¼ teaspoon pepper

Rinse shrimp in cool water, pat dry and place in a shallow bowl. Mix
remaining ingredients and pour over shrimp. Cover and chill 3 hours,
turning twice in marinade. Pre-heat broiler. Place shrimp on foil-lined
broiler pan and brush with marinade. Broil 5-6 inches from heat about
3 minutes per side, basting often with marinade. About 170 calories per
serving.

Preparation: 3 hours
Cooking: 6 minutes

Serves: 2
Serve immediately

Shrimp and Crab Au Gratin

1 pound shrimp, shelled and
   deveined
¼ cup butter
½ pound fresh mushrooms,
   cleaned
2 tablespoons onion, finely
   chopped
1 clove garlic, crushed
¼ cup all-purpose flour
½ teaspoon pepper

1 tablespoon dill (optional)
¾ cup milk
8 ounces sharp Cheddar cheese,
   grated
⅔ cup dry white wine
2 (7½ ounce) cans crabmeat
1 (9 ounce) package frozen
   artichokes, thawed
2 tablespoons cornflake crumbs
½ tablespoon butter

Cook shrimp, drain, and if very large, cut in two. Sauté mushrooms in butter for a few minutes. Add onions and garlic and continue to sauté. Remove from heat. Stir in flour, pepper, dill, and milk. Bring to a boil, and again remove from heat. Add ½ of cheese, stir until melted. Add the wine. Drain crab and remove any cartilage. In a 2-quart casserole combine sauce, crab, shrimp, artichoke hearts, and rest of cheese. Mix lightly. Sprinkle with cornflakes and dot with butter. Bake at 375°F. for 30 minutes.

Preparation: 30 minutes
Cooking: 30 minutes

Serves: 6
Serve immediately

Shrimp Creole

5 tablespoons vegetable oil or
   bacon fat
3 tablespoons all-purpose flour
2 pounds onions, minced
3 ribs celery, minced
1 medium green pepper, minced
1 lemon, grate zest, remove white
   and chop rest

3 cloves garlic, crushed
A few dashes of: Worcestershire
   sauce, Tabasco sauce, thyme
   and MSG
2 (6 ounce) cans tomato paste
3 pounds raw shrimp, cleaned,
   peeled and deveined
Salt, to taste

In a large skillet, heat oil and flour, stirring constantly to brown the flour. Add onions and fry slowly until well browned. Add remaining ingredients, except shrimp. Continue to cook slowly at least 30-40 minutes. Add shrimp. Continue cooking 15-20 minutes more. Serve with rice.

NOTE: Prepare and let cool so flavors blend. Reheat slowly before serving.

Preparation: 30 minutes
Cooking: 1 hour

Serves: 6-8
Can do ahead

Shrimp Elegante

3 pounds fresh or frozen shrimp
  (50 large)
3 chicken bouillon cubes
2½ cups boiling water
½ cup sliced green onions
3 tablespoons soy sauce

1 teaspoon salt
¼ cup cold water
¼ cup cornstarch
4 medium tomatoes, cut in
  eighths
2½ cups fresh snow pea pods

Peel and devein shrimp. In a large saucepan, dissolve bouillon cubes in 2½ cups of boiling water. Add shrimp, green onions, soy sauce, and salt. Return to boiling and cook for 3 minutes, stirring constantly. Blend cold water with cornstarch and stir into shrimp mixture. Cook, stirring constantly, until mixture is thick and bubbly. Add tomatoes and pea pods. Cook until heated through, about 3 minutes longer. Serve over cooked rice.

Preparation: 30 minutes
Cooking: 15 minutes

Serves: 12
Serve immediately

Shrimp in Garlic Butter

2 cups deveined fresh jumbo
  shrimp
½ cup butter

1 can anchovy fillets, drained on
  paper toweling
1 full head garlic, finely chopped

Sauté garlic in ¼ cup of the butter over low heat. Add additional butter as needed. When garlic is softened well and combined with butter, raise heat and add shrimp. Turn frequently and baste with garlic butter for 3-4 minutes or until done. Serve over rice (cooked ahead and kept warm, about 2 cups for six people). Garnish with anchovies and a few sliced green olives.

Tom Whalen

Thomas M. Whalen, III
Mayor of Albany, New York

Shrimp with Broccoli and Macaroni
It's all in one pan.

2-3 tablespoons oil
2 cloves garlic, minced
1 small onion, chopped
1 pound shrimp, shelled,
    deveined, and cut into pieces
1 small head broccoli, cut into
    small pieces

Salt and pepper, to taste
¾ pound macaroni twists, cooked
1 small can pitted black olives
    sliced or green olives sliced
Parmesan cheese, to taste

In a large skillet heat oil and sauté garlic and onion. Add shrimp and cook 3-5 minutes. Add broccoli and sauté on low heat approximately 5 minutes, adding salt and pepper to taste. Strain cooked macaroni (it should be slighly wet) and add to skillet. Simmer 4-5 minutes. Add sliced olives and enough Parmesan cheese so that it sticks lightly to the shrimp, broccoli, and macaroni.

Preparation: 20 minutes
Cooking: 10 minutes

Serves: 4-5
Serve immediately

Sweet and Sour Shrimp

1 pound medium shrimp,
    cleaned, shelled, and deveined
1½ tablespoons sweet butter
¼ teaspoon black pepper
¼ cup white vinegar
2 tablespoons soy sauce
6 whole cloves
1 bay leaf

½ red pepper, cut into 1-inch
    cubes
½ green pepper, cut into 1-inch
    cubes
1 (8 ounce) can pineapple tidbits,
    drain and reserve juice
1½ tablespoons cornstarch

In a large skillet, sauté shrimp in melted butter until shrimp turns pink. Add black pepper, vinegar, soy sauce, cloves, bay leaf, red and green peppers, and pineapple tidbits. In a small bowl, mix 2 tablespoons pineapple juice with cornstarch until smooth. Gradually add remainder of pineapple juice to mixture. Pour cornstarch mixture into shrimp mixture. Stir constantly over medium heat until sauce thickens.

Preparation: 20 minutes
Cooking: 10-15 minutes

Serves: 4
Serve immediately

EGGS, RICE,
& PASTA

Heldebergs and Rent Wars

In the early 1600's, a Dutchman named Van Rensselaer became the Patroon, or owner, of the Heldeberg Mountains just to the southwest of Albany. The Dutch tenant farmers worked for the colony and supplied Holland with beaver skins and farm produce. In return, Holland gave the farmers protection as well as imported products, such as fabric for clothes. By the 1700's, persecuted immigrants from Europe (German, Swiss, and French Huguenots) had begun to settle the farmland. Britain won control of the Heldeberg area and continued to treat the settlers as tenant farmers. If the crop was poor that year, payment was expected in other valuable personal items. All across the hills, from one rooftop to another, people would sound tin horns to announce the arrival of the rent collector. Quickly, men would hide and valuables would be buried. Thus, the farmers escaped paying what they felt was an unfair tax. These actions led to violent rent wars which eventually freed the farmers from their repressive landlords and their medieval methods of land ownership.

As the Dutch and British had known, the Heldebergs were a cornucopia of farm produce. Cheese factories in the mountain counties utilized dairy products from the farms. Individual households made their own cheese by mixing rennet from a calf's stomach with warm cow's milk and setting it in a warm place to curdle. Homemade cheese was much like our present-day cottage cheese.

Grist mills were scattered throughout the Heldebergs; they ground rye and wheat into flours for making breads, pastries, and noodles.

Because life on the farm was physically strenuous, farmers were not concerned with counting calories. Meals were bountiful and full of starch. A favorite supper dish consisted of homemade noodles in a cream and egg sauce enriched with ample amounts of cheese.

While Modern folk may have to watch their starch consumption more carefully than their ancestors did, the selection of recipes presented here will prove quite a delicious temptation.

Egg and Artichoke Casserole

3 (6½ ounce) jars marinated
    artichoke hearts
2 bunches green onions, thinly
    sliced
3 cloves garlic, crushed
12 ounces fresh mushrooms,
    sliced

8 eggs, beaten
8 ounces Cheddar cheese, grated
12 saltine crackers, crushed
6½ ounces Canadian bacon, cut
    in ½-inch cubes
Bacon curls and parsley, to
    garnish

Drain artichokes, reserving 2-3 tablespoons of oil, and cut in half. In artichoke oil, sauté onions, garlic, and mushrooms for about 10 minutes. Combine with all other ingredients. Pour into a greased 9 x 13-inch baking dish. Cover and refrigerate until ready to use or overnight, if desired. Bake at 350°F. for 40-45 minutes. Garnish with bacon curls and parsley, if desired. Cut into squares to serve.

Preparation: 40 minutes
Cooking: 40-45 minutes

Serves: 10
Can do ahead

Eggs New Orleans

6 large fresh artichokes or 12
    canned artichoke bottoms
2 tablespoons vinegar
1 (10 ounce) package chopped
    spinach, cooked and drained

2 tablespoons unsalted butter,
    melted
2 tablespoons all-purpose flour
1 cup milk
6 eggs

HOLLANDAISE SAUCE:
3 egg yolks
½ cup unsalted butter, melted
2 tablespoons lemon juice

¼ teaspoon salt
⅛ teaspoon pepper
Dash of cayenne

Boil fresh artichokes in salted water with 2 tablespoons vinegar until tender. Drain and remove leaves and choke. Make a cream sauce with 2 tablespoons butter, flour, and milk. Add spinach to cream sauce. Poach eggs.

HOLLANDAISE SAUCE: Add all sauce ingredients to a blender and process until thick, about 3 minutes.

TO ASSEMBLE: Place artichoke bottom on a plate with the curve up. Top with spinach mixture, poached egg, and cover with Hollandaise sauce.

Preparation: 45 minutes
Cooking: 15-20 minutes

Serves: 6
Serve immediately

Elegant Curried Eggs
It's been a secret recipe for over 12 years

15 hard-cooked eggs
1½ pounds fresh mushrooms,
  sliced
3 tablespoons butter
¾ cup butter
12 tablespoons all-purpose flour
6 cups milk

¾ cup grated Parmesan cheese
4½ teaspoons curry powder
6 tablespoons chopped pimiento
6 tablespoons chili sauce
6 tablespoons sliced water
  chestnuts
Salt and pepper, to taste

TOPPING:
3 slices whole wheat bread

2 tablespoons butter

Peel eggs and slice in half lengthwise. Sauté mushrooms in 3 table-spoons butter. Set aside. Heat 1½ cups butter and blend in flour. Add milk slowly, stirring constantly until smooth and thick like heavy cream. Add cheese, curry powder, pimiento, chili sauce, salt, and pepper. Bring to a boil. Add mushrooms, water chestnuts, and eggs. Stir gently and pour into a 3-quart baking dish. It can be refrigerated up to 1 day before baking.

TOPPING: In a food processor, blend bread to make soft crumbs. Sauté bread crumbs in butter. Sprinkle over egg mixture. Bake at 350°F. for 45-60 minutes. Pass under broiler to brown.

NOTE: Serve with baked ham and sourdough bread.

Preparation: 45 minutes
Cooking: 45-60 minutes

Serves: 12
Can do ahead

Breakfast Bake
The work is done the night before

1 pound bulk breakfast sausage
6 slices bread
1 heaping cup grated sharp
  Cheddar cheese

6 eggs
2 cups milk
1 teaspoon salt
1 teaspoon dry mustard

Sauté sausage and drain. Tear bread into pieces and place in the bottom of 9 x 13-inch baking dish. Cover with sausage and then cheese. Beat eggs with the rest of the ingredients and pour over layers. Cover and refrigerate overnight. Place in a cold oven. Bake at 350°F. for 40-45 minutes.

Preparation: Overnight
Cooking: 40-45 minutes

Serves: 6-8
Must do ahead

Quiche Lorraine

1 (9 inch) pie pastry shell,
   unbaked
1 egg white
8 bacon slices, crisp cooked and
   crumbled
2 cups (8 ounces) shredded
   natural Swiss cheese

1 tablespoon all-purpose flour
½ teaspoon salt
¼ teaspoon nutmeg
2 eggs, whole
1 egg yolk
1⅓ cups milk

Brush sides and bottom of unbaked pie shell with egg white which was beaten until frothy. Sprinkle bacon over bottom of pie shell. Spread cheese over the bacon. Combine remaining ingredients and mix well. Carefully pour over the cheese and bacon. Bake at 325°F. for 35-45 minutes. Allow to cool 10-15 minutes before serving.

VARIATIONS: Add onion, sautéed in butter, to the bacon. Or, sauté mushrooms with the onion and omit the bacon. Also, broccoli and/or zucchini, crisp-cooked, can be substituted for the bacon. But don't have too many flavor combinations at once or you'll lose the cheese and custard flavors of the quiche.

Preparation: 20 minutes
Cooking: 35-45 minutes

Serves: 6
Can do ahead

Spinach Quiche

1 (9 inch) unbaked pie shell
8 slices bacon, cooked and
   crumbled
1 large onion, thinly sliced
6 ounces Swiss cheese, grated
1 (10 ounce) package frozen
   spinach, cooked and drained

3 eggs, beaten
1½ cups half and half cream
Salt and pepper, to taste
Grated Parmesan cheese

Sprinkle bacon in pie shell. Sauté onion in bacon drippings and place over bacon. Layer Swiss cheese and then spinach. Beat eggs with cream, season with salt and pepper, and pour over the layers. Sprinkle with Parmesan cheese. Bake at 450°F. for 10 minutes. Then reduce to 300°F. and bake 50 minutes more.

Preparation: 20 minutes
Cooking: 1 hour

Serves: 6
Can do ahead

Bacon and Tomato Quiche

6 slices bacon
¼ cup butter
2 medium onions, finely chopped
2 pounds tomatoes, peeled,
  seeded, and chopped

Pinch of thyme
1 bay leaf
6 eggs
1 (9 inch) baked pie shell
Freshly ground pepper, to taste

Preheat oven to 350°F. Chop bacon into small pieces. In heavy saucepan, melt butter. Add chopped bacon and onions and sauté over moderate heat until golden in color. Add tomatoes, herbs, and black pepper. Cover pan and simmer for 20 minutes. In bowl, beat eggs until well mixed. Discard bay leaf, allow tomato mixture to cool slightly. Combine in bowl with eggs, mix well. Pour mixture into pre-baked pie shell and bake for 25-30 minutes until filling is set and golden. Serve hot or cold. Serves 6-8.

Mario M. Cuomo

Mario M. Cuomo
Governor, State of New York

Sausage and Green Chili Strata

1 pound lean bulk pork sausage
2 tablespoons butter
5 slices firm white bread
1 pound Monterey Jack cheese,
  grated
1 pound sharp Cheddar cheese,
  grated

1 (4 ounce) can green chilies,
  chopped
4 eggs
2 cups milk
¾ teaspoon salt
¾ teaspoon chili powder
¼ teaspoon pepper

Brown sausage, drain, and set aside. Lightly butter one side of each bread slice and cut into ½-inch cubes. Sprinkle half the bread cubes evenly in the bottom of a buttered 7 x 11-inch baking dish. Sprinkle half the cheeses and half the chilies over bread cubes. Cover with sausage. Repeat layering with remaining bread, cheeses, and chilies. Combine eggs, milk, and seasonings. Pour evenly over layers. Cover and chill at least 8 hours or overnight. Bake, uncovered, at 350°F. for 1 hour until golden brown. Let stand 15 minutes before cutting.

Preparation: 1 hour
Cooking: 1 hour

Serves: 6
Must do ahead

Crunchy Bran Waffles with Orange Butter Syrup
Uniquely different

BATTER (WAFFLE OR PANCAKE):

½ cup all-purpose flour
½ cup whole wheat flour
¼ cup brown sugar
1 teaspoon baking powder
1 teaspoon baking soda
¼ teaspoon salt

1 cup buttermilk
2 egg yolks
1 cup whole bran cereal, crushed
10 tablespoons melted butter
2 egg whites, stiffly beaten
½ cup chopped pecans

SYRUP:

½ cup unsalted margarine
½ cup sugar

½ cup frozen orange juice
 concentrate, undiluted
2 tablespoons fresh lemon juice

BATTER: Sift flours, sugar, baking powder, baking soda, and salt into a large mixing bowl. Stir in buttermilk, egg yolks, cereal, and 6 tablespoons butter just until moistened. Lightly stir in pecars. Do not overmix. Fold in egg whites.

TO COOK: Heat waffle iron according to manufacturer's directions. Brush iron with remaining butter. Pour batter into center of iron to cover part of bottom. Bake according to manufacturer's directions, until crisp and golden. Remove from iron. Serve with syrup.

SYRUP: Mix all ingredients in medium saucepan. Heat to boil. Cook and stir 2-3 minutes, until thickened and sugar is dissolved. Serve warm.

NOTE: The waffle can be cooled completely and sandwiched together with ½-inch thick layer of ice cream for dessert. It is always good with sausage or fruit too.

Preparation: 30 minutes
Cooking: 1-1½ minutes

Serves: 6
Can be frozen

Tortilla Español

5 small potatoes, peeled and
    thinly sliced
1 medium onion, thinly sliced
½ cup oil

5 eggs
Salt and pepper, to taste
Crumbled bacon (optional)
Shredded cheese (optional)

In an 8-inch skillet, sauté potatoes and onions in oil. Drain off excess oil.
In a bowl, beat eggs and add salt and pepper. Stir in potato mixture and
optional bacon and cheese. Pour into a skillet with 1 tablespoon oil. Cook
over low heat until set. Invert onto a large dish and slide back into skillet
to brown on other side.

Preparation: 15 minutes
Cooking: 40 minutes

Serves: 4-6
Can do ahead

Fran's Pancakes

2 cups all-purpose flour
2 tablespoons sugar
4 teaspoons baking powder
1 teaspoon salt

2 eggs, beaten
2 cups milk
¼ cup oil

Combine flour, sugar, baking powder, and salt in a large bowl. Add eggs
and milk. Mix well. Blend in the oil. Pour batter on a hot, greased grill
and brown on both sides.

NOTE: This batter can be used for waffles too.

Preparation: 10 minutes
Cooking: 2-3 minutes

Yield: 24 (3 inch) pancakes
Serve immediately

Cottage Cheese Pancakes
The cottage cheese makes them very light and airy

4 eggs, well beaten
1 cup cottage cheese
6 tablespoons all-purpose flour

Pinch of salt
6 tablespoons melted butter,
    cooled

Combine beaten eggs with cottage cheese. Blend in flour and salt. Add
butter and mix well. Cook over moderate-high heat on buttered griddle.
Serve with maple syrup.

Preparation: 10 minutes
Cooking: 2-3 minutes

Yield: 12 pancakes
Serve immediately

Spectacular Brunch Puff
Similar to a giant popover

½ cup all-purpose flour
½ cup milk
2 eggs
Pinch of nutmeg
Salt, to taste

¼ cup butter
Juice of ½ lemon
2-4 tablespoons red currant jelly
Confectioners' sugar, to sprinkle

Preheat oven to 450°F. In a medium bowl, mix flour, milk, and eggs. Add nutmeg and salt. Blend, but it is not necessary to remove all lumps. Melt butter in heavy 8-9-inch ovenproof skillet (cast iron). When butter is foaming and beginning to brown, add the batter all at once to the skillet. Immediately put skillet in oven. Bake at 450°F. for 20 minutes. Do not open oven door during baking. After 20 minutes, remove skillet and lightly sprinkle the pancake puff with confectioners' sugar. Return to oven for 3-5 minutes to brown lightly. When browned, remove and sprinkle lemon juice over pancake. Lightly spread currant jelly over total pancake (use enough, it provides sweetening for pancake). Cut into wedge-shaped servings.

Preparation: 5 minutes
Cooking: 25 minutes

Serves: 3-4
Serve immediately

French Toast in the Oven

1 (10 ounce) loaf French bread
8 eggs
3 cups milk
2 teaspoons white sugar
2 teaspoons brown sugar

¾ teaspoon salt
1 tablespoon vanilla extract
1 tablespoon cinnamon
2 tablespoons butter

Cut bread in 1-inch thick slices and arrange in one layer in a greased 9 x 13 x 2-inch pan. Beat eggs with milk, sugars, salt, and vanilla. Pour over bread. Sprinkle with cinnamon. Cover and refrigerate 4-24 hours. Uncover and dot with butter. Bake at 350°F. for 50 minutes.

Preparation: 10 minutes
Cooking: 50 minutes

Serves: 6
Must do ahead

Barley Mushroom Pilaf

3 cups chicken bouillon
1 tablespoon lemon juice
1½ teaspoons salt
1 bay leaf
¼ teaspoon white pepper

½ cup barley
½ cup regular rice
1 small onion, chopped
½ cup sliced mushrooms

In an ovenproof 2½-quart casserole, combine 2 cups bouillon, lemon juice, salt, bay leaf, and pepper. Bring to a boil. Add barley and rice. Cook, covered, approximately 35 minutes over low heat. Meanwhile, in a non-stick skillet, bring ½ cup bouillon to a boil. Add mushrooms and onions. Cook until liquid evaporates. Add onions, mushrooms, and remaining bouillon to cooked barley-rice mixture. Cover. Bake at 350°F. for 10 minutes or until liquid has been absorbed. Fluff with a fork before serving.

Preparation: 40 minutes
Cooking: 10 minutes

Serves: 6
Serve immediately

Risotto Alla Milanese

7 cups chicken stock, fresh
   or canned
4 tablespoons butter
½ cup finely chopped onions
¼-½ cup chopped uncooked
   beef marrow (optional)

2 cups uncooked white rice,
   preferably Italian Arborio rice
½ cup dry white wine
⅓ teaspoon powdered saffron

In a 2-3-quart saucepan, bring chicken stock to a boil. Lower heat to gently simmer. Melt butter in a 3-quart, flameproof casserole. Add onions; cook until tender. Stir in optional marrow. Stir in rice. Add wine. Gently boil until wine is absorbed by rice. Add 2 cups chicken stock to rice mixture. Cook, uncovered, until most of the liquid is absorbed, stirring occasionally. Add 2 more cups chicken stock and continue to cook and stir. Meanwhile, add saffron to 2 cups chicken stock and let it steep for a few minutes. Then pour it over rice. Cook until stock is completely absorbed. Rice should be tender and ready to serve.

NOTE: If rice is firm, add remaining stock, ½ cup at a time, and continue cooking and stirring until tender.

Preparation: 10 minutes
Cooking: 60 minutes

Serves: 6-8
Serve immediately

Minnesota Wild Rice
Try this when plain rice just won't do

¼ cup butter, melted
1 (4 ounce) can button
 mushrooms, drained
2 tablespoons chopped chives
½ teaspoon basil
6 juniper berries, crushed
 (optional)

2 (10½ ounce) cans beef
 consommé
Maderia, sherry, or orange
 curaçao
1 cup wild rice

Melt butter in a 1½-quart casserole. Add mushrooms, chives, basil, and juniper berries. Measure beef consommé and add enough Maderia or other liqueur to equal 3 cups liquid. Add liquid and rice to mushroom mixture. Cover. Bake at 350°F. for 1½-2 hours or until liquid is absorbed.

VARIATION: Add orange slices in a decorative pattern on top of rice 15 minutes before done.

Preparation: 10 minutes
Cooking:1½-2 hours

Serves: 6
Can do ahead

Wild Rice

½ cup butter
1 cup wild rice
½ cup slivered blanched almonds
2 tablespoons chopped chives or
 green scallions

½ pound fresh mushrooms,
 sliced
3 cups chicken broth

Melt butter in a heavy 12-inch skillet. Add rice, almonds, chives or scallions, and mushrooms. Over medium heat, sauté, stirring frequently, until wild rice turns yellow. Pour into a greased 1-quart casserole and add chicken broth. Stir and cover tightly. Bake at 325°F. for 1 hour.

NOTE: It may stand, uncovered, up to ½ hour after baking.

Preparation: 20 minutes
Cooking: 1 hour

Serves: 6-8
Serve immediately

Midnight Buffet Lasagna

10 ounces lasagna noodles

SAUCE:

2 pounds Italian sausage
1 tablespoon dried basil, crushed

2 teaspoons salt
2 (16 ounce) jars spaghetti sauce

FILLING:

3 cups cream-style cottage cheese
1 cup Ricotta cheese
¾ cup grated Parmesan cheese

3 tablespoons parsley flakes
2 eggs, beaten
½ teaspoon pepper

2 pounds Mozzarella cheese,
   thinly sliced

Cook noodles according to package directions. Drain. Set aside noodles.

SAUCE: Brown sausage slowly. Spoon off excess fat. Add next three ingredients and simmer, uncovered, for 30 minutes, stirring occasionally.

FILLING: Combine all ingredients and mix thoroughly.

TO ASSEMBLE: Place half the noodles in a 9 x 13 x 2-inch baking dish. Spread with half the cheese filling mixture, half the Mozzarella cheese, and half the meat sauce. Repeat the layers. Bake at 375°F. for 30 minutes. Let stand 10 minutes before cutting.

NOTE: This dish can be refrigerated up to 1 day before baking. After baking, it can be frozen for a month before serving.

Preparation: 25 minutes
Cooking: 30 minutes

Serves: 8-10
Can be frozen

Tortellini Della Nonna

200 (4 packages) tortellini
¾ cup unsalted butter
1 cup heavy cream
5 slices prosciuto, thinly sliced

½ cup peas
1 cup grated Parmesan cheese
Pepper, to taste

Cook tortellini in salted boiling water for 7 minutes. Drain. Melt butter in large pan and add tortellini. Mix well. Blend in cream. Mix in prosciuto slices, peas, Parmesan cheese, and pepper. Blend thoroughly. Serve hot with additional cheese and fresh ground pepper.

Preparation: 15 minutes
Cooking: 10 minutes

Serves: 6-8
Serve immediately

Italian Spaghetti with Caruso Sauce

5 tablespoons oil
½ cup chopped onion
1 large clove garlic, minced
2 (29 ounce) cans Italian tomatoes
2 (6 ounce) cans tomato paste
1¼ cups water
1½ tablespoons salt
½ teaspoon pepper
1 teaspoon oregano or basil
2 bay leaves

1 tablespoon sugar
¼ cup grated Parmesan cheese
1 pound chicken livers, cut in
   ½-inch pieces
1 teaspoon salt
1½ cups sliced canned
   mushrooms, drained
1½ pounds spaghetti
3 tablespoons butter
Black olives (optional)

Heat 3 tablespoons oil in a heavy pot. Add onions and garlic and sauté until brown. Add tomatoes and break up slightly with a fork. Add tomato paste, water, salt, pepper, oregano or basil, bay leaves, sugar, and cheese. Mix well and simmer over low heat for 1½ hours, stirring occasionally. Sauté chicken livers and mushrooms in 2 tablespoons oil. Sprinkle with 1 teaspoon salt and add to sauce. Cook ½ hour longer. Cook spaghetti according to package directions, drain, and toss with butter. Serve with hot sauce. Garnish with additional cheese and black olives.

Preparation: 30 minutes
Cooking: 2 hours

Serves: 8
Can be frozen

Fettucini Alfredo Plus
The artichokes and pimiento are the "plus"

1 egg yolk
½ cup sweet butter, softened
1 cup grated Parmesan cheese
1 cup heavy cream
19 ounces fettucini

2 (6 ounce) jars marinated
   artichoke hearts, drained
1 (2 ounce) jar chopped pimiento
Salt and pepper, to taste

Combine egg yolk, butter, cheese, and cream in a small saucepan. Heat thoroughly. Combine artichoke hearts and pimiento in a small skillet and heat through. Cook the fettucini according to package directions and drain. Pour sauce over the hot pasta and toss until well coated. Add salt and pepper. Spoon artichoke mixture over the top before serving.

Preparation: 20 minutes
Cooking: 15 minutes

Serves: 6
Serve immediately

Manicotti Marvel
This takes some time to make but is well worth the effort

SAUCE:

¼ cup salad oil
1½ cups finely chopped onion
2 cloves garlic, crushed
1 pound mushrooms, chopped
2 pounds chuck roast
1 (2 pounds, 3 ounce) can Italian
   plum tomatoes, undrained
1 (6 ounce) can tomato paste
2 tablespoons chopped parsley
1 tablespoon salt

1 tablespoon sugar
1 teaspoon dried oregano
1 teaspoon basil
2 bay leaves
¼ teaspoon pepper
⅟₁₆ teaspoon each: thyme,
   rosemary, fennel, marjoram
2 cups water or 1½ cups water
   plus ½ cup Burgundy wine

MANICOTTI SHELLS:

6 eggs, at room temperature
1½ cups all-purpose flour
1½ cups water

¼ teaspoon salt
Butter for frying

FILLING:

2 pounds Ricotta cheese
8 ounces Mozzarella cheese
⅓ cup grated Parmesan cheese
2 eggs

1 teaspoon salt
¼ teaspoon pepper
1 tablespoon chopped parsley

Parmesan cheese, to garnish

SAUCE: In a Dutch oven, heat oil and sauté onion, garlic, and mushrooms for 3 minutes. Add chuck roast and brown on all sides. Add rest of sauce ingredients (mash the tomatoes). Bring to a boil, then reduce heat to a simmer. Cover and cook, adding more water, if necessary, until meat is tender, about 4-5 hours. Remove meat and trim off fat and gristle. Flake meat and add back to sauce, mixing well.

MANICOTTI SHELLS: Combine eggs, flour, water, and salt and beat until smooth. Let stand ½ hour. Heat crêpe pan or non-stick skillet and wipe with butter. Pour in 3 tablespoons batter. Rotate skillet to spread batter evenly over bottom. Cook over medium heat until top is dry but bottom is not brown. Turn out on wire rack to cool. Continue until all of batter is used. Stack with wax paper until ready to use. Can refrigerate overnight.

FILLING: Combine all ingredients, mixing until well blended.

TO ASSEMBLE: Spoon 1½ cups sauce into bottoms of two 9 x 13-inch baking pans. Place ¼ cup filling in center of each shell and roll up. Place ½ of manicotti, seam side down, in each pan. Cover with remaining sauce. Sprinkle with Parmesan cheese. Bake, uncovered, at 350°F. for 45-60 minutes or until bubbly.

NOTE: If you prefer, one pan may be frozen before baking.

Preparation: 2-3 hours
Cooking: 45-60 minutes

Serves: 8-10
Can be frozen

South of the Border Macaroni

1 package macaroni
1 large onion, diced
1 large can solid pack tomatoes
2 teaspoons chili powder

2 cups grated cheese
Cayenne pepper
Salt
Cumin

Cook macaroni according to directions. Drain, and run cold water over it. Brown onions in skillet, add can of tomatoes (broken into small pieces). Add grated cheese, a pinch of cayenne pepper and salt to taste. Bring this to a boil, then mix in the macaroni. Put entire mixture in well-buttered casserole. Sprinkle more grated cheese over all, and bake in 450-degree oven for 45 minutes.

Mrs C. V. Whitney

Mrs. Cornelius Vanderbilt Whitney
The Whitneys, well-known in social circles and the thoroughbred racing world, reside at Cady Hill House, Saratoga Springs.

Quick White Clam Sauce

¾ cup butter
¼ teaspoon basil
½ teaspoon garlic powder
¼ teaspoon black pepper

¼ teaspoon parsley flakes
½ teaspoon chopped chives
2 (6½ ounce) cans minced clams

In a saucepan, melt butter over low heat. Add basil, garlic, pepper, parsley, and chives. Stir well. Add clams and clam liquid. Heat thoroughly. Serve over linguini.

Preparation: 5 minutes
Cooking: 10 minutes

Serves: 4
Serve immediately

Stuffed Shells with Cheese Sauce
No tomatoes are in this dish!

SHELLS:

20 jumbo macaroni shells
½ cup chopped celery
2 tablespoons chopped onion
2 tablespoons cooking oil
2 cups cream-style cottage cheese
1 (10 ounce) package frozen
   chopped spinach, cooked and
   drained

1 egg, slightly beaten
½ teaspoon salt
⅛ teaspoon dried oregano,
   crushed
Dash of pepper

SAUCE:

2 tablespoons chopped onion
2 tablespoons cooking oil
3 tablespoons all-purpose flour
½ teaspoon salt

Dash of pepper
1½ cups milk
¾ cup chicken broth
¼ cup grated Parmesan cheese

SHELLS: Cook shells according to package directions. Drain. Cook celery and onion in hot oil until tender. Drain. Mix with cheese, spinach, egg, salt, oregano, and pepper. Fill shells with this mixture.

SAUCE: Sauté onion in oil until soft. Blend in flour, salt, and pepper. Stir in milk and chicken broth stirring until thick and bubbly. Stir in cheese.

TO ASSEMBLE: Pour half of sauce into a 12 x 7 x 2-inch baking dish. Arrange filled shells in dish. Drizzle remaining sauce over shells. Bake, covered, at 375°F. for 15 minutes and uncovered for 10 minutes more.

Preparation: 45 minutes
Cooking: 25 minutes

Serves: 4-6
Can do ahead

Quick Tomato Sauce with Fettucini
No cooking! The heat of the pasta warms the sauce

2 (6 ounce) cans tomato paste
½ cup olive oil
1 cup grated cheese, Romano
   or Parmesan or both
1-2 teaspoons hot pepper,
   crushed (optional)

8-12 cloves garlic, finely chopped
1½ cups chopped fresh parsley
½ cup chopped fresh basil
1 pound fettucini, cooked

Combine all ingredients. Mix with hot cooked fettucini.

Preparation: 15 minutes

Serves: 4-6
Can do ahead

Super Spaghetti Sauce

3 tablespoons butter
3 tablespoons olive oil
1 large green pepper, chopped
4-5 medium mushrooms, chopped
1 clove garlic, mashed
1 (28 ounce) can tomato purée
1 (12 ounce) can tomato paste
2 (35 ounce) cans peeled tomatoes
1 (29 ounce) can tomato sauce

3 tablespoons crushed oregano
2 tablespoons Italian seasonings
2 bay leaves
2 teaspoons basil
1½ cups dry red wine
½ cup grated Romano or Parmesan cheese
12 hot Italian sausages
2 pounds ground round beef
2 teaspoons sugar, if needed

Place butter and oil in skillet and sauté pepper, onions, mushrooms, and garlic until tender. Drain. Put all tomato ingredients in a large pot with the oregano, Italian seasonings, bay leaves, and basil. Bring to a boil, breaking down large chunks of tomato. Cover and simmer about 30 minutes. Add sautéed ingredients and boil. Simmer, covered for 30 minutes more. Bake sausages on rack in a baking pan for 1 hour at 325°F. Turn to brown evenly and pierce with a fork to allow grease to drain. Cut sausages into thirds and drain on paper towels. While sausages bake, brown ground beef and break into small chunks. Add cooked beef to tomato mixture. Simmer, uncovered, for 30 minutes. Add sausage, cheese, and red wine. Simmer until desired consistency is reached, about 1-2 hours. If sauce is acidic, add sugar to taste. Serve over cooked linguini or vermicelli.

Preparation: 2 hours
Cooking: 4 hours

Serves: 16
Can be frozen

Spaghetti Alla Carbonara

½ pound bacon, thick cut
1 pound spaghetti
⅓ cup dry white wine or dry vermouth

2 eggs, well beaten
½ cup freshly grated Parmesan cheese
Freshly ground pepper, to taste

Cut bacon into ½-inch squares and sauté in a large skillet until cooked through but not crisp. Remove bacon from pan and add wine. Cook down and keep hot. Cook spaghetti and drain. Mix spaghetti with bacon, wine, and bacon fat in skillet. Add eggs and cheese. Toss until eggs cook. Add pepper. Serve with additional cheese.

Preparation: 5 minutes
Cooking: 15 minutes

Serves: 4
Serve immediately

Curried Spaghetti Sauce
The soy sauce and curry powder are a fun twist
to traditional spaghetti sauce

1 green pepper, chopped
1 medium onion, chopped
2 tablespoons cooking oil
1 pound ground beef or Italian
  sausage
3 teaspoons cooking sherry
3 teaspoons soy sauce

2 tablespoons curry powder
2 teaspoons sugar
¼ pound fresh mushrooms, sliced
2 (16 ounce) cans stewed
  tomatoes
1 (6 ounce) can tomato paste
Dash of salt

Sauté green pepper and onion in oil. In separate pan, sauté meat. Add sherry, soy sauce, curry powder, and 1 teaspoon sugar to meat. Mix well. Add to pepper and onion mixture. Then add mushrooms, tomatoes, and tomato paste. Stir and heat until sauce boils. Cover and simmer 1-2 hours. Add extra sugar for taste. Serve over cooked spaghetti or mix sauce with partially cooked, broken spaghetti and top generously with grated cheese. Cook in oven or microwave until bubbly.

Preparation: 30 minutes
Cooking: 2 hours

Serves: 4
Can do ahead

Pesto
A lovely summer condiment with fresh-grown basil

2 cups firmly packed basil leaves,
  rinsed and drained
½ cup olive oil
2 tablespoons pine or pignolia
  nuts

2 large cloves garlic, split
½ cup grated Parmesan cheese
3 tablespoons butter, divided
  into thirds
Salt, to taste

Combine basil, oil, nuts, and garlic in a food processor and purée thoroughly. Add grated cheese and continue blending. Add butter and blend again. Taste and add salt, if needed. Just before serving, add 1-2 tablespoons hot water in which pasta was cooked. Pour over pasta and serve with extra Parmesan cheese and pepper. If freezing, do not add cheese or butter.

Preparation: 10 minutes

Serves: 4-6
Can be frozen

CAKES &
COOKIES

A Baker's Dozen

The Dutch settlers of Albany, originally called Ft. Orange, were known for the bounty of their dining tables and for "a good-natured temperament that sprung from a full belly."

The Dutch brought many foods to this new land, including a large "cruller" named for an early mayor of Albany, the Honorable Mr. Crol. Another pastry, a small, fruit-filled doughnut called "oliekoecken" (oil cake), and the little Dutch town of Ft. Orange played leading roles in the origin of the term "baker's dozen."

It seems that a witch visited the bake shop of Volchert Jan Pietersen late one New Year's Eve. She asked for thirteen "oliekoecken" to a dozen and was refused by the baker. The witch left in a rage, casting a curse of ill fortune on the poor baker. As might have been predicted, the next year was a disaster for the unfortunate baker–everything went wrong. So, when the witch appeared at his shop the next New Year's Eve, the baker, without argument, counted out thirteen cakes for the witch. The witch left, promising good luck hereafter to all those who gave a "baker's dozen."

The following recipes are sure to delight family and guests alike. But always remember to allow for generous servings–especially on New Year's Eve!

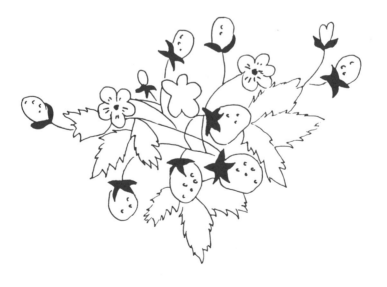

Apple, Chocolate Chip, Walnut Cake

2 cups all-purpose flour
Pinch of salt
1 teaspoon cinnamon
1 teaspoon baking soda
¾ cup vegetable oil
1 cup sugar
2 eggs

2 teaspoons vanilla or almond
  extract
½ cup chopped walnuts
½ cup semi-sweet chocolate
  chips
3 cups apples, peeled and sliced
Confectioners' sugar, to sprinkle

Sift flour, salt, cinnamon, and baking soda together and set aside. Using a wooden spoon only, mix oil, sugar, and eggs. Add vanilla or almond extract, nuts, and chocolate. Mix well. Add flour mixture and blend well. Fold in apples. Mixture will be very thick. Pour mixture into a greased tube or bundt pan. Bake at 325°F. for 1 hour or until done. Sprinkle top with confectioners' sugar when cool.

Preparation: 30 minutes
Cooking: 1 hour

Serves: 8-10
Can do ahead

Carrot Spice Cake
It improves after chilling and is still good days later

CAKE:
2 cups all-purpose flour
2 cups sugar
2 teaspoons cinnamon
½ teaspoon salt
1 teaspoon baking powder

2 teaspoons baking soda
1½ cups corn oil
4 eggs
1 teaspoon vanilla
3 cups grated carrots

FROSTING:
1 (8 ounce) package cream
  cheese, softened
½ cup butter, softened
1 (1 pound) box confectioners'
  sugar

1 teaspoon vanilla
1 cup chopped pecans

CAKE: Mix all dry ingredients. Add oil, eggs, and vanilla. Blend well. Fold in carrots. Bake at 350°F. for 30 minutes in three 9-inch pans.

FROSTING: Cream the cheese and butter. Add sugar and vanilla. Blend well after each addition. Add pecans and mix. Add milk, if needed, for spreading consistency. Spread between layers and on top of cake.

Preparation: 40 minutes
Cooking: 30 minutes

Serves: 8
Can do ahead

Sauced Apple Cake

The brandy soaked apples add a special touch to this holiday cake

4 cups apples, peeled and
   chopped
6 tablespoons brandy
2 cups sugar
½ cup cooking oil
2 eggs
2 cups all-purpose flour

2 teaspoons cinnamon
2 teaspoons baking soda
1 teaspoon nutmeg
1 teaspoon salt
½ teaspoon cloves
1 cup chopped walnuts
1 cup raisins

Combine apples and brandy and set aside. Blend sugar, oil, and eggs. Add flour and spices. The batter will be thick and dry. Mix in nuts and raisins. Add apple mixture and mix well. Pour into greased tube pan. Bake at 350°F. for 1 hour or until done.

NOTE: Serve warm or cold, with or without, whipped cream.

Preparation: 30 minutes
Cooking: 1 hour

Serves: 10
Can do ahead

Vanilla-Almond Cheesecake

CRUST:
1¾ cups fine graham cracker
   crumbs
¼ cup finely chopped walnuts

½ teaspoon cinnamon
½ cup butter, melted

FILLING:
3 eggs
2 (8 ounce) packages cream
   cheese, softened
1 cup sugar

¼ teaspoon salt
2 teaspoons vanilla
½ teaspoon almond extract
3 cups sour cream

CRUST: Combine all ingredients. Then press them on bottom and about ⅔ up the sides of a 9-inch spring-form pan.

FILLING: Mix all the ingredients in given order with an electric mixer. Mix after each addition to insure smoothness. Pour into crust. Bake at 375°F. for 35-45 minutes or until set. Cool. Chill 4-5 hours.

Preparation: 30 minutes
Cooking: 35-45 minutes

Serves: 12
Must do ahead

Mocha Cream Roll

MOCHA ROLL:
5 eggs, separated
1 cup confectioners' sugar

3 tablespoons cocoa
Cocoa, for coating

FILLING:
1½ cups heavy cream
½ cup cocoa

¼ cup confectioners' sugar
3 tablespoons coffee-flavored
  liqueur

ICING:
6 ounces semi-sweet
  chocolate chips
2 tablespoons butter

2 tablespoons white corn syrup
3 tablespoons milk

MOCHA ROLL: Grease 10 x 15-inch jelly roll pan. Line with wax paper. Grease and flour wax paper. Beat egg whites stiff and add ½ cup confectioners' sugar. Beat egg yolks at high speed adding ½ cup confectioners' sugar and cocoa. With wire whisk, gently fold yolk mixture into whites mixture. Spread evenly in jelly roll pan. Bake at 400°F. for 15 minutes. Sprinkle clean towel with cocoa. Invert pan onto towel. Gently peel wax paper away. Roll cake with towel, jelly roll-style. Cool.

FILLING: With an electric mixer, whip heavy cream with cocoa, sugar, and liqueur until thick. Unroll cake and spread with filling mixture. Roll up again and place seam side down on serving plate.

ICING: Melt chocolate chips with butter in top of double boiler over hot water. Remove from heat. Beat in corn syrup and milk until smooth. Spread over roll.
NOTE: Roll may also be decorated with a glaze. Combine ¾ cup confectioners' sugar, 4 tablespoons water, and food coloring of your choice.

Preparation: 1 hour
Cooking: 15 minutes

Serves: 8-10
Can be frozen

Chocolate Rum Cake

CAKE:

¼ cup raisins
¼ cup rum
7 ounces sweet chocolate
3 tablespoons water
½ cup butter
3 eggs, separated

⅔ cup sugar
4½ tablespoons all-purpose flour
⅔ cup almonds, blanched and
 pulverized
Pinch of salt

ICING:

3 ounces sweet chocolate
3 tablespoons confectioners' sugar

3 tablespoons butter

CAKE: Soak raisins in rum until moist and plump. In a double boiler, melt chocolate with water. Stir until smooth. Remove from heat. Stir in butter until melted. Beat egg yolks with sugar until pale and creamy. Combine with chocolate mixture. Blend in flour and nuts. Stir in raisins and rum. Beat whites with a pinch of salt until stiff. Stir ⅓ of whites into mixture to lighten. Fold chocolate into remaining whites. Pour batter into greased 8-inch round pan lined with greased wax paper. Bake in middle level of oven at 375°F. for 20-25 minutes. Let cool 10 minutes in pan, then turn onto rack. Cake will be quite moist.

ICING: Melt chocolate. Add sugar and butter. Stir until smooth. Frost top and sides of cooled cake.

Preparation: 20 minutes
Cooking: 20-25 minutes

Yield: 1 cake
Can do ahead

Chunky Apple Cake
There are chunks of apple in every bite

1 cup sugar
½ cup butter or margarine
1 egg
½ teaspoon vanilla
3 cups apples, peeled and diced

½ cup chopped walnuts
1 cup all-purpose flour
½ teaspoon each: cinnamon,
 baking powder, baking soda,
 salt, nutmeg

Cream sugar and butter. Add egg and vanilla and mix with electric mixer. Add apples, nuts, and dry ingredients. Mix well. Spread into greased 9-inch square pan. Bake at 350°F. for 45 minutes.

Preparation: 30 minutes
Cooking: 45 minutes

Serves: 9
Serve immediately

Black Bottom Cupcakes

Kids love them for after school treats or lunch box snacks

BATTER:

1½ cups sifted all-purpose flour
1 cup sugar
1 teaspoon baking soda
¼ cup cocoa
½ teaspoon salt

1 cup water
⅓ cup oil
1 tablespoon vinegar
1 teaspoon vanilla

FILLING:

1 (8 ounce) package cream
   cheese, softened
⅓ cup sugar
1 egg

⅛ teaspoon salt
1 (6 ounce) package semi-sweet
   chocolate chips

BATTER: Blend all ingredients together in listed order. Place liners in cupcake pans and fill to ⅓ full.

FILLING: Mix cream cheese with sugar. Add egg, salt, and chocolate chips. Mix well. Top cake batter (in liners) with one heaping teaspoon of filling. Bake at 350°F. for 25-30 minutes.

NOTE: After baking, sprinkle with a little confectioners' sugar.

Preparation: 10-15 minutes
Cooking: 25-30 minutes

Yield: 24 cupcakes
Can do ahead

Italian Cheesecake

16 ounces Ricotta cheese
16 ounces cream cheese
1½ cups sugar
4 eggs
3 tablespoons all-purpose flour

3 tablespoons cornstarch
Juice of ½ lemon
½ cup butter, melted
1 pint sour cream
2 teaspoons vanilla

Mix Ricotta and cream cheese. Add sugar gradually. Add eggs, one at a time, beating after each addition. Add flour, cornstarch, lemon juice, and butter. Mix well. Add sour cream and vanilla. Blend well. Grease and flour a 10-inch spring-form pan. Pour mixture into pan. Bake at 350°F. for 1½ hours. Turn oven off. Leave in oven 2 hours longer. Remove from oven. Cool.

NOTE: It may be sprinkled with confectioners' sugar or served with a topping of your choice.

Preparation: 15 minutes
Cooking: 1½ hours

Serves: 10-12
Can do ahead

Raspberry Cheesecake

CRUST:
¼ cup butter, melted
⅛ cup sugar

1⅓ cups crushed graham crackers
Dash of cinnamon

FILLING:
1 (3 ounce) package raspberry-
  flavored gelatin
1 cup boiling water
1 (8 ounce) package cream
  cheese, softened

1 cup sugar
3 teaspoons lemon juice
6½ ounces chilled evaporated
  milk

CRUST: Melt butter in a small saucepan. Add sugar, graham cracker crumbs, and cinnamon. Mix until blended. Reserve 3 tablespoons of mixture. Press the rest into a 10-inch pie plate. Bake at 350°F. for 10-15 minutes. Remove from oven and cool.

FILLING: Put the raspberry-flavored gelatin in a large bowl and add boiling water. Let cool. In a separate bowl, cream cheese with sugar. Add to cooled gelatin and blend thoroughly. This thickens as it cools. Mix the lemon juice with evaporated milk and beat until peaks form. Fold into gelatin mixture. Then pour it into crust. Sprinkle with crumbs reserved from crust. Chill thoroughly.

NOTE: This is nice with fresh strawberries or peaches chopped and added to filling.

Preparation: 4 hours
Cooking: 10-15 minutes

Serves: 8
Must do ahead

Peché au Chocolat (Chocolate Sin)
As sinful as the name implies

Butter
Flour
10 ounces semi-sweet chocolate,
  broken into small pieces
½ cup unsalted butter,
  cut in 8 pieces

6 large eggs, separated,
  at room temperature
1 cup sugar
2½ teaspoons coffee-flavored
  liqueur
Confectioners' sugar

Place oven rack in lower third of oven. Preheat oven to 375°F. Butter and flour bottom and sides of 8-inch spring-form pan. Melt chocolate and butter pieces in heavy saucepan over low heat. Beat egg yolks in large bowl at high speed, or use wire whisk. Gradually add ¾ cup sugar until mixture is pale yellow and thick. Add chocolate mixture and beat until smooth. Add liqueur and beat until well blended. Beat egg whites in

medium bowl at high speed until soft peaks form. Gradually add remaining ¼ cup sugar into whites and continue to beat until stiff peaks form. Fold whites thoroughly into chocolate mixture. Pour batter evenly into pan. Bake at 375°F. for 15 minutes. Then reduce oven temperature to 350°F. and bake 15 minutes more. Reduce oven temperature to 250°F. and continue baking 30 minutes longer. (Total baking time is 1 hour) Turn off oven, open oven door, leave pan in oven 30 minutes. Remove cake from oven, cover top with damp paper toweling, and let stand 5 minutes. Remove toweling and cool cake completely. Dome of cake with crack and collapse. This is normal. Press top of cake down lightly to smooth top. Remove side of spring-form pan. Dust top of cake with confectioners' sugar, transfer to plate and serve.

NOTE: Cake will rise very high in the oven but collapses as it cools. Also, it may be served with whipped cream on the side.

Preparation: 30 minutes
Cooking: 1 hour

Serves: 8
Can do ahead

Chocolate Chip Cheesecake

1½ cups all-purpose flour
¼ cup unsweetened cocoa
½ teaspoon salt
½ cup oil
½ cup sugar
1 teaspoon vanilla
1 teaspoon baking soda
1 cup water

1 tablespoon vinegar
1 (8 ounce) package cream
  cheese, softened
½ cup sugar
1 egg
⅛ teaspoon salt
6 ounces semi-sweet chocolate
  chips

FROSTING:
½ cup semi-sweet chocolate
  chips

2 tablespoons butter
3 tablespoons hot coffee

Mix flour, cocoa, salt, oil, sugar, vanilla, baking soda, water, and vinegar. It will be thin. Pour into an 8 x 8-inch square pan. Combine cream cheese, sugar, egg, and salt. Beat until well blended. Stir in chocolate chips. Pour this mixture over mixture in square pan and swirl through. Bake at 350°F. for 50-60 minutes.

FROSTING: Melt chocolate chips and butter in small saucepan. Add coffee and mix well. Spread over cake.

NOTE: You can use confectioners' sugar on top if you don't want frosting.

Preparation: 20 minutes
Cooking: 50-60 minutes

Yield: 12-16 squares
Can do ahead

Chocolate Bread with Honey Butter

BREAD:
1 cup sugar
½ cup margarine, softened
2 eggs, beaten
1 cup buttermilk
1¾ cups unbleached flour

½ cup cocoa
½ teaspoon each: baking powder,
    salt, baking soda
½ cup chopped walnuts or
    pecans (optional)

BUTTER:
½ cup butter, softened
2 tablespoons chocolate syrup

2 tablespoons honey

BREAD: In a large bowl, cream sugar and margarine. Add eggs and buttermilk. Mix well. Sift the dry ingredients together. Add to liquid mixture, stirring until the dry particles disappear. Stir in nuts. Pour into greased 9 x 5-inch loaf pan. Bake at 350°F. for 55-60 minutes. Cool upright in pan for 15 minutes. Then remove from pan and cool completely.

BUTTER: In a small bowl, combine all ingredients. Beat with mixer at highest speed until light and fluffy. Serve with bread.

Preparation: 20 minutes
Cooking: 55-60 minutes

Yield: 1 loaf
Can be frozen

Oatmeal Chocolate Chip Cake
A good dessert to take to a party

1 cup quick oats
1¾ cups boiling water
1 cup sugar
1 cup brown sugar, firmly packed
½ cup margarine, softened
2 large or 3 medium eggs

1¾ cups all-purpose flour
1 teaspoon baking soda
½ teaspoon salt
1 tablespoon cocoa
1 (12 ounce) package semi-sweet
    chocolate chips

Soak oats in boiling water for 10 minutes. Stir in sugars, margarine, and eggs. Add flour, baking soda, salt, and cocoa. Stir in half of chocolate chips. Pour into greased and floured 9 x 13-inch pan. Sprinkle remaining chips on top. Bake at 350°F. for 40 minutes.

NOTE: You may want to sprinkle chopped walnuts on top or serve with whipped cream or ice cream.

Preparation: 20 minutes
Cooking: 40 minutes

Serves: 12
Can do ahead

Chocolate Date Cake

CAKE:

1 (8 ounce) package
  chopped dates
1¼ cups boiling water
½ cup shortening
1 cup sugar
2 eggs

1¼ cups plus 2 tablespoons
  all-purpose flour
1 tablespoon cocoa
1 teaspoon baking soda
1 teaspoon vanilla

TOPPING:

½ cup sugar
6 ounces chocolate chips, sweet
  or unsweetened

½ cup chopped pecans

CAKE: Mix dates and water. Let cool. Cream shortening and sugar. Add eggs, one at a time, beating after each addition. Add flour, cocoa, and soda in ⅓ portions alternating with liquid from the dates. Stir in dates and vanilla. Batter will be thin. Pour into greased and floured 9 x 13-inch pan.

TOPPING: Sprinkle on topping in order listed. Bake at 350°F. for 35-45 minutes.

VARIATION: Substitute butterscotch chips for chocolate chips in the topping.

Preparation: 40 minutes
Cooking: 35-45 minutes

Serves: 12
Can be frozen

Coconut Pound Cake

1 cup butter
¾ cup shortening
3 cups sugar
5 eggs
3 cups all-purpose flour

1 teaspoon baking powder
1 cup milk
2 teaspoons vanilla
1⅓ cups coconut

Cream butter, shortening, and sugar together. Add eggs, one at a time, beating after each addition. Add flour, baking powder, milk, vanilla, and coconut. Mix until well blended. Pour into a greased and floured 10-inch tube pan. Bake at 350°F. for 1 hour. Cool. Turn onto serving plate.

Preparation: 30 minutes
Cooking: 60 minutes

Serves: 12-16
Can be frozen

Mary Kay's Fabulous Chocolate Mousse Cake

DIPPING MIXTURE:

10 tablespoons crème de cacao
3 cups strong coffee
⅓ cup sugar

⅓ cup water
2 tablespoons cinnamon

CAKE:

2 (9½ x 5½ inch) pound cakes,
   homemade or purchased

FILLING:

8 eggs, separated
2 cups confectioners' sugar
4 ounces unsweetened baking
   chocolate, melted and cooled

4 ounces German sweet
   chocolate, melted and cooled

FROSTING:

1 ounce unsweetened baking
   chocolate
¼ cup butter

½ cup confectioners' sugar
2-4 tablespoons milk

DIPPING MIXTURE: Combine ingredients and set aside.

CAKE: Cut the pound cake into ¼-½-inch slices. Dip enough slices into the dipping mixture to line the bottom and sides of a large tube pan (angel food cake pan). Set the leftover cake aside temporarily.

FILLING: Beat egg yolks until thickened, about 8 minutes. Add sugar gradually while beating. Then add cooled, melted chocolates. Beat egg whites until they stand in peaks. Fold into chocolate mixture. Fill center of "pound cake mold" with chocolate mixture. Dip remaining slices of pound cake into dipping mixture and completely cover chocolate filling. Refrigerate overnight, at least 12 hours. Turn cake onto plate. It will be very moist. Refrigerate, uncovered, for several hours more.

FROSTING: Melt chocolate and butter together. Remove from heat and gradually add confectioners' sugar while mixing well. Add milk, one tablespoon at a time, until icing is the consistency of a heavy glaze. Spread on top of cake so that frosting drips down sides but not completely to bottom. Refrigerate until ready to serve. It can be safely refrigerated up to 3-4 days.

NOTE: Add a helping of whipped cream when serving, if you dare. Also, this recipe may be halved, using a loaf pan.

Preparation: 1 hour, plus

Serves: 16-24
Must do ahead

Rusty Red Devil's Food

1¼ teaspoons baking soda
½ cup sour milk
½ cup butter
2 cups sugar
4 squares unsweetened chocolate

1 cup water
2 eggs, well beaten
2 cups all-purpose flour
1 teaspoon vanilla

Dissolve baking soda in sour milk. Add butter and sugar to sour milk mixture. In a saucepan, melt chocolate with water, stirring constantly, until chocolate is melted. Remove from heat, cool, and add to sour milk mixture. Add eggs, flour, and vanilla. Mix thoroughly. Pour into a greased and floured 9 x 13-inch pan. This is a very liquid batter. Bake at 350°F. for 30-35 minutes.

NOTE: You could use two 9-inch round cake pans for a layered cake. When cool, frost with a white, caramel, chocolate frosting or your favorite topping.

Preparation: 25 minutes
Cooking: 30-35 minutes

Serves: 10
Can do ahead

Oatmeal Cake with Broiled Icing

CAKE:
1¼ cups boiling water
1 cup quick oatmeal
½ cup margarine, softened
1 cup sugar
1 cup brown sugar, firmly packed

2 eggs, beaten
1½ cups sifted all-purpose flour
½ teaspoon salt
1 teaspoon baking soda
½ teaspoon cinnamon

FROSTING:
6 tablespoons butter, softened
⅔ cup brown sugar,
  firmly packed

4 tablespoons half and half cream
1 cup coconut
½ cup chopped nuts

CAKE: Pour boiling water over oatmeal. Let stand. Cream margarine with sugars. Add eggs. Sift together dry ingredients. Add to sugar mixture. Stir in oatmeal. Pour into 9 x 13-inch pan. Bake at 350°F. for 35-40 minutes.

FROSTING: Cream butter and sugar. Add all other ingredients. Mix well. Spread over warm cake in pan. Broil at 300°F. or put cake on second shelf down and broil until frosting bubbles. Watch very carefully.

Preparation: 25 minutes
Cooking: 35-40 minutes

Serves: 10-12
Can do ahead

Strawberry Shortcake

2 cups all-purpose flour
¼ cup sugar
2½ teaspoons baking powder
½ teaspoon salt

¼ teaspoon nutmeg
⅓ cup butter
1 egg or 2 egg yolks, well beaten
⅓ cup milk

TOPPING:
1 pint strawberries, sliced

½ pint heavy cream, whipped

Mix dry ingredients and sift twice. Place dry ingredients in a medium bowl and work in butter with finger tips. Add egg or egg yolks and milk. Stir with fork until all ingredients are mixed well. Press lightly into ungreased 8 x 8-inch pan. Bake at 400°F. for 15 minutes. Cut into square serving size pieces. Then split each piece in half so as to have a top and bottom half.

TOPPING: Spoon strawberries over bottom half of cake. Replace top half of cake and spoon on more strawberries. Top with whipped cream.

Preparation: 15 minutes
Cooking: 15 minutes

Serves: 9
Can be frozen

Alex's Apricot Brandy Pound Cake
This won the grand prize in a local newspaper recipe contest!

1 cup butter, softened
3 cups sugar
6 eggs
1 teaspoon each: vanilla, orange
    extract, rum extract

2¾ cups all-purpose flour
¼ teaspoon baking soda
½ teaspoon salt
1 cup sour cream
½ cup apricot brandy

Cream butter and sugar until light. Add eggs, one at a time, beating thoroughly after each addition. Stir in vanilla, orange, and rum extracts. Sift flour, baking soda, and salt. Add sifted flour alternately with the sour cream and apricot brandy to the egg-sugar mixture. Pour into a buttered, floured, large bundt pan. Bake at 325°F. for 1 hour and 10 minutes or until tester comes out clean from cake. It stays very moist when wrapped and refrigerated.

NOTE: This can also be baked in three 3 x 5-inch or six 2 x 4-inch loaf pans. Bake about 1 hour. It is good with fresh strawberries or raspberries.

Preparation: 25-30 minutes
Cooking: 1 hour and 10 minutes

Serves: 12-16
Can be frozen

Forgotten Meringue Cake

CAKE:

1½ cups egg whites
   (about 12 eggs)
¼ teaspoon cream of tartar

2½ cups sugar
1 teaspoon vanilla
¾ teaspoon almond extract

ICING:

2 cups heavy cream

½ cup sugar

GARNISH:

2 (10 ounce) packages frozen
   raspberries, defrosted

CAKE: Preheat oven to 450°F. Beat egg whites with cream of tartar until fluffy. Add sugar, one tablespoon at a time, beating after each addition until whites are glossy. Add vanilla and almond extract. Mix well. Put into an ungreased angel food cake pan. Place pan in oven and turn heat off immediately. Leave cake in oven overnight. Do not open the oven door until morning.

ICING: Next day, whip heavy cream with sugar until stiff. Turn cake out onto plate and frost with whipped cream. Serve with raspberries.

NOTE: Remove any racks above the cake from oven as it rises considerably.

Preparation: 30 minutes
Cooking: Overnight

Serves: 8-10
Must do ahead

Cream Cheese Pound Cake

1 cup margarine, softened
½ cup butter, softened
1 (8 ounce) package cream
   cheese, softened

3 cups sugar
6 eggs
3 cups all-purpose flour
1 tablespoon vanilla

Cream margarine, butter, and cream cheese until fluffy. Add sugar and mix well. Add eggs and flour alternately, ending with the flour. Add vanilla. Pour into greased and floured tube pan. Bake at 325°F. for 70-75 minutes. Do not open oven to peek.

NOTE: Serve with berries or ice cream.

Preparation: 30 minutes
Cooking: 70-75 minutes

Serves: 12
Can do ahead

Lemon Chiffon Cake

Excellent served after a heavy meal or on hot days.

CAKE:

2 cups all-purpose flour
1½ cups sugar
3 teaspoons baking powder
1 teaspoon salt
½ cup vegetable oil

7 eggs, separated
¾ cup cold water
2 teaspoons grated lemon peel
2 teaspoons vanilla
½ teaspoon cream of tartar

FROSTING:

⅓ cup butter, softened
3 cups confectioners' sugar

½ teaspoon grated lemon peel
2 tablespoons lemon juice

CAKE: Mix flour, sugar, baking powder, and salt in large bowl. Make a well in center of dry ingredients and add oil, egg yolks, water, lemon peel, and vanilla. Beat until smooth. Beat egg whites and cream of tartar in a large bowl with an electric mixer on high speed until stiff peaks form. Gently fold egg yolk mixture over beaten egg whites with spatula until just blended. Pour into an ungreased 10-inch tube pan. Bake at 325°F. for 1¼ hours or until the top springs back when touched lightly. Remove from oven. Invert on funnel and let hang until cake is cold. Remove from pan.

FROSTING: Mix all ingredients until smooth. Frost cooled cake.

NOTE: Sweetened whipped cream may be substituted for frosting.

Preparation: 30 minutes
Cooking: 1¼ hours

Serves: 12
Can be frozen

Fingerklgtschen (Almond Cookie)

⅔ cup butter, softened
½ cup sugar
2 egg yolks
½ teaspoon almond extract
1¾ cups sifted all-purpose flour

½ teaspoon salt
Red jelly, strawberry, raspberry,
  currant, etc.
Confectioners' sugar,
  to sprinkle

Cream butter and sugar. Add egg yolks and beat until light. Add extract, flour, and salt. Mix well. Shape into balls and put on cookie sheet. Press tip of finger into center of each ball. Bake at 325°F. for 8 minutes. When cool, fill fingerprints with jelly and sprinkle confectioners' sugar over cookies.

Preparation: 15 minutes
Cooking: 8 minutes

Yield: 3 dozen
Can be frozen

Greek Butter Cookies
Not too sweet and very attractive

2 cups sweet butter, softened
¾ cup sugar
1 egg, separated
½ cup milk
1 teaspoon vanilla

1½ ounces whiskey or cognac
3 teaspoons baking powder
5 cups all-purpose flour
   (approximately)
½ cup sesame seeds

Cream butter and sugar beating until fluffy. Continue beating while adding egg yolk, milk, vanilla, and whiskey. Add baking powder. Then slowly add flour. Continue adding flour until dough is no longer sticky. Remove from bowl and knead about 5 minutes. Using approximately 1 tablespoon of dough for each cookie, roll it into a thin piece and twist or make a small loop at the top and braid right end under left, then left over right. The finished cookie should be about 3 inches long. Place on greased cookie sheet. Brush with beaten egg white and sprinkle with sesame seeds. Bake at 350°F. for 12 minutes or until golden brown.

Preparation: 1¼ hours
Cooking: 12 minutes

Yield: 4½ dozen
Can be frozen

Date-Nut Treat
These cookies are chewy and delicious

1 cup butter
1½ cups sugar
3 eggs, lightly beaten
1 pound pitted dates, finely cut
2 cups chopped nuts

2½ cups all-purpose flour
1 teaspoon cinnamon
½ teaspoon ground cloves
1 teaspoon baking soda
3 teaspoons hot water

Cream butter and sugar. Add eggs and beat mixture lightly. Stir in dates and nuts. Sift flour and spices together. Dissolve soda in hot water. Add flour and soda mixture to creamed mixture. Beat well. Drop by spoonfuls on greased cookie sheets. Bake at 350°F. for 10-12 minutes or until lightly browned.

Preparation: 20 minutes
Cooking: 10-12 minutes

Yield: About 6 dozen
Can be frozen

Cereal Cookies

1 cup butter or margarine
1 cup sugar
1 cup brown sugar, firmly packed
2 eggs
1 teaspoon vanilla
1 teaspoon baking soda
2 cups all-purpose flour

½ teaspoon baking powder
½ teaspoon salt
2 cups rolled oats (1 minute or
    regular, not instant)
2 cups crisped rice cereal
1 cup shredded coconut

Cream butter or margarine and sugars. Add eggs and vanilla. Sift dry ingredients together and add to mixture. Mix in oats, cereal, and coconut. Dough will be crumbly. Roll into 1-inch balls or drop by teaspoons onto greased cookie sheets. Bake at 350°F. for 10-11 minutes.

NOTE: This recipe halves beautifully.

Preparation: 30 minutes
Cooking: 10-11 minutes

Yield: 8 dozen
Can be frozen

Date Balls

½ cup butter
1 cup sugar
½ pound dates, finely chopped
1 egg, well beaten
1½ cups crisped rice cereal

½ cup walnuts or pecans
Pinch of salt
½ teaspoon vanilla
1 cup shredded coconut

Melt butter and sugar in top of double boiler (or heavy saucepan over moderate-low heat). Cool. Add dates and well-beaten egg. Cook for 15 minutes over rapidly boiling water or until mixture thickens. Stir carefully to avoid scorching. Add remaining ingredients, except coconut. Mix well. Refrigerate for 1 hour. Roll mixture into 1-inch balls. Then coat with coconut.

NOTE: These keep best if refrigerated as they tend to soften too much at room temperature. Also, they may be frozen for up to 3 months.

Preparation: 15 minutes
Cooking: 20 minutes

Yield: 3-4 dozen
Can be frozen

Chocolate Dipped Tea Logs
Rich and nutty

COOKIES:

1 cup sugar
1 cup butter or margarine,
  softened
3 ounces cream cheese, softened
1 egg yolk

2½ cups all-purpose flour
1 cup finely chopped walnuts
½ teaspoon salt
½ teaspoon lemon peel,
  fresh or dried

DIP:

6 ounces semi-sweet chocolate
1 tablespoon orange-flavored
  liqueur

Ground nuts, for dipping

COOKIES: Cream sugar, butter or margarine, and cream cheese in a large bowl until light and fluffy. Beat in egg yolk. Stir in flour, walnuts, salt, and lemon peel. Cover and refrigerate at least 2 hours. Shape about 1 tablespoon of dough into a log, 2-inches long and 1-inch thick. Repeat with remaining dough. Place on ungreased cookie sheets. Bake at 325°F. for 12 minutes or until light brown. Cool on wire racks.

DIP: Melt chocolate and orange-flavored liqueur together. Dip ends of baked logs into chocolate, then ground nuts. Let stand on wire racks until chocolate sets.

Preparation: 15 minutes
Cooking: 12 minutes

Yield: About 8 dozen
Can be frozen

Chocolate Macaroons

1 (14 ounce) can sweetened
  condensed milk
2 ounces unsweetened chocolate
2 cups coconut, shredded
1 cup chopped nuts

1 tablespoon coffee,
  strongly brewed
1 teaspoon vanilla
⅛ teaspoon salt

Combine milk and chocolate in top of double boiler. Place over boiling water on high heat and stir constantly until mixture thickens, about 5 minutes. Add remaining ingredients and stir to blend. Drop by teaspoons onto oiled or greased baking sheet. Bake at 350°F. for 10 minutes or until bottoms are set. Be careful not to burn as macaroons should be soft and chewy. Transfer to wax paper lined rack and cool completely.

Preparation: 30 minutes
Cooking: 8-10 minutes

Yield: 2-2½ dozen
Can be frozen

Lemon Melting Moments

⅔ cup cornstarch
1 cup all-purpose flour

½ cup confectioners' sugar
1 cup unsalted butter

FROSTING:

6 tablespoons unsalted butter
1½ tablespoons lemon juice

1½ cups confectioners' sugar
1-2 drops yellow food coloring

With an electric mixer, cream sugar and butter. Add cornstarch and flour which have been sifted together. Refrigerate cookie dough until cool enough to form a log about 1½-inches round. Cut cookies about ⅛-¼-inch wide. Place on ungreased cookie sheet. Bake at 325°F. for 10-12 minutes. Cookies should not be brown.

FROSTING: Mix ingredients in food processor. When cookies are cool, frost by either spreading frosting on top or using two cookies and frosting in between, sandwich-style.

Preparation: 45 minutes
Cooking: 10-12 minutes

Yield: 50 cookies
Can do ahead

Mandel Kager

Spicy cardamom flavor

COOKIES:

½ cup + 6 tablespoons
   margarine, softened
6 tablespoons sugar
1 egg
1⅔ cups all-purpose flour

½ teaspoon baking powder
1 tablespoon cinnamon
1½ teaspoons powdered
   cardamom
½ cup chopped toasted almonds

GLAZE:

1 egg yolk

1 tablespoon water

Mix margarine, sugar, and egg. Sift flour, baking powder, cinnamon, and cardamom. Stir into margarine mixture. Mix in toasted almonds. Chill dough 1 hour. Shape into 1-inch balls. Place on ungreased baking sheet. Mix egg yolk and water. Flatten cookies slightly and brush with glaze. Bake at 375°F. for 10-12 minutes.

NOTE: If desired, top with almond half or sliver before baking.

Preparation: 20 minutes
Cooking: 10-12 minutes

Yield: 3-4 dozen
Can be frozen

Swedish Oatmeal Cookies

COOKIE:

½ cup shortening or margarine
½ cup sugar
½ cup brown sugar, firmly packed
1 egg
½ teaspoon vanilla

¾ cup all-purpose flour
½ teaspoon salt
½ teaspoon baking soda
1½ cups rolled oats (quick or old-fashioned)

TOPPING:

⅓ cup sugar
¼ cup butter or margarine
1 tablespoon light corn syrup

⅓ cup chopped almonds
⅛ teaspoon almond extract

COOKIE: In large bowl, cream shortening, sugars, egg, and vanilla. Combine flour, salt, and baking soda. Stir into creamed mixture. Stir in rolled oats. Drop cookie dough by rounded teaspoonfuls 2 inches apart onto ungreased baking sheets. Bake at 350°F. for 8 minutes.

TOPPING: In small pan, combine sugar, butter, and corn syrup. Bring to a boil. Remove from heat. Stir in almonds, and extract. Remove cookies from oven. Spoon scant ½ teaspoon topping onto center of each cookie. Return to oven and bake an additional 6-8 minutes until bubbly and brown. Cool before removing from cookie sheets.

NOTE: If toppping bubbles over top of cookie, use less on each. Toasting almonds before chopping makes cookies doubly delicious.

Preparation: 45 minutes
Cooking: 14-16 minutes

Yield: 3 dozen
Can be frozen

Madeleines

1 cup butter
¾ cup sugar
2 eggs, separated
1 cup all-purpose flour

1 tablespoon lemon juice
1 tablespoon lemon rind
Confectioners' sugar, to coat cookie

Cream butter, sugar, and egg yolks in mixer at medium speed. Add flour, egg whites, lemon juice, and lemon rind. Beat on low speed. Butter madeleine pans well. Fill each shell to half its height (about 1 heaping teaspoon). Bake at 325°F. for 20 minutes. When done, let cool for 5 minutes before removing cookies from pan. Cover each cookie completely with confectioners' sugar when cool.

Preparation: 20 minutes
Cooking: 20 minutes

Yield: 3 dozen
Can be frozen

Rugalach
It's not the easiest cookie to make but it's worth the time and effort

DOUGH:

1 cup butter, softened
8 ounces cream cheese, softened
¼ cup sugar

Pinch of salt
2 cups all-purpose flour

FILLING:

1 (12 ounce) jar apricot jam
Raisins, to sprinkle

1 egg, beaten

TOPPING:

1 cup crushed walnuts
½ cup sugar

1 teaspoon cinnamon

DOUGH: Cream butter, cream cheese, sugar, and salt. Gradually beat in flour. The dough will be very stiff. Divide dough in half and chill for at least 1 hour. Roll out ½ of the dough at a time on a well floured board (dough is very sticky). Roll to ⅛-inch thickness.

FILLING: Spread apricot jam on the dough. Sprinkle on a handful of raisins. Cut the dough into strips 1½ x 3-inches. Roll each strip up and brush with egg.

TOPPING: Mix walnuts, sugar, and cinnamon. Roll each strip in the nut mixture and place on ungreased cookie sheet. Bake at 325°F. for 20 minutes. Remove from sheet immediately.

Preparation: 2 hours
Cooking: 20 minutes

Yield: 3-4 dozen
Can be frozen

Pecan Puffs

½ cup butter, beat until soft
2 tablespoons sugar, added until creamy

1 cup pecan nut meats, ground
1 cup sifted cake flour

Stir pecans and flour into butter mixture. Roll dough into small balls. Place on greased baking sheet. Bake in slow oven (300°F.) for 45 minutes. Roll while hot in powdered sugar. When cool, roll again.

NOTE: These burn very easily, so check them while they are baking.

Mrs. C. V. Whitney

Mrs. Cornelius Vanderbilt Whitney
The Whitneys reside at Cady Hill House, Saratoga Springs.

Chocolate Nut Heaven

BROWNIE:

1 cup butter or margarine
1½ cups sugar
3 eggs
1 teaspoon vanilla
2½ squares unsweetened
   chocolate, melted

1 cup sifted all-purpose flour
½ teaspoon baking powder
1 cup coarsely chopped walnuts

ICING:

1½ cups sifted confectioners'
   sugar
2 tablespoons sweet butter,
   melted

1 square unsweetened chocolate,
   melted
1 teaspoon vanilla
2 tablespoons sour cream

BROWNIE: Cream margarine or butter and sugar thoroughly in a large mixing bowl. Gradually add eggs, vanilla, and melted chocolate. In a separate bowl, combine flour and baking powder. Add dry ingredients to wet ingredients. Mix thoroughly by hand. Stir in walnuts. Spread into a greased 6 x 11-inch glass baking pan. Bake at 400°F. for 15 minutes. Reduce heat to 350°F. and bake an additional 15 minutes. Brownies should not be very wet or very dry but should be firm. Test consistency with a toothpick. Remove from oven. Cool and cut into squares. Top with icing.

ICING: Mix all icing ingredients together thoroughly. Spread on brownies.

Preparation: 30 minutes
Cooking: 30 minutes

Yield: 2 dozen
Can be frozen

Grandma Creble's Lacy Oatmeal Cookies
This is a light, delicate cookie

½ cup margarine, softened
1 cup sugar
1 egg, beaten
1 cup quick oats
4 tablespoons all-purpose flour

⅓ teaspoon salt
1 teaspoon vanilla
1½ teaspoons baking powder
½ cup chopped nuts (optional)

Cream margarine and sugar. Add egg and all other ingredients. Mix well. Cover cookie sheet with aluminum foil. Drop by ⅓ teaspoonfuls onto cookie sheet, 2-3 inches apart. Bake at 350°F. for 10 minutes. Let cookies cool on foil and then peel off. Use new foil for each batch.

Preparation: 30 minutes
Cooking: 10 minutes

Yield: 5 dozen
Can do ahead

Sugar Cookies
The nutmeg makes the difference

4 cups all-purpose flour	1½ cups sugar
1 teaspoon baking powder	1 egg
½ teaspoon each: baking soda, salt, nutmeg	½ cup sour cream
	1 teaspoon vanilla
1 cup butter or margarine, softened	¼ cup sugar

Sift flour with baking powder, baking soda, salt, and nutmeg. Set aside. In large bowl, beat butter, sugar, and egg until light and fluffy. Beat in sour cream and vanilla. Add flour mixture gradually. Combine well. Form dough into ball. Wrap in foil. Refrigerate overnight. Using ¼ dough at a time, roll on floured surface to ¼-inch thickness. Cut out cookies with 2½-inch cookie cutters. Sprinkle tops with sugar. Lightly grease cookie sheet. Bake at 375°F. for 10-12 minutes. Cool on wire racks.

Preparation: 30 minutes
Cooking: 10-12 minutes

Yield: 5-6 dozen
Can be frozen

Oatmeal Crunchies
Great for snacks and lunch boxes

1 cup sifted all-purpose flour	½ cup shortening
½ cup sugar	1 egg
½ teaspoon baking powder	¼ teaspoon vanilla
½ teaspoon baking soda	¾ cup quick-cooking, rolled oats
¼ teaspoon salt	¼ cup chopped walnuts
½ cup brown sugar, firmly packed	Sugar, for dipping (optional)

Sift together flour, sugar, baking powder, baking soda, and salt. Add brown sugar, shortening, egg, and vanilla. Beat well. Stir in rolled oats and walnuts. Form dough into small balls (dough will be crumbly). Dip tops in a little additional sugar if desired. Place cookies on ungreased cookie sheet. Bake at 375°F. for 10-15 minutes.

Preparation: 15 minutes
Cooking: 10-15 minutes

Yield: About 3½ dozen
Can be frozen

Nighty-Nights

2 egg whites
⅔ cup sugar
1 cup walnuts, chopped

1 cup semi-sweet chocolate chips
1 teaspoon vanilla
Pinch of salt

Preheat oven to 350°F. Beat egg whites in medium bowl until stiff peaks form. Gradually beat in sugar. Stir in walnuts, chocolate chips, vanilla, and salt. Line two cookie sheets with aluminum foil or brown paper cut to fit sheet. Drop batter by teaspoons onto cookie sheet (no more than 12 to a sheet). Place cookie sheets in oven, close door, and <u>turn oven off.</u> Leave in overnight. Remove fully baked cookies in the morning.

NOTE: If in a hurry, these can be baked at 250°F. for 40 minutes, removed to a wire rack, cooled, served or stored in an airtight container. Do not make these when the weather is humid.

Preparation: 15 minutes
Cooking: 8-10 hours

Yield: 15-24 cookies
Can do ahead

Aunt Carrie's Sand Tarts

1 cup butter, softened
2 cups sugar
2 eggs, reserving 1 egg white
2½-3 cups all-purpose flour

Cinnamon, to sprinkle
Sugar, to sprinkle
Walnut pieces, for centers

Cream butter, sugar, and eggs (reserving 1 egg white) until light and fluffy. Add flour gradually mixing well to form a soft dough. Form dough into a ball and chill in refrigerator at least ½ hour. Roll out on floured surface to about ½-inch thickness. Cut out in circles with the floured edge of a glass or cookie cutter. Brush tops with reserved egg white. Sprinkle with cinnamon and sugar. Place a walnut piece in the center of each cookie. Bake on ungreased cookie sheet at 350°F. for 8-10 minutes.

NOTE: Cookies may be cut into other shapes and decorated as desired.

Preparation: 2 hours
Cooking: 8-10 minutes

Yield: 5-6 dozen
Can be frozen

Caramel Oatmeal Squares

2 cups rolled oats
2 cups all-purpose flour
1½ cups brown sugar, firmly
   packed
½ teaspoon salt
1 teaspoon baking soda

1 cup margarine, melted
1 (14 ounce) package caramels
½ cup evaporated milk
1 (6 ounce) package semi-sweet
   chocolate chips

Mix all dry ingredients. Add in the margarine. Press half of this mixture into bottom of a greased 9 x 13-inch baking pan. Bake at 350°F. for 10 minutes. Meanwhile, melt caramels in saucepan with evaporaed milk. Remove baking pan from oven. Spread all of caramel mixture evenly on top of the baked oatmeal mixture. Sprinkle chocolate chips on top of caramel mixture. Then cover with remaining half of oatmeal mixture. Bake at 350°F. for 20 minutes or until golden brown. Cool before cutting into desired size squares.

Preparation: 20 minutes
Cooking: 30 minutes

Yield: 2-3 dozen squares
Can do ahead

Raspberry Squares

BOTTOM LAYER:
1 cup all-purpose flour
1 teaspoon baking powder
½ cup butter or margarine,
   softened

1 tablespoon milk
½ cup raspberry jam

TOP LAYER:
1 egg
4 tablespoons melted butter
1 cup sugar

2 cups coconut
1 teaspoon vanilla

BOTTOM LAYER: Sift flour and baking powder together. Add butter and milk, mixing well. Spread mixture in ungreased 8 x 8-inch pan. Cover with raspberry jam.

TOP LAYER: Beat egg with melted butter. Mix in sugar, coconut, and vanilla. Spread mixture over jam. Bake at 375°F. for 30 minutes or until top is golden brown. Cool at least 1 hour. Cut into squares.

Preparation: 20 minutes
Cooking: 30 minutes

Yield: 16 squares
Can be frozen

Frosted Pumpkin Bars

BARS:

4 eggs	2 cups all-purpose flour
1⅔ cups sugar	2 teaspoons baking powder
1 cup oil	2 teaspoons cinnamon
1 (16 ounce) can pumpkin pie filling	1 teaspoon salt
	1 teaspoon baking soda

FROSTING:

3 ounces cream cheese, softened	1 teaspoon vanilla
½ cup butter, softened	2 cups sifted confectioners' sugar

BARS: Beat together eggs, sugar, oil, and pumpkin filling until light and fluffy. Stir together flour, baking powder, cinnamon, salt, and soda. Add to pumpkin mixture and mix thoroughly. Spread batter in ungreased 15 x 10 x 1-inch cookie sheet. Bake at 350°F. for 25-30 minutes.

FROSTING: Cream together cream cheese and butter. Stir in vanilla. Add confectioners' sugar. Beat well until mixture is smooth. Frost cooled pumpkin layer and cut into bars.

Preparation: 30 minutes

Cooking: 30 minutes

Yield: 6 dozen bars

Serve immediately

Pecan Bars
Like mini-pecan pies

CRUST:

½ cup dark brown sugar, firmly packed

1 cup all-purpose flour

½ cup butter, melted

FILLING:

2 eggs

1 cup dark brown sugar, firmly packed

1 cup chopped pecans

¼ teaspoon salt

½ teaspoon baking powder

CRUST: Mix together dark brown sugar, flour, and melted butter. Pat into greased and floured 8 x 8-inch baking pan. Bake at 350°F. for 15 minutes.

FILLING: Beat eggs and add remaining ingredients, mixing well. Spread over crust. Bake at 350°F. for 15 minutes. When cool, cut into bars. They should be moist and chewy.

NOTE: These will keep in a covered tin indefinitely.

Preparation: 15 minutes

Cooking: 30 minutes

Yield: 2 dozen bars

Can be frozen

Nicholas Brownies
It's an unbeatable combination of flavors

BROWNIES:
1¼ cup butter, melted
¾ cup baking cocoa
½ cup instant cocoa mix
1 cup sugar

1½ cups brown sugar, firmly
   packed
5 eggs, slightly beaten
2 cups all-purpose flour
1½ teaspoons baking powder

FILLING:
¾ cup butter
3 cups confectioners' sugar

4 tablespoons crème de menthe

TOPPING:
6 tablespoons butter

6 ounces semi-sweet chocolate
   chips

BROWNIE: Mix butter, cocoa, instant cocoa mix, sugars, and eggs in a large bowl. Add the flour and baking powder. Mix well. Bake in greased 9 x 13-inch pan at 325°F. for 30-40 minutes. Cool.

FILLING: Melt butter and mix sugar. Stir in crème de menthe. Spread over cooled brownies.

TOPPING: Melt butter and chocolate chips together. Spread over filling.

Preparation: 20 minutes
Cooking: 30-40 minutes

Yield: 48 small brownies
Can do ahead

Grace's Brownies

½ cup raisins
Water
½ cup butter
2 squares unsweetened chocolate
1 cup sugar

2 eggs
½ cup all-purpose flour
1 teaspoon baking powder
1 cup walnuts
1 teaspoon vanilla

Cook raisins about 5 minutes in small saucepan with enough water to cover. Drain. Melt butter and chocolate. <u>By hand,</u> cream sugar and eggs together. Add flour and baking powder. Add chocolate mixture. Mix well. Add nuts, vanilla, and raisins. Pour batter in a greased and floured 8 x 8-inch pan. Bake at 350°F. for 25-30 minutes. Cool and cut into squares.

Preparation: 10 minutes
Cooking: 25-30 minutes

Yield: 12-16 squares
Can do ahead

George Washington's Secrets
A nice change from chocolate

CRUST:

2¼ cups sifted all-purpose flour
½ cup sugar

1 cup butter, softened

FILLING:

2 eggs
1 cup brown sugar, firmly packed
½ teaspoon each: salt, baking
  powder, vanilla

½ cup chopped maraschino
  cherries (about 20 cherries,
  drained, liquid reserved)
½ cup chopped walnuts
½ cup flaked coconut (optional)

FROSTING:

1 tablespoon butter
1 cup confectioners' sugar

Cherry liquid
Additional coconut, if desired

CRUST: Mix flour, sugar, and butter until crumbly. Press into an ungreased 9 x 13-inch pan. Bake at 350°F. for 20 minutes or until lightly browned.

FILLING: Blend eggs, brown sugar, salt, baking powder, and vanilla. Add cherries, walnuts, and coconut. Place on baked crust. Bake at 350°F. for 25 minutes. Cool.

FROSTING: Combine butter, confectioners' sugar, and enough cherry liquid to make mixture spreadable. Frost when filling is cooled. Sprinkle with additional coconut if desired. When frosting has set, cut into bars.

Preparation: 30 minutes
Cooking: 45 minutes

Yield: About 2 dozen bars
Can be frozen

DESSERTS & PIES

Pie à la Mode

Desserts have always held a special place in the tastes of Albany residents. A world-famous dessert, pie à la mode, had its origin in a small town, Cambridge, not far from Albany.

The story goes that one day in the 1890's, a Professor Townsend was eating his dinner at the Hotel Cambridge. The waitress, Mrs. Berry Hall, observed that he was eating ice cream with his apple pie. Perhaps because of his scholarly, continental background, Professor Townsend replied that, yes he enjoyed his pie "à la mode."

Shortly thereafter, the professor visited New York City, taking with him a yearning for his favorite dessert, new name and all. At the fashionable Delmonico's, he nonchalantly ordered Pie à la Mode. When the waiter stated that he had never heard of such a thing, the professor expressed great astonishment.

"Do you mean to tell me that so famous an eating place as Delmonico's has never heard of Pie à la Mode, when the Hotel Cambridge, up in the village of Cambridge, New York, serves it every day? Call the manager at once. I demand as good service here as I get in Cambridge!"

The manager came running, and Professor Townsend repeated his remarks.

"Delmonico's never intends that any other restaurant shall get ahead of us," said the manager, and ordered that Pie à la Mode be featured on the menu every day.

A newspaperman representing the *New York Sun* was seated at a nearby table and heard the conversation. The next day, the *Sun* carried a feature story of the incident, and it was picked up by many other newspapers. In no time at all, Pie à la Mode became standard on menus all over the country.

While world fame cannot be assured, the desserts presented here are bound to enhance the reputation of any cook.

Easy and Quick Baklava

BAKLAVA:

1 cup butter, melted	1 teaspoon cinnamon
2 cups ground nuts	¼ teaspoon nutmeg
½ cup sugar	1 pound phyllo pastry

SYRUP:

1½ cups water	6-8 whole cloves
1 cup sugar	2 cinnamon sticks
½ cup honey	Peel of ½ orange or lemon
1 teaspoon lemon juice	

BAKLAVA: Brush bottom of 9 x 13-inch baking pan with some butter, reserving remainder to paint phyllo leaves. Mix together nuts, sugar, cinnamon, and nutmeg. Fold four leaves of phyllo in half. Fit in pan and paint with butter. Sprinkle with some of nut mix. Repeat, using two leaves of phyllo each time until nut mixture is finished. End with phyllo. Paint with butter and score into squares with sharp knife. Bake at 350°F. for 1 hour or until golden.

SYRUP: Combine all ingredients in saucepan. Bring to boil. Reduce heat and simmer 10 minutes. Cool to room temperature. Cut through scored lines of baklava. Strain syrup and pour over (it will bubble a little). Let stand 8-24 hours before serving.

NOTE: Frozen phyllo pastry leaves can be purchased at specialty food stores. Thaw before using. Keep covered with a damp towel to prevent them from drying.
Do not refrigerate baked baklava. It will keep 10 days tightly wrapped at room temperature.

Preparation: 30 minutes   **Yield:** 20-40 pieces
Cooking: 1 hour   Can do ahead

Pots de Crème

1¼ cups half and half cream or milk	1 (12 ounce) package semi-sweet chocolate chips
2 eggs	3 tablespoons brandy

Scald cream or milk. Beat eggs in blender or food processor. Add remaining ingredients and blend until smooth. Spoon into small dessert glasses or dishes. Chill for at least 3 hours before serving.

Preparation: 5 minutes   **Serves:** 6-8
Cooking: 5 minutes   Must do ahead

Bananas Foster

½ cup butter
½ cup brown sugar, firmly packed
4 firm bananas, peeled and cut
   lengthwise

½ teaspoon ground cinnamon
½ cup banana-flavored liqueur
1 cup rum
1 pint vanilla ice cream

In a medium saucepan, heat butter and sugar until mixture becomes a smooth syrup. Add bananas and stir until they are well coated. Sprinkle on cinnamon. Quickly pour in liqueur and rum, heat and ignite, burning off alcohol. After flames burn out, serve banana mixture over vanilla ice cream.

NOTE: Heat the mixture quickly after adding liqueur and rum, and light immediately, or the alcohol will burn off from the stove heat. If you don't want to flambé at the table, heat the liqueur and rum thoroughly, then add to banana mixture. If alcohol isn't cooked out either by flambé-ing or heating, the whole mixture tastes of alcohol.

Preparation: 15 minutes
Cooking: 15 minutes

Serves: 4
Serve immediately

Crème Brûlée

3 cups heavy cream
6 tablespoons sugar
6 egg yolks

2 teaspoons vanilla
Peanut brittle, to garnish

In a double boiler, heat cream. Add sugar, stirring until dissolved. In a separate bowl, beat egg yolks until light. Gradually, pour hot cream into egg yolks, mixing constantly to blend. Add vanilla. Pour into individual baking dishes (custard cups or ramekins). Place dishes in a larger baking pan filled with enough water to nearly reach the top of the individual baking dishes. Bake at 300°F. for 35 minutes or until a clean knife inserted comes out clean. Remove from oven, cool individual dishes, and refrigerate until ready to use. Just before serving, sprinkle crushed peanut brittle on top.

NOTE: You may substitute 1 teaspoon vanilla and 1 teaspoon rum or orange-flavored liqueur instead of 2 teaspoons vanilla.

Preparation: 20 minutes
Cooking: 35 minutes

Serves: 6-8
Must do ahead

Crêpe Soufflé

CRÊPE:

3 eggs
½ cup all-purpose flour
½ cup milk

¼ teaspoon salt
2 tablespoons butter, melted
2 tablespoons sugar

TOPPING:

1 tablespoon butter
1 tablespoon lemon juice
2 tablespoons sliced almonds
2 tablespoons confectioners' sugar

1 pound fresh strawberries or
  raspberries, cleaned, sliced,
  and sweetened in ¼ cup sugar
1 cup heavy cream, whipped

CRÊPE: Beat eggs well. Slowly add flour, beating constantly. Stir in milk, salt, melted butter, and sugar. Grease a 9-inch quiche dish or pie pan. Pour batter in pan. Bake at 450°F. for 12-15 minutes until brown and puffy. Remove crêpe from oven and add topping.

TOPPING: Melt butter with lemon juice in a small pan while the crêpe is cooking. When crêpe is removed from oven, quickly sprinkle it with the almonds and confectioners' sugar. Drizzle the lemon juice-butter mixture over the crêpe and cut into quarters at the table. Top with berries and serve. Pass whipped cream separately.

Preparation: 15 minutes
Cooking: 15 minutes

Serves: 4
Serve immediately

Cherry Cheese Custard

1 (21 ounce) can cherry pie filling
2 cups creamed cottage cheese
1 cup sour cream
½ cup sugar

2 teaspoons grated orange rind
1 teaspoon vanilla
2 eggs

Spoon pie filling into 8 x 8-inch baking dish. Set aside. In blender, at medium speed, blend cottage cheese and remaining ingredients until smooth. Carefully pour cheese mixture over pie filling, covering filling completely. Bake at 350°F. for 1 hour or until custard is set.

NOTE: It is best if served within 2 hours

Preparation: 30 minutes
Cooking: 1 hour

Serves: 6
Can do ahead

Strawberry Ginger

3 (10 ounce) packages frozen
  strawberries
3 cups heavy cream

1 cup brown sugar
½ teaspoon ground ginger

Defrost and drain strawberries. Whip cream until stiff. Mix brown sugar with ginger and fold into whipped cream. Fold berries in lightly. Chill for at least 1 hour.

NOTE: Frozen raspberries may be substituted for strawberries.

Preparation: 20 minutes

Serves: 8-12
Must do ahead

Cranberry Yogurt Pops

1 (16 ounce) container plain
  yogurt
1 (6 ounce) can frozen
  concentrate cranberry juice,
  thawed

2 tablespoons honey
1 teaspoon vanilla
12 freezer popsicle containers

Combine all the ingredients and blend together with wire whisk until mixture is smooth. Pour into containers. Freeze about 6 hours.

Preparation: 10 minutes

Yield: 12 pops
Must do ahead

Café Suprème

2 cups heavy cream
1 teaspoon instant coffee powder
½ cup coffee-flavored liqueur
4 tablespoons sugar

2 egg whites
4 teaspoons sugar
Cinnamon, for decoration

Beat heavy cream with coffee powder until stiff but not dry. Add coffee liqueur and 4 tablespoons sugar and beat until <u>very</u> stiff. Beat egg whites to soft peaks in a separate, small bowl. Add 4 teaspoons sugar to egg whites and beat until stiff. Fold egg whites into whipped cream mixture. Mound the mixture in 12 dessert glasses. Decorate with cinnamon to taste.

NOTE: This can be made a day ahead and chilled until ready to serve.

Preparation: 25 minutes

Serves: 12
Can do ahead

Lemon Parfait

½ cup fresh lemon juice   1 cup sugar
    (about 3 lemons)   Pinch of cream of tartar
1 tablespoon grated lemon rind   1 cup heavy cream
3 eggs, separated   3 tablespoons confectioners' sugar

Combine lemon juice, half of lemon rind, egg yolks, and ½ cup sugar in a small saucepan. Beat well. Cook over moderate heat, stirring constantly until thick (do not boil). Transfer to a large bowl and cool. In a small bowl, beat egg whites with cream of tartar until they hold soft peaks. Add remaining sugar, 1 tablespoon at a time, until stiff peaks are formed. Fold egg white mixture into egg yolk-lemon mixture. Whip cream until it holds stiff peaks. Beat in confectioners' sugar. Fold whipped cream into lemon mixture. Pour into dessert glasses or dishes. Garnish with remaining lemon rind. Chill in freezer at least 2 hours.

NOTE: Keep in freezer for several months until needed and thaw before using.

Preparation: 30 minutes   **Serves:** 8
                                      Can be frozen

Aesop's Grapes

3 pounds seedless green grapes   Dark brown sugar, to sprinkle
1 pint sour cream

Wash and drain grapes. Add sour cream to cover. Chill for about 3 hours. Serve in individual bowls. Pass brown sugar to sprinkle on grapes.

Preparation: 15 minutes   **Serves:** 4-6
                                      Must do ahead

Petite Raspberry Tarts

½ cup butter, softened   1 cup all-purpose flour
3 tablespoons confectioners' sugar   ¼ cup good quality raspberry jam

Cream butter and sugar. Add flour. Mix well. Press dough into the bottom of 24 mini-cupcake tart pans. Bake at 350°F. for 10-15 minutes until light brown. Cool. Remove from pan. Fill with jam.

Preparation: 15 minutes   **Yield:** 24
Cooking: 15 minutes   Can do ahead

Dacquoise au Chocolat
"One of the finest and most elusive desserts in any great city,
it is a joy to look at and heavenly to eat."

MERINGUE:

8 egg whites, at room temperature
11 tablespoons granulated sugar

1⅓ cups finely ground hazelnuts

BUTTER CREAM:

6 extra large egg whites, at room
   temperature
1¾ cups superfine sugar
2 cups sweet butter, at room
   temperature

3 ounces sweet chocolate, melted
1 tablespoon water

TOPPING:

⅓ cup finely ground hazelnuts

MERINGUE: Beat 8 egg whites with an electric beater until they stand in peaks. Very gradually, add ½ of the granulated sugar. Continue beating meringue until it feels smooth, not grainy, when rubbed between fingers. Fold in ground hazelnuts and the remaining granulated sugar into the meringue. Place meringue in a pastry bag with a number 4 star tip. Squeeze out meringue in a neat spiral to completely fill three 9-inch circles. Use 2 greased and floured cookie baking sheets. Fill in any empty spots in the meringue circle. Smooth over the meringue with a spatula. Each circle should be of equal thickness and equal size. Do not discard any unused meringue, but squirt it out onto the baking sheet with the one circle on it (extra meringue can be crumbled and used later for garnish). Place both baking pans in a <u>preheated</u> 350°F. oven. Immediately turn off the oven heat. Leave in oven for 8-10 hours or overnight. Remove from oven and gently run a spatula under the meringue to free it from the pan. Each meringue will be ¼-½-inch high.

BUTTER CREAM: With a wire whisk, beat egg whites in a bowl which is set in a basin of hot water. Gradually add sugar. Continue beating rapidly until the mixture is somewhat thickened. The mixture temperature must be 105°F. A ribbon should form from the lifted whisk when it is done. Next, place bowl holding egg whites in a bowl of ice water. Start beating now with an electric mixer at high speed. Beat for 20 minutes or until the meringue is at room temperature. Very gradually, add butter, one pat at a time, beating constantly. Combine melted chocolate and water and blend it into the butter cream. If it gets too soft, put it in the refrigerator to firm. It makes 5-6 cups butter cream.

TO ASSEMBLE: Select the nicest of the 3 meringue circles for the top layer. Set it aside. Spread a layer of butter cream on one of the meringue circles. Add a second circle on top and spread butter cream on top. Add the reserved top meringue circle. Spread butter cream on the top and sides of the dacquoise. Return butter cream to refrigerator if it becomes too soft to hold its shape while assembling the dacquoise layers. Crush any leftover meringue pieces into fine crumbs and mix with remaining ⅓ cup ground hazelnuts. Coat sides of dacquoise with this mixture and sprinkle any leftover nuts on top. Last, sprinkle the top with confectioners' sugar. Chill the dacquoise for 2 hours to facilitate slicing. It may also be wrapped tightly and frozen up to 2 months.

NOTE: The meringue may also be baked on greased and floured, foil-lined cookie sheets in a 275°F. oven for 1 hour. At the end of the 1 hour, turn off the oven and let meringues remain in oven, with door closed, for 2½ hours. Then remove from oven and carefully peel off the foil from the baked meringue.

Preparation: 3½ hours   **Serves:** 12-16
Cooking: 3½ hours plus   Can be frozen

Minetry's Miracle
Sinfully delicious

2 cups sweet butter
2 cups sugar
1 dozen eggs, separated
4 dozen (10 ounces) small
   amaretti (Italian macaroons)
1 cup bourbon

4 squares unsweetened chocolate,
   melted
1 teaspoon vanilla
1 cup chopped pecans
2 dozen lady fingers, split
1½ cups heavy cream, whipped

Cream butter and sugar together until light and fluffy. Beat egg yolks until light and whisk them into the creamed mixture. Soak the amaretti in bourbon until soft. Beat chocolate into the butter mixture. Add vanilla and pecans. Beat egg whites until stiff but not dry and fold into the chocolate mixture. Line a 10-inch spring-form pan around the sides and bottom with split lady fingers. Alternate bourbon-soaked amaretti with chocolate mixture in the lined pan. Chill overnight. Remove sides of pan and decorate top with whipped cream.

NOTE: Shaved semi-sweet chocolate makes a nice garnish. Make 5-7 days ahead so the bourbon taste mellows!

Preparation: 45 minutes   **Serves:** 16-20
Cooking: 5 minutes   Can be frozen

Flan
"It's always been a big hit."

¾ cup sugar for caramel
5 eggs
1 cup sugar

1 (13 ounce) can evaporated milk
1 teaspoon vanilla
1 teaspoon salt

Make caramel by placing ¾ cup sugar in frying pan and heat very slowly to melting point, breaking lumps of sugar with wooden spoon. Cook till golden brown, thick and clear. Clarity is crucial, for if caramel becomes dark it is bitter. Pour hot caramel into mold or baking pan. Tip mold to coat bottom and all sides. Set aside.

Put all other ingredients into blender, blend thoroughly. Pour into mold. Put 1 inch of water in larger baking pan. Set mold inside this pan. Bake at 350°F. for 1½ hours or until set. Test with knife. When knife comes out dry, flan is ready.

Dana Kennedy

Wife of Pulitzer Prize winner, William Kennedy,
author of *Ironweed* and other books about Albany

Strawberry Yogurt Sherbet

1½ cups water
½ cup honey
8 teaspoons lemon juice
1 (10 ounce) package frozen
  strawberries

1 (¼ ounce) envelope
  unflavored gelatin
1½ cup yogurt, plain
  or strawberry-flavored

In a saucepan, combine water, honey, lemon juice, and strawberries. Cook a few minutes to combine ingredients. Drain, from the strawberry mixture, ½ cup strawberry syrup into a small saucepan. Sprinkle gelatin evenly over syrup. Cook over low heat, stirring constantly, until gelatin is dissolved. Stir gelatin mixture, strawberries, and remaining syrup with yogurt until well combined. Cover bowl and freeze mixture until partially frozen, about 1½ hours. With a mixer at medium speed, beat mixture until smooth but still frozen. Be sure to scrape bowl with rubber spatula. Cover and freeze 2 hours longer or until firm.

NOTE: If too firm, let sherbet stand at room temperature for 10 minutes for easier serving.

Preparation: 20 minutes

Serves: 6
Can be frozen

Spiced Fruit Compote

1 (15¼ ounce) can pineapple
  chunks
1 (1 pound 13 ounce) can peach
  halves
1 (1 pound) can apricot halves
½ cup butter, melted

⅔ cup brown sugar, firmly packed
¼ teaspoon ground cloves
¼ teaspoon cinnamon
1 teaspoon curry powder,
  or to taste

Drain fruits well. Arrange in layers in a medium casserole or 9-inch pie plate. Combine butter, sugar, and spices and sprinkle over fruit. Bake at 350°F. for 1 hour. Serve hot over vanilla ice cream.

NOTE: Can also be served as a side dish with ham or beef.

Preparation: 15 minutes
Cooking: 1 hour

Yield: 8 servings
Can do ahead

Cold Peach Soufflé

1 (12 ounce) package frozen
  sliced peaches, thawed
1 envelope gelatine
½ cup peach syrup
4 eggs, separated
¼ cup water
1 tablespoon lemon juice

⅛ teaspoon salt
¼ teaspoon almond extract
½ cup sugar
1 cup heavy cream, whipped,
  or substitute whipped topping
  mix whipped with milk

Drain syrup from peaches into top of double boiler and set slices aside. Sprinkle gelatine on peach syrup to soften. Beat egg yolks and water together. Add to gelatine mixture. Cook over boiling water, stirring constantly until gelatine is dissolved, about 5 minutes. Remove from heat and stir in lemon juice, salt and almond extract. Chill slightly. Sieve peaches or mash in blender. Mix into gelatine mixture. Beat egg whites until stiff. Beat in sugar. Fold in gelatine mixture. Fold in whipped cream (or whipped topping mix). Turn into a 1½-quart soufflé dish and chill until firm.

NOTE: To serve soufflé with a collar, use a 1-quart soufflé dish. Cut a strip of brown paper about 4 inches deep and long enough to go around dish. Fasten strip around outside edge and secure with scotch tape, allowing to extend 2 inches above the top of dish. Brush inside of strip with oil. When soufflé is firm, loosen tape and peel paper away gently.

Mrs C. V. Whitney

Mrs. Cornelius Vanderbilt Whitney
The Whitneys, well-known in social circles and the thoroughbred racing world, reside at Cady Hill House, Saratoga Springs

Michigan Hot Fudge Sauce

1 (14 ounce) can sweetened
    condensed milk
14 ounces light corn syrup (use
    milk can as a measure)

12 ounces milk chocolate
½ pound butter

Combine ingredients in saucepan over low heat. Stir constantly until combined and thickened. Do not boil.

NOTE: Mixture thickens as it cools. Reheat over low heat. Refrigerate and use for up to 2 weeks.

Preparation: 5 minutes
Cooking: 10 minutes

Yield: 4 cups
Can do ahead

Pistachio Cream Eclairs

ÉCLAIRS:
1 cup water
½ cup butter
¼ teaspoon salt

1 cup all-purpose flour
4 eggs

FILLING:
1 (3 ounce) package pistachio
    instant pudding

1 cup milk
1½ cups heavy cream, whipped

GLAZE:
½ cup semi-sweet chocolate
    chips
1½ teaspoons milk

1 teaspoon butter
1½ teaspoons light corn syrup

ÉCLAIRS: Heat water, butter, and salt until mixture boils. Reduce heat and stir in flour until it forms a ball. Let cool and beat in eggs, one at a time, with a wooden spoon. By hand or using a pastry bag, make éclairs about 3 inches long and 1 inch wide. Place éclairs on a greased cookie sheet. Bake at 375°F. for 40 minutes. Remove éclairs from oven and cut a slit in the top of each. Return to oven and bake 10 minutes more. Cool.

FILLING: Combine pudding mix and milk until slightly thick. Add whipped cream and chill.

GLAZE: Combine all ingredients in a double boiler and melt.

TO ASSEMBLE: Fill éclairs with filling and frost tops with glaze. They can be safely frozen up to 3 months before serving.

Preparation: 45 minutes
Cooking: 1 hour

Serves: 12
Can be frozen

Lustrous Chocolate Frosting
A smooth, shiny, and rich frosting

2 (1 ounce) squares unsweetened
   chocolate
1 cup sugar
3 tablespoons cornstarch

Dash of salt
1 cup boiling water
3 tablespoons butter
1 teaspoon vanilla

Melt chocolate squares in double boiler. Combine sugar, cornstarch, and salt in a bowl. When chocolate is melted, place top part of double boiler directly on burner. Quickly add boiling water, then sugar-cornstarch-salt mixture, stirring constantly. Bring to a boil. Remove from heat when thickened. Blend in butter and vanilla.

NOTE: When frosting boils, it will "spit" so wearing a glove will protect your hand. Combining of ingredients should be done quickly. Ice cake while frosting is warm.

Preparation: 5 minutes
Cooking: 20 minutes

Yield: Frosts 1 (2-layer) cake
Can be frozen

Tart Strawberry Mousse

¼ cup orange juice
1 (¼ ounce) envelope unflavored
   gelatin
1 pint strawberries, cleaned and
   hulled

4 tablespoons sugar,
   to taste
1 cup sour cream

In a small saucepan, mix orange juice with unflavored gelatin. Heat until gelatin is dissolved and the juice mixture is clear. Purée the hulled strawberries in a food processor or blender. Add sugar and gelatin mixture. Continue to process until well blended. Add sour cream and process to thoroughly blend. Taste the mixture and blend in more sugar, if you wish. Remove mousse into soufflé dishes or stemmed wine glasses. Refrigerate at least 3 hours before serving.

Preparation: 25 minutes
Cooking: 10 minutes

Serves: 4
Must do ahead

Zula Inglese

VANILLA PUDDING:

⅓ cup sugar
2 tablespoons cornstarch
⅛ teaspoon salt
2 cups milk

2 egg yolks, slightly beaten
2 tablespoons butter, softened
2 teaspoons vanilla

CHOCOLATE PUDDING:

½ cup sugar
⅓ cup cocoa
2 tablespoons cornstarch
⅛ teaspoon salt

2 cups milk
2 egg yolks, slightly beaten
2 teaspoons vanilla

LIQUEUR MIXTURE:

½ cup sweet vermouth
¼ cup Grand Marnier, crème de
   cacao, or your favorite liqueur

¼ cup water

1 package lady fingers, about 24

VANILLA PUDDING: In a 2-quart saucepan, blend sugar, cornstarch, and salt. Combine milk and egg yolks. Gradually stir egg-milk mixture into sugar mixture. Cook over medium heat until mixture thickens and boils. Stir constantly. Boil for 1 minute. Remove from heat. Add butter and vanilla.

CHOCOLATE PUDDING: In a 2-quart saucepan, blend sugar, cornstarch, and salt. Combine milk and egg yolks. Gradually stir egg-milk mixture into sugar mixture. Cook over medium heat until mixture thickens and boils. Stir constantly. Boil for 1 minute. Remove from heat. Add vanilla.

LIQUEUR MIXTURE: Mix all ingredients in a bowl. Soak lady fingers in liqueur mixture (they soak up quickly so be careful not to have them fall apart).

TO ASSEMBLE: In a clear glass bowl, alternate layers of vanilla pudding, lady fingers soaked in liqueur mixture (arrange as many as you can fit close together), chocolate pudding, and then another layer of liqueur soaked lady fingers. Repeat layers until the glass bowl is filled. Spoon some extra liqueur on top and chill.

Preparation: 30-45 minutes
Cooking: 10-15 minutes

Serves: 8-10
Can do ahead

English Plum Pudding

A sensational, rich, fruity, "meaty" dessert. The contributor's family tradition holds that it is the same recipe used by Mrs. Bob Cratchit in Dickens' *A Christmas Carol*

PUDDING:

1 pound beef suet, membranes
  removed, chopped fine
1 pound seedless raisins
1 pound dried currants
1 pound sugar
1 pound all-purpose flour
¾ pound mixed citron, orange,
  and lemon peel, dried and
  cut fine

4 eggs, beaten
2 teaspoons ground cinnamon
2 teaspoons ground nutmeg
1 teaspoon ground allspice
  (optional)
1¾ cups milk

HARD SAUCE:

1 egg, beaten
1 cup sugar

⅓ cup sweet butter, melted
1 teaspoon vanilla

PUDDING: Mix all ingredients in a large bowl. Cover lightly and refrigerate overnight to swell. Pour contents onto a 1-yard square, clean cloth. Gather the corners of the cloth around to form a bag allowing room for swelling, and tie tightly around gather with string. Place in a large 3-4-gallon pot and cover with boiling water. Boil gently for 7 hours. Remove pudding in bag, drain, and hang at least 1 week. Three hours before serving, repeat boiling process. Remove bag from pot, cut away cloth, and place pudding on platter to serve with hard sauce.

HARD SAUCE: Combine beaten egg and sugar. Beat in melted butter. Add vanilla and beat until stiff. Chill for at least 1 hour. Pass in a separate bowl to top plum pudding.

NOTE: A loop in the string after tying the cloth can be fastened to the handle of the pot to assist in the removal of the hot pudding when boiling has been completed. The pudding may be hung for months if kept in a dark place. To flame for serving, heat ½ cup brandy gently, light it, pour over pudding, and serve while still ablaze.

Preparation: 2 hours
Cooking: 7 hours

Serves: 14-20
Must do ahead

Raisin and Rice Custard Pudding

¼ cup butter, softened
½ cup sugar
½ cup brown sugar, firmly packed
4 eggs
1 teaspoon vanilla

2 cups milk
1 teaspoon cinnamon
2 cups cooked rice
1 cup raisins

Mix butter, sugars, eggs, vanilla, milk, and cinnamon in a blender. Grease a 2-quart casserole or soufflé dish and pour in mixture. Stir in cooked rice and raisins. Bake at 350°F. for 45 minutes.

NOTE: Top with a dab of whipped cream or maple syrup, to serve.

Preparation: 10 minutes
Cooking: 45 minutes

Serves: 10
Serve immediately

Raspberry Bavarian Pie

CRUST:
⅓ cup butter
½ cup sugar
⅓ teaspoon salt

1 egg yolk
1 cup all-purpose flour
⅓ cup finely chopped almonds

FILLING:
1 (10 ounce) package frozen
  raspberries, partially thawed
  and drained
2 egg whites
1 cup sugar

1 tablespoon lemon juice
¼ teaspoon vanilla
¼ teaspoon almond extract
⅛ teaspoon salt
1 cup heavy cream

CRUST: Cream butter, sugar, and salt until fluffy. Add yolk and beat thoroughly. Mix in flour and almonds. Press into greased 10-inch pie pan. Bake at 400°F. for 12 minutes. Cool.

FILLING: Place all ingredients for filling, except cream, in large bowl. Beat up to 15 minutes until mixture thickens and expands in volume. Whip cream and fold into raspberry mixture. Spoon into pastry crust. Freeze for at least 8 hours. Remove from freezer 15-20 minutes before serving.

NOTE: Garnish with raspberries if desired. Pie may be made with strawberries instead of raspberries.

Preparation: ½ hour
Cooking: 12 minutes

Serves: 8
Must be frozen

Peggy's Pie
A rich mocha, mousse-like dessert

CRUST:
1¼ cups ground amaretti or ground coconut macaroons
⅓ cup sugar
⅓ cup unsalted butter, melted

½ square (½ ounce) unsweetened chocolate, melted
½ cup finely chopped Macadamia nuts

FILLING:
½ cup unsalted sweet butter, softened
¾ cup brown sugar, firmly packed
1 square (1 ounce) unsweetened chocolate, melted and cooled

2 teaspoons instant coffee powder
2 eggs

TOPPING:
1¼ cups heavy cream
2 tablespoons strong coffee, cold
1 tablespoon confectioners' sugar

¼ teaspoon vanilla
Shaved sweet chocolate, for garnish (optional)

CRUST: Mix amaretti crumbs, sugar, and butter. Stir in chocolate and nuts. Spread over bottom and sides of a well-buttered 9-inch pie plate. Bake at 400°F. for 40 minutes. Cool.

FILLING: In a large mixing bowl, cream butter and sugar until light and fluffy. Add chocolate and coffee powder. Beat well. Beat in eggs, one at a time, beating for 5 minutes after each egg. Spoon into prepared crust. Cover and refrigerate 6 hours or overnight.

TOPPING: Whip cream until soft peaks form. Add coffee, sugar, and vanilla. Beat until stiff. Spread over pie before serving. Garnish with shaved sweet chocolate, if desired.

NOTE: This pie must be made at least 6 hours before serving. The crust and filling can be made up to 2 days in advance.

Preparation: 30 minutes
Cooking: 5 minutes

Serves: 8
Must do ahead

Irish Coffee Pie
Light, flavorful and dietetic

Vegetable cooking spray
⅓ cup graham cracker crumbs
¼ cup skim milk
1 (¼ ounce) envelope unflavored
  gelatin
⅔ cup skim milk
2 eggs, separated
¼ cup plus 3 tablespoons sugar
Dash of salt

1 tablespoon instant coffee
  powder
2 tablespoons Irish whiskey
1 teaspoon vanilla
1⅔ cups cottage cheese
⅛ teaspoon cream of tartar
1 tablespoon sliced almonds
1 tablespoon semi-sweet
  chocolate chips, chopped

Spray 9-inch pie pan with vegetable cooking spray. Spread graham cracker crumbs in bottom of pan. Set aside. Pour ¼ cup skim milk in blender or food processor. Add gelatin. Scald ⅔ cup skim milk. Pour in and process about 2 minutes until gelatin is dissolved. Add egg yolks, ¼ cup plus 1 tablespoon sugar, salt, instant coffee, whiskey, and vanilla. Process 30 seconds. Add cheese. Process 1 minute until smooth. Pour into bowl. Chill 1 hour. Beat egg whites and cream of tartar with electric mixer in small bowl. Add remaining 2 tablespoons sugar and beat until stiff peaks form. Fold in cottage cheese mixture. Blend well. Pour into prepared pan. Chill until firm. Garnish with almonds and chocolate chips.

Preparation: 1½ hours

Serves: 8
Must do ahead

Brownie Bourbon Pie

BROWNIE:

1 package brownie mix (or your
  own recipe)

2 tablespoons bourbon

TOPPING:

5 egg yolks
¾ cup sugar
2 (¼ ounce) envelopes
  unflavored gelatin

¼ cup cold water
⅔ cup bourbon
4 cups heavy cream

BROWNIE: Bake brownie mix according to package directions in 10-inch pie pan. DO NOT OVERBAKE. When slightly cool, drizzle about 2 tablespoons bourbon over brownie. Set aside.

TOPPING: Beat egg yolks until thick and lemon-colored. Slowly beat in sugar. Soften gelatin in cold water. Add ⅓ cup bourbon and heat mixture

in double boiler until gelatin is dissolved. Pour mixture into yolks, stirring briskly. Stir in remaining bourbon. Whip heavy cream and fold into egg mixture. Refrigerate cream mixture until firm, about 20-30 minutes. Then put mixture into a pastry bag, if available, and pipe on top of brownie, or spread over brownie with a large spoon. Return to refrigerator briefly to set.

Preparation: 1 hour
Cooking: ½ hour

Serves: 8
Must do ahead

Chocolate Mousse Pie

CRUST:
3 cups chocolate wafer crumbs (or 2 packages of chocolate wafers)

½ cup unsalted butter, melted

FILLING:
1 pound semi-sweet chocolate squares
2 whole eggs
4 egg yolks

2 cups heavy cream
6 tablespoons confectioners' sugar
4 egg whites, at room temperature

TOPPING:
1-2 cups heavy cream

Grated or shaved chocolate, for garnish

CRUST: Combine crumbs and butter. Press onto bottom and completely up sides of a 10-inch spring-form pan. Refrigerate 30 minutes.

FILLING: Soften chocolate in top of a double boiler. Let cool to lukewarm (95°F.). Add 2 whole eggs and 4 egg yolks. Beat until thoroughly blended with a whisk or, if possible, use an electric mixer. Whip cream and confectioners' sugar until soft peaks form. Beat 4 egg whites until stiff but not dry. Stir a little of the cream and egg whites into chocolate to lighten. Fold remaining cream and egg whites into chocolate mixture until completely incorporated. Turn into shell. Chill 6 hours or overnight.

TOPPING: Top with 1-2 cups of whipped cream. Decorate with grated or shaved chocolate or leftover chocolate wafer crumbs.

NOTE: Whip the cream ahead of time. Pie can be frozen without whipped cream topping and removed to refrigerator 2 hours before serving.

Preparation: 1-1½ hours

Serves: About 12
Can be frozen

Chocolate-Walnut Pie
Good after a light meal or as part of a dessert buffet

1 (9 inch) unbaked pie shell
¾ cup semi-sweet chocolate
   chips
1 cup chopped walnuts
½ cup butter
⅔ cup brown sugar, firmly packed

½ cup all-purpose flour
2 eggs
1 teaspoon vanilla or bourbon
½ cup heavy cream
Confectioners' sugar

Sprinkle chocolate chips evenly over bottom of pie shell. Sprinkle walnuts over the chocolate chips. In a medium saucepan, melt butter. Remove from heat. Add brown sugar and flour, beating with a wire whisk until smooth. Add eggs, vanilla or bourbon and beat again until glossy and smooth. Pour mixture over walnuts and chocolate chips, spreading carefully to cover the walnuts. Bake at 350°F. for 30-35 minutes. Do not overbake! Allow to cool. Whip cream with confectioners' sugar and serve with pie.

NOTE: This is a rich pie so small servings are best.

Preparation: 10 minutes
Cooking: 30-35 minutes

Serves: 8-10
Can be frozen

Tarte Tatin
It's deceivingly simple yet elaborately delicious

PIE:
2 tablespoons butter
1½ cups sugar
6-7 tart apples, peeled, sliced

1 crust pie dough, prepared
   or your own

TOPPING:
½ cup heavy cream

1 teaspoon vanilla

Butter glass baking dish, 9 inches in diameter, with 1 tablespoon of butter. Cover bottom of dish with 1 cup sugar. Arrange one neatly overlapping row of apple slices on sugar. Fill dish with remaining apples, level, not heaped. Sprinkle sugar with remaining ½ cup sugar, or to taste. Dot with remaining 1 tablespoon butter. Press pie dough with fingers into 9-inch circle on wax paper. It is not necessary to roll it. Cover dish with dough. Bake at 375°F. about 45 minutes until apples are golden and sugar begins to carmelize. Watch carefully as carmelization happens quickly. Remove from oven and loosen crust all around with a knife. Immediately put a serving platter upside down over dish, turn over, and remove baking dish.

TOPPING: Whip heavy cream with vanilla. Serve pie hot or at room temperature and pass whipped cream to top.

NOTE: Glass dish is necessary to preserve taste of the apples and to aid in determining carmelization time. You may wish to line oven rack with foil as apple liquid may overflow dish.

Preparation: 20 minutes
Cooking: 45 minutes

Serves: 8
Can do ahead

Mocha Magic

PIE:
24 chocolate sandwich cookies, crushed
⅓ cup butter, melted

½ gallon coffee ice cream, softened

SAUCE:
3 ounces unsweetened chocolate
2 tablespoons butter
1 cup sugar
Dash of salt

2 (5½ ounce) cans evaporated milk
½ teaspoon vanilla

TOPPING:
1½ cups heavy cream
1½ ounce coffee-flavored liqueur

Confectioners' sugar, to taste

PIE: Butter a 9-inch pie plate. Combine cookie crumbs with butter and press into pie plate. Refrigerate ½ hour. Spoon softened ice cream onto cookie crumbs and freeze.

SAUCE: Melt chocolate and butter in double boiler. Add sugar, salt, and evaporated milk. Bring mixture to a boil, stirring. When thickened, remove from heat and add vanilla. Chill for ½ hour. Spread on top of ice cream and freeze for at least 4 hours.

TOPPING: Whip cream with coffee-flavored liqueur and confectioners' sugar. Serve on top of pie.

NOTE: The pie and sauce can be frozen for at least 1 week. Add topping just before serving.

Preparation: 30 minutes
Cooking: 15 minutes

Serves: 12
Must do ahead

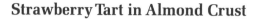

Strawberry Tart in Almond Crust

CRUST:

5 ounces finely ground blanched almonds (can be ground in food processor)

½ cup unsalted butter, at room temperature

4 tablespoons sugar

1½ cups all-purpose flour

1 egg, beaten

½ teaspoon vanilla

FILLING:

Approximately 3 pints of perfectly ripe strawberries

1 (6 ounce) jar red currant jelly

1 tablespoon unflavored gelatin

¼ cup orange-flavored liqueur

CRUST: Thoroughly blend all the crust ingredients together. Press into a 9-inch tart pan with a removable bottom, taking care to keep the crust thickness uniform. Chill for 30 minutes. Bake at 350°F. for 15-20 minutes. Crust should be golden. Cool.

FILLING: Hull berries and arrange them upside down in the tart pan. If you have enough berries, you may put one on top of another toward the center. Prepare a glaze by melting the jelly, gelatin, and liqueur in a saucepan. Stir over low heat until jelly is melted. Spoon or brush over berries.

NOTE: The tart can be decorated at the last minute with a few flowers. Do not refrigerate unless necessary; bring to room temperature before serving.

Preparation: 45 minutes
Cooking: 20 minutes

Serves: 6-8
Can do ahead

Frozen Strawberry Pie

4 egg whites
⅛ teaspoon salt
½ cup sugar
1½ tablespoons lemon juice
1½ cups mashed and sweetened
  strawberries, fresh or frozen
1 cup heavy cream

⅓ cup sugar
1 teaspoon vanilla
1 (9 inch) graham cracker
  pie crust
Strawberries, for garnish
  (optional)

Beat egg whites with salt, sugar, lemon juice, and berries until stiff (about 15 minutes). Whip cream with ⅓ cup sugar and vanilla. Fold whipped cream into strawberry mixture. Pour into the graham cracker pie crust. Freeze. Cut just before serving. Garnish with sliced strawberries if desired.

NOTE: This recipe makes a lot of filling so there will be some left over from a 9-inch pie. A 10-inch pie crust can be substituted or the extra filling can be put into a freezer pan or individual cups and frozen to be eaten as ice cream.

Preparation: 40 minutes

Serves: 6-8
Must be frozen

Velvet Hammer

1 quart vanilla ice cream
3 tablespoons coffee-flavored
  liqueur

3 tablespoons dark rum
Fresh whole coffee beans,
  for garnish

Use the metal blade in a food processor to combine ice cream, liqueur, and rum. Process until ice cream is soft and creamy. Transfer the mixture to a container and freeze 4-6 hours or overnight. At serving time, spoon mixture into brandy snifters or glass dessert bowls. Top each with a coffee bean.

NOTE: Shiny coffee beans look best. This may be made in a blender but if doing so, soften the ice cream first and process in 2 batches.

Preparation: 15 minutes

Serves: 6-8
Must do ahead

Snappy Pumpkin Pie
This tastes even better the second day—if it lasts that long

CRUST:

1½ cups gingersnap cookie crumbs (about 35 cookies)

4 tablespoons butter, melted

FILLING:

1 (¼ ounce) envelope unflavored gelatin

½ cup water

⅓ cup sugar

½ teaspoon each: salt, cinnamon, allspice

¼ teaspoon ginger

¼ teaspoon nutmeg

½ cup milk

3 eggs, separated

1 cup pumpkin pie filling

¼ cup sugar

2 cups heavy cream

Vanilla, to taste

Confectioners' sugar

CRUST: Combine crumbs and melted butter. Press into 9-inch pie plate. Bake at 350°F. for 10-15 minutes. Set aside. You may wish to reserve some crumbs for garnish.

FILLING: Dissolve gelatin into the ½ cup water in large saucepan over medium heat. Add ⅓ cup sugar, salt, and all the spices. Stir well. Add milk, slightly beaten egg yolks, and pumpkin filling. Cook and stir over medium heat until mixture comes to a boil. Remove from heat and stir vigorously for a few moments. Allow this mixture to cool in the refrigerator (in saucepan) while you beat egg whites until soft peaks form. Gradually blend in ¼ cup sugar. Fold egg white-sugar mixture into cooked pumpkin mixture. Set aside. Whip heavy cream, adding confectioners' sugar and vanilla to taste. To layer, spoon ½ of pumpkin mixture into crust, then ½ the whipped cream. Repeat layers ending with whipped cream. Garnish with gingersnap cookie crumbs, if desired, or a bit of nutmeg.

Preparation: 1¼ hours

Cooking: 10-15 minutes

Serves: 10-12

Can do ahead

Cape Cod Pie
A zingy Thanksgiving favorite

3½ cups cranberries, chopped
1½ cups sugar
1½ tablespoons all-purpose flour
¼ teaspoon salt
3 tablespoons water

2 tablespoons butter
¼-½ cup chopped walnuts
2 (9 inch) pie crusts, for top
   and bottom

Mix cranberries, sugar, flour, salt, and water. Melt butter and add to cranberry mixture. Add walnuts. Pour filling into a 9-inch unbaked pie crust. Criss-cross strips of pie crust dough on top of filling, moistening edges if necessary so that top crust will adhere to bottom crust. Then press edges with fork. Bake at 450°F. for 10 minutes. Then bake at 350°F. for 40 minutes more.

Preparation: 30 minutes
Cooking: 50 minutes

Serves: 6-8
Can do ahead

Strawberry Parfait Pie

1 (3 ounce) package lemon-
   flavored gelatin
Hot water
1 pint strawberry ice cream,
   softened

1 (10 ounce) package frozen
   strawberries, thawed and
   drained, reserve juice
1 (9 inch) pie crust, baked
Fresh strawberries, garnish
Whipped cream, garnish

Dissolve gelatin in hot strawberry juice to which enough hot water has been added to make 1¼ cups. Add ice cream by spoonfuls, stirring until melted. Add thawed strawberries (halve any large berries). Place in refrigerator to set and stir every 30 minutes until almost firm. Pour into baked crust. Garnish with fresh strawberries and whipped cream.

Preparation: 20 minutes
Cooking: 5 minutes

Serves: 6
Can do ahead

Praline Pumpkin Custard Pie

SHELL:

⅓ cup pecans, chopped

⅓ cup brown sugar

3 tablespoons butter

1 (9 or 10 inch) unbaked pie shell

FILLING:

3 eggs, slightly beaten

½ cup sugar

½ cup brown sugar, firmly packed

2 tablespoons all-purpose flour

¾ teaspoon salt

¾ teaspoon cinnamon

½ teaspoon ginger

¼ teaspoon ground cloves

¼ teaspoon mace

1½ cups cooked pumpkin

1½ cups half and half cream, warmed

SHELL: Combine pecans, sugar, and butter. Press gently into bottom of pie shell. Prick with fork. Bake at 450°F. for 10 minutes. Cool.

FILLING: Combine eggs, sugars, flour, salt, and spices. Add pumpkin and mix well. Mix in half and half cream. Turn into baked and cooled pie shell. Bake at 350°F. for 50-60 minutes or until knife inserted in center of pie comes out clean.

Preparation: 30 minutes

Cooking: 60-70 minutes

Serves: 8

Can be frozen

GIFTS FROM THE KITCHEN

The Cider Industry, Pretzels

In colonial Albany, people had to be self-sufficient. They built their own houses and barns; they spun, wove, and sewed their own clothing; and, of course, they grew, processed, cooked, and preserved their own food.

One example of a widely-used homemade product is cider. When the early Dutch discovered that their transplanted European apple trees produced fruit useful only when pressed and made into cider, the industry blossomed. Cider became hard naturally and was stored easily. One only needed to add sugar to increase potency and improve keeping quality.

Over 100 drinks and home remedies were made from cider. A 1767 survey in the Colonies estimated cider consumption at "more than a keg (5 gallons) a day for each person." In the kitchen, cider was used for jellies, pies, soups, and sauces. It basted hams and moistened mincemeat. As a curative, it was believed to strengthen the heart and alleviate hay fever, hardening of the arteries, insomnia, and nervous breakdowns. It supposedly would stop gangrene, ease childbirth, and, served hot, cure bronchitis. No social function or special celebration was complete without it. A toast with hard cider was frequently offered at weddings, baptisms, and funerals. And, a barrel of cider awaited all voters emerging from the polling place.

Concern over excessive drinking began to mount in the early 1800's. John Adams is reported to have said, "If the ancients drank wine as our people drink rum and cider, it is no wonder we hear of so many possessed with devils." Churches, employers, and housewives all rejoiced when an apple blight, nicknamed "Temperance," wiped out almost all the cider orchards in New York State.

During the course of the 19th century, expanding industries freed people from the necessity of having to produce everything for themselves. More and more goods were available ready-made, and "store-bought" became the norm. Recently, there has been a trend to valuing handmade, homemade things again. And what could be a nicer gift than one which requires personal time?

The recipes for homemade gifts presented here run the gamut from simply fun to simply elegant. One recipe, for Soft Pretzels, has an historic footnote in Albany. In 1652, Jochem Wassels, an Albany baker, and his wife were arrested for selling the salty twists to the local Indians, who would pay almost any price for them. The Wassels' crime? Using good flour to make pretzels for "the heathen." One thing is sure: your homemade gift, whether pretzels or otherwise, will be warmly received–with no threat of reprisals from the authorities!

Candy Strawberries
You can still serve "strawberries" even if they're not in season

2 (3 ounce) packages wild
    strawberry-flavored gelatin
1 cup ground pecans
1 cup flaked coconut
½ teaspoon vanilla

¾ cup sweetened condensed milk
A few drops red food coloring
Red decorator's sugar
Slivered almonds
A few drops green food coloring

Mix thoroughly gelatin, pecans, coconut, vanilla, milk, and red food coloring. Chill for 1 hour. Mold into strawberry shape and roll in decorator's sugar. Tint almonds with green food coloring. Add to strawberries as leaves.

NOTE: They can be attractively presented on top of green cellophane grass in a fruit straw basket as if they were real berries.

Preparation: 1½ hours

Yield: 1-2 dozen
Can do ahead

Herbal Stocking Stuffers
A simple, attractive gift

1 (2 ounce) bottle dried parsley
    flakes
1 (2 ounce) bottle dried leaf
    chervil
1 (2 ounce) bottle freeze-dried
    chives
1 (2 ounce) bottle dried leaf
    tarragon

4 (6 inch) wooden taster spoons
4 (12 inch) pieces decorative
    ribbon, no wider than ¾-inch
4 gummed labels about 1-inch
    wide by 2-inches long

Combine parsley, chervil, chives, and tarragon. Mix well. Soak empty spice bottles in warm water to remove labels. Dry bottles and place ¼ of spice mixture in each bottle. Put the following label on each bottle: FINE HERBS–for scrambled eggs and omelettes, herbed butter, meat, vegetable or fish sauces, broiled chicken. Tie wooden spoon to neck of spice bottle with decorative ribbon.

Preparation: 15 minutes

Yield: 4 gifts

Cranberry and Fruit Relish
It's zesty, tasty, and pretty on the table

4 cups fresh cranberries
1 navel orange, unpeeled and
  quartered
1 apple or pear, quartered and
  cored

½ cup dates, pitted
1-1½ cups sugar

Pick over cranberries. Coarsely chop orange, apple or pear, and dates. You may use a meat grinder or food processor. Sweeten to taste. Refrigerate up to 1 week until ready to use.

Preparation: 20 minutes

Yield: 4 cups
Can do ahead

Italian Seasoning
Adds pizzazz

¼ cup grated Parmesan cheese
¾ teaspoon oregano

¼ teaspoon parsley
½ teaspoon salt

Combine all ingredients. Store in closed glass container in a cool place for 2-3 weeks.

NOTE: Adds dimension to buttered noodles, salads, clear soups, and meatloaf.

Preparation: 3 minutes

Yield: ¼ cup
Can do ahead

Swedish Nuts

4 cups (1 pound) walnut halves
2 egg whites
1 cup sugar

Dash of salt
½ cup butter or margarine

Toast nuts on cookie sheet in 325°F. oven for 10-15 minutes or until light brown. Cool nuts. Beat egg whites, adding sugar and salt, until stiff peaks form. Mixture will be grainy. Fold toasted nuts into meringue. Melt butter or margarine on cookie sheet. Spread nuts over melted butter. Bake at 325°F. for 30-40 minutes. Stir every 10 minutes, or until nuts are coated and no butter remains on pan. Cool.

Preparation: 10 minutes
Cooking: 50 minutes

Yield: 4 cups
Can be frozen

Homemade Vanilla

5 whole vanilla beans
1½ cups dark rum

1 jar, 8 inches high and 3 inches
in diameter

Place vanilla beans loosely in bottom of jar. Pour dark rum on top. Mark the liquid level on the jar. Cover jar tightly and place in cupboard or other dark place for eight weeks. Do not peek or open jar. After the beans have soaked, use the vanilla according to recipes. When the vanilla gets half way down from the level marked on jar, add enough dark rum to reach the original level again. You do not have to wait to use the vanilla.

NOTE: The beans will last many years. Discard only when they lose their color or no longer color the liquid.

Preparation: 5 minutes   Must do ahead

Kids' Claydough
It occupies children for hours

1 cup all-purpose flour
1 cup water
½ cup salt

1 tablespoon oil
2 tablespoons cream of tartar
Food coloring

Mix ingredients in a saucepan over medium heat. Work it until stiff. Cool on a cookie rack. If desired, leave out food coloring until after dough cools and let the children mix in a drop or two of coloring with their fingers.

NOTE: This keeps for 2-3 months in a plastic bag or airtight container.

Preparation: 5 minutes   **Serves:** 1 child
Cooking: 5 minutes   Can do ahead

Soft Pretzels
The entire family, young and old, can enjoy making pretzels

7-8 cups unsifted all-purpose
    flour
2 tablespoons sugar
1 tablespoon salt
2 packages dry yeast
¼ cup margarine or shortening,
    softened

2⅔ cups very hot tap water
    or milk
Vegetable oil
1 egg yolk
2 tablespoons water
Coarse salt

In a large bowl, thoroughly mix 2½ cups flour, sugar, salt, and undissolved yeast. Add margarine and very warm tap water or milk. Beat with electric mixer at medium speed for 2 minutes. Scrape down sides of bowl. Add 1 cup more of flour. Beat with electric mixer at high for 1 minute. Keep scraping bowl sides. Stir in the remaining 3½ cups flour. Measure 1 more cup of flour. Use this flour, if necessary, to turn dough into stiff dough and for flouring the board and your hands. This is the eighth cup. DO NOT use more than 8 cups of flour. Knead dough for 10 minutes. Cover with plastic wrap and then a dry towel. Let dough rise for 20 minutes. Punch down. Place dough in a plastic bag and refrigerate a minimum 45 minutes or up to a maximum 2 days.

TO FORM PRETZELS: Remove dough from refrigerator and bring dough to room temperature. Lightly flour a board or cloth and roll dough to measure 12 x 15 inches. Using a long, sharp knife, cut dough into 30 strips, each measuring 12 x ½ inches. Line cookie sheets with foil and lightly grease them. One at a time, form the pretzels as shown in the diagram below: Be sure to leave about 1 inch between the pretzels on the cookie sheet. Brush tops with oil or egg mixture (1 egg yolk and 2 tablespoons water). Sprinkle lightly with coarse salt (not table salt). Bake at 375°F. for 20-25 minutes, or until nicely browned. Serve warm with mustard or store in airtight container or freezer.

Preparation: 25 minutes
Cooking: 20-25 minutes

Yield: 30
Must do ahead

Strawberry Jam
Surprise everyone with fresh strawberry jam in the middle of winter

2 (10 ounce) packages frozen
   strawberries, thawed
2¾ cups sugar
1 (1¾ ounce) package powdered
   fruit pectin

¾ cup water
4-6 (½ pint) jelly glasses

Mash or finely chop strawberries (do not purée). Mix in sugar until dissolved. Set aside for 20 minutes, stirring occasionally. In a large saucepan, mix pectin with water. Boil 1 minute stirring constantly. Add sugared berries to the hot pectin. Stir 3 minutes. Pour into sterilized jelly glasses. Cover and let stand 24 hours. Refrigerate until ready to use.

NOTE: Jam may also be frozen.

Preparation: 1 hour
Cooking: 1 minute

Yield: 4-6 half pints
Must do ahead

Three Berry Jam

1 pound fresh sweet dark red
   cherries, pitted and coarsely
   chopped
1 quart fresh raspberries, washed
1 quart fresh strawberries, hulled
   and coarsely chopped

5 cups sugar
Juice of 1 large or 2 small
   fresh lemons
8 (½ pint) jelly glasses

Put fruit in a large pot and cover with sugar. Let stand overnight. In morning, bring fruit to a rolling boil. Boil hard for 10 minutes, stirring as needed. Add lemon juice and boil for 5 more minutes. Pour into sterilized jelly glasses and seal.

Preparation: 24 hours
Cooking: 15 minutes

Yield: 8 half pints
Must do ahead

Hot Pepper Jelly
It goes well with lamb

½ cup hot peppers, seeded and ground
¾ cup bell peppers, seeded, and ground
6½ cups sugar

1½ cups apple cider vinegar
Green food coloring
1 (6 ounce) bottle liquid fruit pectin
8 (½ pint) jelly glasses

In a large saucepan, combine hot peppers, bell peppers, sugar, and vinegar. Bring to a hard boil. Remove from heat and let stand 5 minutes. Add a few drops of green food coloring and stir. Pour into 8 sterilized jelly glasses and seal.

NOTE: Spread a bit of this on cream cheese and serve with crackers for an easy, delicious appetizer.

Preparation: 1 hour
Cooking: 10 minutes

Yield: 8 half pints
Must do ahead

Red Pepper Relish
Festive looking for the holidays

12 medium sweet red peppers
1¼ teaspoons salt
2½ cups sugar

2 cups white vinegar
6 (½ pint) jelly glasses

Finely chop red peppers. Add salt and let stand for 3 hours. Add sugar and vinegar. Cook, stirring frequently, for 2½ hours. It will thicken. Pour relish, boiling hot, into sterilized jelly jars and seal.

NOTE: Serve over cream cheese with crackers.

Preparation: 3 hours
Cooking: 2½ hours

Yield: 6 half pints
Must do ahead

RESTAURANTS & CATERERS

Immigration

One undeniable fact about the population of Albany is its astonishing diversity. From 1609, when Henry Hudson established the presence of the Dutch here, an endless parade of ethnic and racial groups has passed through. The settlement of Fort Orange, which was to become Albany, was predominantly Dutch through the colonial period, even after the British had taken over. This heritage remains evident in the names of local towns and streams—Coeymans, Watervliet, Colonie, Guilderland, Normanskill, Foxenkill.

The Dutch, however, were not the only settlers. The first immigrants to arrive, in fact, were French-speaking Walloons. The Swiss and Germans settled in the hill town of Berne, the Scots in New Scotland. Jews came to the colony with the Dutch, seeking religious freedom, as did so many others. And the Dutch also brought black slaves.

Even as these early settlers supplanted native Americans and so altered the world to suit their customs, additional waves of immigration came to the Albany area changing it still more, making it a cosmopolitan cross-section of an everchanging nation. New Englanders came in the late 18th century, bringing with them Yankee stubbornness and agricultural expertise. The Irish and Germans in the 1840's, and the Poles and Italians later in the century came after jobs, first building the Erie Canal, then the railroad, and finally working in textile mills, in an ever-growing metropolitan area. In the 20th century, Chinese, Filipinos, Hispanics, Vietnamese, and Indians have added new dimensions to the mosaic that makes up our heritage.

Some people claim that our area is a "melting pot" where all immigrants blend to become Americans. In fact, it is more like a wonderful stew in which each group enriches the whole, but retains its own unique characteristics.

We celebrate our patchwork culture and welcome the diversity it has brought to our restaurants. The recipes that follow, from local chefs, and some of our own "celebrities," emphasize this variety. We hope you will enjoy them.

Beverwyck Restaurant

A beautifully restored Albany restaurant, it takes its name
from Beverwyck, the first official name for the settlement that later
became Albany.

Shrimp Scampi Beverwyck

2 pounds butter
⅓ cup flour
⅓ cup tomato sauce
2 ounces lemon juice
¾ ounce Worcestershire sauce
1 ounce crushed garlic
   (by weight)

½ ounce crushed fennel
1 ounce oregano
1 ounce basil
½ ounce crushed red pepper
1 ounce chopped fresh parsley
Pinch of salt

Leave butter at room temperature for 2 hours or until soft enough to work with. Combine all ingredients and mix evenly. Roll up in a stick and cover with wax paper. This is a compound butter and can keep up to several weeks in the freezer.

Peel and devein shrimp leaving on the tail piece. Use approximately 5 shrimp per serving. The jumbo shrimp would be the best choice.

Put butter mixture in a sauté pan and heat at a low temperature, add shrimp and cook until done. Serve over rice. Serves 4.

Rice Pilaf

1 cup rice
1 medium-size onion,
   finely diced
4 chicken bouillon cubes
2 bay leaves

1 tablespoon thyme
¼ cup butter
Pinch of salt
1⅓ cups water

Sauté onions in butter and add thyme, bay leaves, bouillon, rice, and water. Cover. Cook until air bubbles appear on surface of rice. Take off heat and allow it to finish cooking on top of the stove.

Serve shrimp over rice with desired vegetable.

Scullen & Meyer
Loudonville

A specialty shop that is "all about food," the owners describe their store as comprised of ten sections all adding up to the American taste.

Lamb in Dill Sauce

4 pounds leg of lamb, cubed
1 cup chopped onion
1 cup Chablis wine
2 cups chicken stock
1 cup heavy cream
2 tablespoons flour

½ teaspoon white pepper
3 teaspoons dill weed
1 clove garlic, minced
¼ cup sour cream
5 tablespoons lemon juice
1 pound mushrooms

In a skillet, brown the lamb in butter and oil. Transfer lamb to a large pot. In the skillet, sauté the onion and garlic. Add onion and garlic to the lamb. Add the wine and chicken stock and simmer 1½ hours. Remove the lamb with a slotted spoon and reduce liquid by 65%. Add heavy cream and 2 tablespoons flour mixed with a little liquid from the pot. In another skillet, sauté the mushrooms in butter. Add mushrooms and seasonings to the pot. Just before serving, whisk in the sour cream and lemon juice taking care that the sauce doesn't curdle. Add the reserved lamb to the sauce. Serves 8.

NOTE: It can be frozen and served later.

Pitts and Pitts…Caterers
Troy

This catering service offers unique progressive food which has been highly acclaimed by local critics.

Chicken and Ham Croquettes

2 tablespoons butter
¼ cup flour
¾ cup milk
½ pound cooked chicken,
   finely chopped
½ pound ham, finely
   chopped

2 small red apples, skinned,
   cored and chopped
Grated rind of 1 lemon
Salt and pepper
1 tablespoon tarragon, dried,
   crumbled and rubbed in
   palm of hand

For coating and frying use beaten egg, bread crumbs, and fat for frying.

Make a thick white sauce with the butter, flour, and milk. Add meats, apple, and lemon rind. Season to taste with salt, pepper, and tarragon. Allow to cool. Form into cork shapes, dust with flour, coat with beaten egg, then roll in bread crumbs. Deep fry about 10 minutes, until golden brown, drain on paper towels. Serve with garnish of parsley. Serves 4.

Garcia's of Scottsdale
Albany
This delightful Mexican favorite from Phoenix has recently made a welcomed entrée into Albany.

Pollo Fundido

BURRO INGREDIENTS:

3 (2 pound) whole chickens
1 tablespoon vegetable shortening
4 large bell peppers, chopped
1 large white onion, diced
Celery stalk, diced
1 (1 pound) can whole tomatoes, peeled

2 teaspoons garlic salt
2 teaspoons salt
1 teaspoon black pepper
4-6 (10-14 inch) flour tortillas

TOPPPING INGREDIENTS:

1 pound mild, aged Cheddar
1 pound cream cheese
⅓ quart whipping cream

1 ounce diced jalapenos
2 ounces chicken stock

Boil chicken until done, cool, and dice or shred meat into pieces no larger than 1 inch. Pre-heat shortening in pot to 300°F. Add vegetables, seasonings, sauté until al dente and remove from heat. Add chicken to vegetable mixture, mix well, strain excess juice.

Slice cheese into 3 x 3-inch squares, 1 ounce each (16 slices). (Fine shredded Cheddar cheese is okay to use.) Mix together: 1 pound cream cheese in mixing bowl with ⅓ quart whipping cream, 1 ounce of diced jalapenos and 2 ounces of chicken stock. Mix until smooth.

Measure 4-4½ ounces of chicken mixture, place in center of tortilla, bring both ends of tortilla even, fold inward and roll a cylinder shape. Fasten with a toothpick. Pre-heat fryer to 350°F. Fry until golden brown (strain). Place on heat-resistant plate or cookie sheet and cut equally into three sections. Put 1 ounce cream cheese mixture on top of each section. Put 1 ounce Cheddar cheese on top of cream cheese on each section. Place into a pre-heated oven (350°F.) until cheese melts evenly. Refasten with toothpick, if necessary. Serves 4-6.

Cafe Capriccio
Albany

An intimate restaurant in the downtown area, Cafe Capriccio
features many chef-owner created specialities as well as a variety
of fresh pasta.

Bouillabaisse

Bouillabaisse, like many classic preparations, is not so much the product
of a precise recipe but rather involves a basic approach to local produce
with a more or less specific outcome. Preparing a Bouillabaisse therefore
requires an understanding of fundamentals but not the rigorous disci-
pline necessary to prepare a delicate French sauce. Bouillabaisse is, con-
sequently, a forgiving delicacy because it allows for great variation and
cannot easily be spoiled.

The distinguishing features of Bouillabaisse are the particular variety of
fish swimming the Mediterranean around Marsailles and the practices
of southern French cooks. Since we must look to Boston Harbor for our
supplies, our preparation will necessarily reflect mid-Atlantic rather than
southern Mediterranean flavors.

The following recipe is intended to provide a general guide. The number
of persons to be served and your personal taste should determine quantities of ingredients.

INGREDIENTS:

Fish heads, tails, bones and other
    parts for stock
At least 6 varieties of fish, such as
    lobster, shrimp, sea bass, blue,
    scallops, clams, mussels, squid

Leeks, onions, garlic, olive oil,
    fennel, bay leaf, parsley, black
    peppercorns, saffron, crushed
    red pepper
Italian plum tomatoes

PREPARATION OF STOCK FOR BROTH: Preparing a fish stock as a
basis for the broth is essential. In a stockpot combine fish heads, tails,
bones and other parts with onions, green stems of leeks, bay leaves, garlic,
parsley stems, black peppercorns. Cover with water and simmer for 2½-
3 hours. Skim as necessary. When finished, strain liquid pressing juices
out of ingredients. At this stage the stock is clear and delicious. Notice
the fresh, subtle scent of the sea.

PREPARATION OF BROTH: In a heavy open pot, large enough to ac-
commodate all of the ingredients to be served, sauté in olive oil chopped
leeks; add garlic after about 3 minutes. Sauté garlic for about 30 seconds

then add tomatoes. Season tomatoes with bay leaf, fennel, red pepper, black pepper, and chopped parsley. Simmer 15 minutes. Then add fish stock in sufficient quantity to double liquid in pot. Add saffron and simmer 5 minutes. At this stage the broth is ready. It will later be used to poach the fish we have selected.

PREPARATION OF FISH: Fish should be cleaned and where appropriate, cut into serving pieces. Mussels and clams must be scrubbed and tested to insure their shells are not filled with mud. Lobsters should be split, shrimp deveined and other fish made ready for cooking.

COOKING THE FISH: Fish for Bouillabaisse will be cooked together in the broth. Since some species require more or less cooking time they should be placed in the pot accordingly. When all fish is cooked it should be arranged on individual plates or on a serving platter, with the broth transferred to a tureen. Fish and broth may be combined or eaten separately.

ONE HINT: I prefer to steam the clams separately because clam broth tends to be strong and to dominate other more subtle flavors.

Chez René
Glenmont

Cuisine Française élégante is served in a country inn just outside Albany. Bon Appétit!

Chez René Fresh Calves' Liver Piquante

4 (5 ounce) slices of fresh
  calves' liver
2 ounces butter
1 ounce salad oil
6 dry shallots, finely chopped
1 garlic clove, finely chopped
5 large fresh mushrooms, cut
  julienne style (long slivers)

1 teaspoon chopped fresh parsley
1 teaspoon chopped fresh chives
1 ounce red wine vinegar
6 ounces Bordelaise sauce
  (or beef gravy)
Worcestershire sauce
Salt
Pepper

In a frying pan, heat butter and salad oil until very hot. Lightly flour the slices of calves' liver on both sides. Sauté the liver according to taste (rare or medium), remove from pan and keep warm.

In the same frying pan, add shallots, garlic, mushrooms, chives and parsley. Brown until golden, then add red wine vinegar, 3 dashes of Worcestershire sauce, Bordelaise sauce, salt and pepper to taste and let simmer for 1 minute. Put back calves' liver for 1 minute. Remove from pan and serve on a plate, garnished with fresh parsley. Serves 4.

Golden Fox Steak House
Albany

Located in central Albany, the Golden Fox hosts four different dining rooms, each with its own unique atmosphere and menu.

Clams Flambé

16 fresh Littleneck clams	2 ounces oil
1 bunch green onions	4 tablespoons butter
1 cup sliced fresh mushrooms	½ jigger of brandy
1 fresh tomato, diced	½ jigger of sherry (or chablis)
1 cup water	1 lemon

Wash clams and place in pan with hot oil. When clams begin to open, flambé with brandy. Add to pan all additional ingredients, and cook rapidly 3-4 minutes. Place equal quantities of clams and vegetables in a hot casserole dish and serve. Serves 4.

Popovers
These are a famous house specialty

1¾ cups flour	1 teaspoon salt
1 dozen eggs	⅓ cup vanilla
3 pints half and half cream	⅓ cup egg whites
3 ounces sugar	

Combine all ingredients. Pour into popover pans and bake at 300°F. for 30 minutes. Turn oven off and leave popovers in oven for an additional hour. Remove and serve. Makes 2 dozen.

Jack's Oyster House
Albany

Serving the finest quality seafood at the most affordable prices, Jack's has been a fixture in downtown Albany for over 70 years.

Baked Schrod

4 (8-9 ounce) fillets of fresh schrod	1 ounce dry Sauterne wine
	Paprika
4 ounces melted butter	Parsley
Juice of ½ of fresh lemon	

Preheat oven to broil for 10 minutes. Mix butter and wine and pour over fresh fillet. Sprinkle with paprika. Sear for 2 minutes, then lower heat to 400-425°F. and continue cooking for 5 to 6 minutes until golden brown. Remove and squeeze with fresh lemon and top with fresh parsley. Serve immediately. Serves 4.

Peking Restaurant
Albany

The authentic Chinese cuisine originiates with the owner from
Tientsin, China where he opened his first restaurant.

Hot and Sour Soup
(Szechuan Cooking)

2 ounces shredded pork
4 cups chicken broth
1 piece soft bean curd, sliced
  and halved
1 ounce bamboo shoots, shredded
Wood ear (as desired)
2 tablespoons soy sauce

2 tablespoons vinegar
½ teaspoon white pepper
⅔ teaspoon sesame oil
1 teaspoon cornstarch
Scallions, chopped
1 egg

Place pork, bean curd, bamboo shoots, and wood ears (softened) in chicken broth and bring to a boil. Add soy sauce, vinegar, white pepper, and cornstarch (after mixing cornstarch with 3 tablespoons of cold water). Stirring to a boil again, add the egg (after beating). Add sesame oil and scallions (chopped) as desired.

NOTE: Soften wood ears by soaking the dried ones in a cup of lukewarm water overnight.

Gideon Putnam Hotel and Conference Center
Saratoga Springs

"The place to be in Saratoga." The formal dining room of this classic hotel, situated in the middle of Saratoga State Park, offers exceptional scenery along with its exciting continental menu.

Chef Otto's Shrimp in Wine and Cream Sauce

10-15 jumbo shrimp, peeled
  and deveined
3 tablespoons butter
1 cup sliced mushrooms
½ cup white wine

½ cup heavy cream
Salt and pepper, to taste
½ teaspoon chopped parsley
1 teaspoon minced shallots

Dredge shrimp in seasoned flour and sauté in butter over medium heat for about 1 minute, add shallots and mushrooms, cook for an additional 2 or 3 minutes. Add wine and reduce by half, add heavy cream, bring to a boil and cook until it thickens slightly. Serve immediately sprinkled with chopped parsley. Serves 2.

The Cranberry Bog
Albany

An exciting atmosphere with a wonderful menu makes this a fine place to dine and "a nice way to end the day."

Cranberry-Nut Bread

1 cup white sugar
½ teaspoon salt
½ teaspoon baking soda
1 egg, unbeaten
1½ teaspoons baking powder
¼ cup chopped nuts

1 cup cranberries
2 cups flour
2 tablespoons shortening
Juice and grated rind of 1 orange
Boiling water

Mix dry ingredients together. Put juice and orange rind in measuring cup. Add shortening, then fill cup to ¾ mark with boiling water. Add to dry mixture. Add unbeaten egg, cranberries and chopped nuts. Bake in greased pan for 1 hour at 350 degrees. Let stand 24 hours before slicing.

The Italian American Community Center
Albany

A favorite of many Albanians, this restaurant proudly offers a wide sampling of regional Italian cooking.

Cavatelli Con Broccoli

Olive oil
2 cloves garlic
4 anchovies, very finely chopped
4 tablespoons melted butter
1 pound broccoli

1 pound cavatelli
Boiling water
Salt and pepper, to taste
Parsley
Parmesan cheese

In a large fry pan add enough olive oil to cover bottom of pan. Heat olive oil, garlic, anchovies, and butter. Sauté broccoli in above. Cook cavatelli for 10 minutes in boiling water. Mix together cavatelli and broccoli in fry pan. Season with salt and pepper. Serve garnished with parsley and Parmesan cheese. Serves 4.

Scholz's Zwicklbauer Hofbrau
East Berne

This restaurant offers friendly German hospitality in the heart of the
Helderberg Mountains

Red Cabbage

1 head red cabbage, finely
   shredded
1½ tablespoons lard
1 onion, diced and fried
3 tablespoons vinegar

1 tart apple, sliced
Dash of sugar
Pepper and salt, to taste
3 or 4 cloves

Place the cabbage in enough water to simmer it and add the remaining
ingredients, cooking until the cabbage is tender enough to eat. Then add
1 tablespoon of flour to the mixture to thicken it. Serve.

The Van Dyck
Schenectady

The Historic Stockade section of Schenectady is the site of this elegant
Victorian-style restaurant.

Seafood Treasure Chest à la Jamaique

½ cup shallots, chopped
1 pound mushrooms, quartered
10 ounces Sauterne wine
1 ounce lemon juice
1 pound small bay scallops
1 pound medium shrimp

1 (12 ounce) can snow crabmeat
1 pound monk fish, diced in ½-
   inch cubes
3 sprigs saffron
¾ cup cornstarch
2 cups converted rice

Mix shallots, mushrooms, wine, and lemon juice in small saucepan and
cook for 15 minutes over medium heat. Set aside. Mix seafood in medium saucepan and poach in 1½ quarts water for 15 minutes or until
shrimp are firm. Add saffron sprigs to mixture while poaching. Drain
seafood mixture and save stock. Set seafood aside. Divide stock in half
and place in 2 medium saucepans. In one pan add rice and stir. Simmer
for 20 minutes until done. Dilute cornstach with water and add half of
mixture to other pan of fish stock. Stir until thickened and smooth (add
more cornstarch mixture if necessary). Add seafood mixture and mushroom and shallot mixture and stir. Serve over rice or in patty shell or puff
pastry. Serves 6-8.

Scrimshaw Room at Americana Inn
Albany

With gracious hospitality in a colonial setting, the Scrimshaw specializes in New England seafood, veal and steaks. Marko Cerezin, Director of Food and Beverage at the Americana Inn, kindly shared the following specialty.

Oysters in Champagne with Sauce Louise

24 oysters (6 oysters with 2
   ounces of sauce per portion)

LIGHT CREAM SAUCE:

¾ ounce butter	1 pint milk
¾ ounce bread flour	1 teaspoon salt

SAUCE LOUISE:

⅛ cup clam juice	1½ teaspoons sweet butter
Salt, to taste	1 teaspoon anchovy paste
Cayenne, to taste	4 egg yolks
Nutmeg, to taste	¾ cup cream
1 teaspoon lemon juice	

COURT BOUILLON:

½ cup clam juice	½ carrot, coarsely chopped
½ cup champagne	4 peppercorns
½ onion, coarsely chopped	1 bay leaf
½ stalk celery, coarsely chopped	

8 ounces Sauce Louise	8 strips pimiento
4 raw mushrooms	4 sprigs parsley

LIGHT CREAM SAUCE: 1. Melt butter in thick bottomed sauce pot. Stir in flour to make a roux. Cook over low heat, stirring constantly for 8-10 minutes. Do not allow to brown.
2. Heat milk to boil, stir in roux gradually, beating briskly until sauce is thickened and smooth.
3. Simmer for 5 minutes, stirring occasionally. Bring to boil.
4. Strain

SAUCE LOUISE: Reduce ⅛ cup clam juice in half, add 4 tablespoons light cream sauce and heat. Add salt, cayenne and nutmeg to taste. Then add lemon juice, sweet butter and anchovy paste, stir. Combine 4 egg yolks and temper with sauce. Add cream; thicken.

PROCEDURE: 1. Poach oysters in court bouillon mixture which consists of ½ cup clam juice, champagne, celery, onion, carrot, bay leaf, and peppercorn for 2 minutes.

2. Cover 7-inch plate with Sauce Louise, place 6 oysters on top of sauce at equal intervals.

3. In center of oysters place thinly sliced mushroom and strips of pimientos with sprig of parsley. Serves 4.

Truffles Restaurant at the Albany Hilton
Albany

Dining elegance and European fare are offered at Truffles in the heart of the capital district.

Medallions of Veal with Sauce Moutarde de Meaux

"To make an exceptional meal, you must start with exceptional ingredients. I suggest buying Provimi veal and for this entrée, have the medallions sliced from the loin."

THE VEAL (for 2):
4 (4 ounce) veal medallions

Dredge veal through flour, shake off excess. In a flat skillet, heat 2 tablespoons clarified butter or oil and heat until almost smoking. Briefly sauté medallions, till browned, then the same on the other side.

SAUCE SUPRÊME (2 cups):

8 ounces chicken backs
8 ounces veal scraps
½ cup sliced shallots
1 cup white wine

2 cups chicken broth (canned is fine, skim off the fat)
2 cups heavy cream

In a wide, flat pot, in 1 tablespoon oil, with high heat, brown veal and chicken scraps. Once browned, skim off excess fat. Add sliced shallots and briefly sauté. Add white wine and completely reduce over high heat. Add chicken stock and reduce until 1 inch of liquid remains. Add heavy cream, bring to a boil. Remove from heat and strain. In a small sauce pot, place 3 tablespoons moutarde de meaux, heat, and add the sauce suprême. Bring to a slight boil and serve over the veal.

SUGGESTED ACCOMPANIMENT: Fresh pasta with julienne of carrot and leeks tossed with garlic and sweet butter. Or, a sauté of snow peas and cherry tomatoes. Or, a salad of Boston lettuce with a vinaigrette.

Twenty-One Restaurant
Albany

Continental cuisine is served in an elegantly restored Victorian brownstone just steps from the Capitol in downtown Albany.

Escallop de Veau au Pistaches

30 (1 ounce) scallops of veal, pounded thin
90 shelled, white pistachios
9 ounces diced prosciutto
2½ cups mushrooms, washed and sliced

1 cup Madiera wine
3¾ cups heavy cream
Salt and white pepper, to taste
Seasoned flour for dredging
Oil to sauté

Dredge veal scallops in seasoned flour. Line a large sauté pan with oil, heat to very hot. Sauté the veal very quickly, 1 minute on each side, and remove to heated serving platter. Drain the oil. Return pan to heat and deglaze with the Madiera wine. Bring to a boil scraping all the bits from the bottom of pan. Must reduce wine by about half. Add the prosciutto and pistachios, then the heavy cream and reduce to medium sauce consistency. The sauce will then nape the back of the spoon. Adjust the seasoning with salt and white pepper. Bring the sauce back to a boil, pour over the veal and serve immediately. Serves 6.

NOTE: Since the pistachios and prosciutto are usually salty, please be advised that you may want to omit the salt in the sauce or if so be careful not to over-salt the sauce.

Quackenbush House
Albany

Unique continental dining is offered in our city's oldest building, dating from the early 1700's.

Veal Quackenbush

1½ pounds veal scallops, sliced thin
½ cup white wine
½ cup tinned beef broth or beef stock
8 ounces Swiss or Gruyere cheese, diced or grated

8 ounces smoked ham, diced or julienne
½ stick butter or margarine
½ cup flour
Salt, to taste
1 tablespoon diced or minced parsley

Mix flour and some salt together. Dredge veal scallops in flour. Melt ¼ stick of butter in sauté pan over medium high heat and add veal to pan (do not overlap). Cook veal 1 minute per side. After veal is cooked, transfer it to a warming pan. After all veal is cooked, deglaze pan with white wine, scraping up bits on the bottom of the pan. Add ham, rest of butter, beef broth and cook over high heat 1 minute. Finally add cheese, stirring constantly. When cheese is melted, check pan juices and add salt if necessary. Spoon mixture over cooked veal; sprinkle with parsley and serve immediately. Serves 4-6.

Mrs. London's Bake Shop
Saratoga Springs

Mrs. London is noted for her delectable desserts and outstanding breads served in her tea room or sold in the adjoining bakery.

"Mrs. London's Eat Your Heart Out" Chocolate Cake

Very very rich…chocolate lovers love this!

1 devil's food cake, either from your own favorite recipe or from a cake-pudding mix

2 cups raspberry jam
2-4 tablespoons Framboise (black raspberry liqueur)

FOR ICING:

3 ounces semi-sweet chocolate
2 tablespoons unsalted butter
2¾ cups sifted confectioners' sugar

2 teaspoons vanilla
6 tablespoons whipping cream
Candied violets or roses (optional)

Make a devil's food cake and cool. Split lengthwise into 3 equal parts. Combine raspberry jam with the Framboise to spreading consistency. Reassemble cake by spreading 1 cup jam between each layer and restacking.

TO MAKE ICING: Melt in double boiler the chocolate and the butter. When melted add the sugar, 1 teaspoon of the vanilla and mix with a mixer. When blended add the cream (add cream off the heat). Mix until smooth. You may need to return to the heat to get completely smooth. Add remaining vanilla and if too stiff 1 more tablespoon of cream. Ice the cake and decorate with candied violets or roses if desired. Serves 10-16.

Deux Amies

The fresh, vibrant flavors of this summer salad are typical of the sophisticated fare developed by Deux Amies, a food consulting firm.

Cold Rice Salad

2 cups raw converted rice
¼ cup oil (mix olive and salad)
1½ tablespoons lemon juice
½ cup mayonnaise
1 tablespoon grated fresh
  ginger root
½ cup scallions, chopped
½ cup golden raisins

½ cup slivered almonds,
  lightly toasted
5 ounces (½ jar) chutney
1 teaspoon cumin
Salt and pepper, to taste
1 cucumber
Lettuce leaves
2 ounces apricots, chopped

Cook rice following instructions on box until done. While rice is hot season with oil, salt, cumin, raisins, grated ginger, and lemon juice. Chill. Add mayonnaise, scallions, almonds, chutney, and apricots. Score 1 whole cucumber with a fork for a decorative touch. Cut cucumber into thin circular slices. If desired, line the bowl with lettuce leaves. Heap rice salad in a mound. Garnish with cucumber slices.

The Gourmet Touch
Delmar

From elegant hors d'oeuvres to hearty snacks, Rosemarie Mosman's made-to-order food adds a festive touch to any party.

Sausage Appetizers

1 (8 ounce) package refrigerator
  butterflake rolls
½ pound hot Italian sausage,
  crumbled
2 lightly beaten eggs
1 cup Ricotta cheese

¼ cup grated Parmesan cheese
¼ cup chopped Mozzarella
  cheese
1 tablespoon chopped parsley
Pepper, to taste

Preheat oven to 375°F. Separate rolls into 8 sections. Press each piece into small greased muffin cups. Brown sausage. Drain well then divide sausage evenly among muffin cups. Mix eggs, cheeses, parsley, and pepper. Spoon over sausage and bake until browned slightly, for approximately 20 minutes. (These appetizers can be frozen before or after baking.)

Potpourri

This index is intended to help you find a recipe
that uses a leftover or an unusual ingredient.

POTPOURRI

Index

INDEX

INDEX

INDEX

INDEX

INDEX

INDEX

INDEX

Junior League of Albany Publications

419 Madison Avenue
Albany, New York 12210
518-463-2015

Please send me_____copies at 14.95 per copy. (Ne
York State residents add local sales tax). Add $1.7
per book for shipping. Make checks payable to Junio
League of Albany Publications.

Shipping address, if different:

Name_____

Address_____

City_____

State_____Zip_____

Name_____

Address_____

City_____

State_____Zip_____

Junior League of Albany Publications

419 Madison Avenue
Albany, New York 12210
518-463-2015

Please send me_____copies at 14.95 per copy. (New
York State residents add local sales tax). Add $1.75
per book for shipping. Make checks payable to Junior
League of Albany Publications.

Shipping address, if different:

Name_____

Address_____

City_____

State_____Zip_____

Name_____

Address_____

City_____

State_____Zip_____

Junior League of Albany Publications

419 Madison Avenue
Albany, New York 12210
518-463-2015

Please send me_____copies at 14.95 per copy. (New
York State residents add local sales tax). Add $1.75
per book for shipping. Make checks payable to Junior
League of Albany Publications.

Shipping address, if different:

Name_____

Address_____

City_____

State_____Zip_____

Name_____

Address_____

City_____

State_____Zip_____

Share the best of Albany's rich tradition blended with recipes for today. Give **THE STENCILED STRAWBERRY COOKBOOK** to a new neighbor or old friend, near or far.

A thoughtful gift for that thoughtful person in your life. **THE STENCILED STRAWBERRY COOKBOOK** is a treasured keepsake.

Beginner cooks and seasoned gourmets will discover a wide range of recipes for every ability and taste. **THE STENCILED STRAWBERRY COOKBOOK** is a versatile wedding, anniversary, hostess and special occasion gift.